American History Through Literature

GETTYSBURG

American History Through Literature

Paul Finkelman
Series Editor

FREEDOM ROAD
Howard Fast
Introduction by Eric Foner

JOHN RANDOLPH
Henry Adams
Introduction by Robert McColley

THE LIFE OF WASHINGTON
Mason L. Weems
Introduction by Peter S. Onuf

GETTYSBURG
Edited by Earl Schenck Miers and Richard A. Brown
Introduction by James I. Robertson, Jr.

CLOTEL; OR, THE PRESIDENT'S DAUGHTER
William Wells Brown
Introduction by Joan E. Cashin

GETTYSBURG

EARL SCHENCK MIERS
RICHARD A. BROWN

A new edition
with a foreword
by JAMES I.
ROBERTSON, JR.

M.E. Sharpe

Armonk, New York
London, England

Library of Congress Cataloging-in-Publication Data

Gettysburg / [edited by] Earl Schenck Miers and Richard A. Brown. —
New ed. / with a foreword by James I. Robertson, Jr.
p.   cm. — (American history through literature)
Originally published: New Brunswick, N.J. : Rutgers University Press, 1948.
Includes bibliographical references and index.
ISBN 1-56324-696-1 (hardcover : alk. paper). — ISBN 1-56324-697-X (pbk. : alk. paper)
1. Gettysburg Campaign, 1863. 2. Gettysburg Campaign, 1863—
Personal narratives. 3. Gettysburg (Pa.), Battle of, 1863.
4. Gettysburg (Pa.), Battle of, 1863—Personal narratives.
I. Miers, Earl Schenck, 1910–1972. II. Brown, Richard A., 1951–
III. Series
E475.51.G37   1996
973.7'349—dc20   96-1729
CIP
Printed in the United States of America

For

Alan E. James

Contents

Maps

Series Foreword

Novelists, poets, and essayists often use history to illuminate their understanding of human interaction. At times these works also illuminate our history. They also help us better understand how people in different times and places thought about their own world. Popular novels are themselves artifacts of history.

This series is designed to bring back into print works of literature—in the broadest sense of the term—that illuminate our understanding of U.S. history. Each book is introduced by a major scholar, who places the book in a context, and also offers some guidance to reading the book as "history." The editor will show us where the author of the book has been in error, as well as where the author is accurate. Each reprinted work also includes a few documents to illustrate the historical setting of the work itself.

Books in this series will primarily fall into three categories. First, we will reprint works of "historical fiction"—books that are essentially works of history in a fictional setting. Rather than simply fiction about the past, each will be first-rate history presented through the voices of fictional characters, or through fictional presentations of real characters in ways that do not distort the historical record. Second, we will reprint works of fiction, poetry, and other forms of literature that are primary sources of the era in which they were written. Finally, we will republish nonfiction such as autobiographies, reminiscences, essays, and journalistic exposés, and even works of history that also fall into the general category of literature.

Paul Finkelman

Foreword

It was just a dot on the map: a small, pleasant town lying amid the rolling hills and broad, shallow valleys of central Pennsylvania. A mountain chain loomed twenty miles to the west. The major reason the little community of twenty-four hundred people existed and flourished was the ten roads leading into it from all points of the compass. Among its few shops and businesses was a warehouse containing shoes. They were badly needed by the barefooted army that Gen. Robert E. Lee guided on a major Confederate invasion of the North in the Civil War's third year.

The name of the town was Gettysburg. For the first three days of July 1863, the principal armies of North and South waged a struggle there—one so furious in its intensity and so important in its consequences that it remains the most famous battle in American history. Some 163,000 soldiers (average age: twenty-four) and their officers (average age: forty-one) engaged in a level of combat none of them had ever imagined war to be. When the smoke cleared, over 51,000 men were dead, wounded, or missing.

Burial details were still at work four months later when President Abraham Lincoln of the Union came to Gettysburg to make a few appropriate remarks at the dedication of a new national cemetery. His Gettysburg Address proved to be timeless in its sentiments. No public utterance in American statesmanship is better known or more deeply revered.

Many consider the struggle at Gettysburg to be the climactic moment of the Civil War. The battle marked the coming-of-age of the Northern Army of the Potomac; it was a stunning rebuff of a Confederate offensive born in great part of desperation. A third of Lee's army melted away in the heat of combat. Seventeen of fifty-two Southern generals were casualties. The spirit of invincibility that had swirled around the Confederate Army of Northern Virginia vanished, along with its offensive mettle. Thereafter, Lee would wage a defensive war against overwhelming resources and newfound Union optimism. It was the very type of war that the South could not hope to win.

Gettysburg may or may not have been the apex of the nation-building contest of the 1860s, but it was unquestionably one of the

Civil War's major turning points. The fighting was filled with courage and fraught with controversy. Strangely, this huge battle was not planned in advance.

Lee's army was driving north through Pennsylvania; Gen. George G. Meade's Union army was giving strong pursuit. Following different roads that led to the junction at Gettysburg, elements of the two hosts collided. Simple contact brought instant combat because the stakes were so high on both sides. For three days thereafter, Confederates launched a series of attacks against a Union line that ran north to south in the shape of an inverted question mark.

The first action occurred west of town along McPherson's Ridge. Confederate assaults from a second front drove the Federals through Gettysburg to Cemetery Ridge, a shallow range of high ground immediately south of the village (and so named because the town burying ground was there). Lee had won the first round, but not by a wide margin.

On the second day, Southern units assailed the flanks of the Northern troops at Culp's Hill and on Little Round Top. The attacks were disjointed and badly timed. Nevertheless, the intense fighting of that day added blood-soaked names to American military annals: Devil's Den, the Wheatfield, the Peach Orchard. Round two went to the Union side, but at great cost.

By that nightfall, both armies were battered but intact. The decision at Gettysburg still hung in the balance. Both generals had to finish the violence that had been unleashed. Lee assumed that the Union center was weak because of the transfer of soldiers to the hard-pressed flanks. The Southern commander determined to renew the offensive the following day by striking the Federal center. Across the way, Meade predicted exactly what Lee's next move would be. He adjusted his lines accordingly.

July 3 brought the most famous assault in the Western Hemisphere. It began shortly before three o'clock on a bright, hot afternoon. Two Confederate divisions under Gens. George Pickett and Johnston Pettigrew moved paradelike across fourteen hundred yards of open ground toward the middle of a reinforced Union line.

It took only forty minutes to decide the issue. The Pickett–Pettigrew Charge was a fight between human gallantry and inhuman machinery—a contest between men charging bravely against massed artillery and concentrated musketry with a clear field of fire. The flower of Southern manhood disappeared in the face of Northern determination. Five of every eight Confederates in the attack were killed, wounded, or captured.

When Meade received word that the assault had been repulsed, all he could say was: "Thank God." A downcast Lee observed: "All this has been my fault. . . . This has been a sad day for us."

After darkness on July 4, as rain drenched the mangled countryside, Lee led his men southward in retreat. The battle of Gettysburg and the Southern hopes for a successful end to the war were history. Yet echoes from Gettysburg would ring through the ages.

Civil War buffs have never tired of arguing over the performances of the major figures in the battle: Lee committing his small army to combat on ground of the enemy's choosing, A.P. Hill's impetuosity, George G. Meade's repeated vacillations, James Longstreet's slowness, Richard Ewell's hesitations, Daniel E. Sickles's recklessness, "Jeb" Stuart's absence, and other modern second-guessing. The three-day engagement offers almost endless fodder for speculation as well as admiration. Small wonder that interest in the struggle has never waned.

One war always calls attention to another. The heroism and heartache of World War II caused Americans to begin reflecting anew on their past, especially the contest between North and South. Gettysburg became an immediate focal point, and Earl Schenck Miers stepped forward as one of the pathbreakers in a new wave of popular interest in the Civil War.

Miers was a remarkable individual. Born May 27, 1910, in Brooklyn, he was the son of a house painter–janitor and an English immigrant. Miers suffered brain damage at birth. The result was athetosis, a form of cerebral palsy. His parents, despite their limited means, pursued every medical avenue in search of a miracle cure for what was then called "the shakes." The quest was in vain. Miers spent a lifetime coping with his affliction.

He adjusted masterfully. While attending public schools in Brooklyn and in Hackensack, New Jersey, Miers learned not only to read quickly and to absorb easily but also to compensate for poor handwriting with a typewriter. That machine became his outlet; his grandmother's stories of the Revolutionary War and her remembrances of the Civil War became his inspirations. Miers determined to become a writer.

Success first came with short stories published before he had reached his fifteenth year. While a junior in high school, he worked part-time as a local newspaper reporter. That ultimately brought Miers eighteen hundred dollars and a chance to go to college. He entered Rutgers University on the eve of the 1929 Great Depression. Not content merely with meeting curriculum requirements, and in spite of his handicap, Miers pursued extracurricular activities to an almost full-time extent. Editing the college newspaper, writing student shows, serving as a member of the student council and honorary society, and working as a correspondent for several New York and New Jersey newspapers were among his "outside" endeavors.

Following graduation with a bachelor's degree in journalism, Miers went to work for the public relations department at Rutgers. He married Starling Wyckoff, who bore him two sons and a daughter. In 1943, Rutgers conferred upon Miers an honorary master of arts degree. The next year, he founded and became first director of the Rutgers University Press. This new duty was quite comfortable for Miers, for by then he had published four books for adults and three others for juveniles. It was while with the Rutgers press that Miers produced his first Civil War study, *Gettysburg*.

The battle had long fascinated him. Recognizing that not much new information existed on the struggle and that the best accounts had already been written by eyewitnesses, Miers settled on a novel approach. He would let those who fought the battle tell its story. His task would be to select and correlate the accounts with headers and a running narrative to provide cohesion. A graduate student and university press colleague, Richard A. Brown, agreed to collect the materials needed.

This approach now goes by many names—compilation history, readers, scissors-and-paste books, to name a few—but Miers was the first in modern times to attempt it with Civil War history. He proved quite good at it. Miers combined some of the more revealing of the old memoirs (by such observers as Arthur J.L. Fremantle, Frank A. Haskell, and James Longstreet) with more recently published recollections (such as those by W.W. Blackford, John Dooley, and Cornelia Hancock). The result was fresh, human, solid history.

Ninety-two excerpts follow the Gettysburg campaign chronologically. The approach to battle by both sides, the many and bloody stages of the conflict itself, and the traumatic aftermath, all receive full attention. Ten maps provide easy reference points for the most amateur of Civil War students.

Praise of *Gettysburg* at its 1948 publication was widespread. The *New York Times Book Review* termed the work "the very best collection of firsthand accounts, written by soldiers and civilians" about the 1863 battle, because the scores of quotations offered a "richness of texture, time and place that most narrative histories fail to achieve." More than that, Miers's composite account served as a model for a number of later works, including Henry Steele Commager's two-volume *The Blue and the Gray*.

It also was but the first of a long line of Civil War studies Miers wrote thereafter. The more notable titles include *The General Who Marched to Hell* (1951), *The Living Lincoln* (1955), *The Web of Victory* (1955), *Robert E. Lee, a Great Life in Brief* (1956), *The Great Rebellion* (1958), *Lincoln Day by Day* (three volumes, 1960), *Tragic Years, 1861–1865* (1960), *Ride to War* (1961), and *New Jersey and the Civil War* (1964).

Among Miers's literary assets was the ability to turn a memorable phrase. "Death," he wrote, "is part of war—sometimes the easiest part." He once spoke of a Union officer who displayed "unflinching duty in an age when, among the battle-scarred hills of Virginia, democracy and freedom stood on trial before the world." In one of his last books, Miers noted: "We live with our memories—these memories which, as Walt Whitman said, are so 'unspeakably and forever precious.' "

Miers's career took an upswing in keeping with his productivity. In 1949 he became an editor, first for New York publisher Alfred A. Knopf and then for the World Publishing Company. After four years of working with other people's manuscripts, Miers saw that he preferred authorship to editorship. He retired to concentrate on historical research and writing.

To say merely that Miers was prolific would be an understatement. In his career, he turned out over a hundred books and pamphlets, plus twenty-four introductions and special articles for other publications. Two of Miers's booklets were for the National Society for Crippled Children and Adults and bore the titles *Why Did This Have to Happen?* and *Cerebral Palsy*. He devoted much time to the Easter Seal Society and never refused an invitation to speak to groups interested in physical handicaps and rehabilitation.

In personality, he was outgoing, intense, and convivial. His friendship was genuine and enduring. A bright sense of humor often appeared in public. Presiding over a Civil War symposium, Miers introduced a speaker by observing that the gentleman was "going to talk about the battle front in twenty minutes, whether he knows it or not."

His unquenchable energy was a leading characteristic. He was always working on a book-length treatment of some historical subject. Honorary degrees from Lincoln College and Rutgers served only to increase his output. Yet failing health in the late 1960s steadily curbed his activities. On November 17, 1972, Miers died at his Edison, New Jersey, home. He was sixty-two.

All authors remember their first book with a special, sentimental fondness. Miers was no exception with his entry into Civil War history. Various aspects of the conflict (especially Gen. William T. Sherman) intrigued him, but he never got completely away from Gettysburg. The battle continued to mesmerize him as it had its participants.

Gettysburg haunts us still. It is the most visited of all the battlefield parks maintained by the National Park Service. Over two million people walk its fields each year, many of them making an "annual pilgrimage." Books and articles on the battle flow regularly from presses. Television productions, a full-length movie, at least one periodical—all are constant reminders of what happened there.

Gettysburg was the largest military engagement ever fought in the Western Hemisphere. The struggle was one of the bloodiest in the annals of man. That battle proved to be the costliest Confederate defeat of the war. On the retreat to Virginia, Lee's ambulance wagons stretched a full seven miles. The Northern Army of the Potomac, having previously suffered one defeat after another, won—and won clearly—a smashing victory. The Southern Army of Northern Virginia began a downward journey that would lead ultimately in 1865 to Appomattox Court House. Lincoln would tell the world what Gettysburg meant for the American dream of union.

For Johnny Rebs and Billy Yanks, Gettysburg was a test of what soldiers can bring themselves to attempt and what they can force themselves to endure. The major lesson from that great contest in Pennsylvania is the unforgettable one of men who demonstrated that they loved their country more than they loved their own lives.

We remember, because it would be profane to forget.

James I. Robertson, Jr.

Introduction

CITIZENS OF PHILADELPHIA: Prepare to defend your homes. The traitors who have spread desolation in the southern counties of your State, and carried into captivity free men and women, because they were black and under your protection, approach your city. Their strategy is sufficiently well understood to make it certain that their object is Philadelphia. Do the citizens of the Quaker City expect more favorable treatment at their hands than others? Arise now in your might; shake off your apathy, and show, by rallying rapidly and arming yourselves to meet the enemy and drive him back, that you deserve the blessings of a home. To stand idly now would invite suspicion either of treachery or cowardice. I urge upon the citizens of Philadelphia that they close all places of manufacture by noon, and all other places of business at three o'clock P.M. of each day, devoting the remainder of the day to military organization and instruction. Let companies of from sixty to a hundred men each be rapidly organized, and having chosen their officers, let them report their organization at headquarters, and stand ready at a moment's notice. There is not a moment to be lost, and therefore let us not squander away valuable time.

N. J. T. DANA, *Major-Gen. Commanding.*

With the issuance of this address on Saturday, June 27, 1863, Philadelphians faced the fact that the invasion of Pennsylvania by the Army of Northern Virginia was more than a succession of ugly rumors. Twelve days earlier Governor Curtin had proclaimed to the State that the Rebel forces, flushed with their victories at Fredericksburg and Chancellorsville, had crossed the Potomac; and even the laconic report in *The New York Times* for June 28 that "the return game between the Army of the Potomac and the Army of Virginia may be played this week" could not disguise the mounting apprehension with which the country awaited the outcome of

Lee's audacious move. When at last the issue was finally resolved the focal point of conflict was a drowsy little college
town of not many more than two thousand inhabitants. Few
periods in American history were to become more indelibly
inscribed upon the nation's heart than the bloody days of
July 1, 2, and 3 at Gettysburg. Said Abraham Lincoln:
". . . we here highly resolve that these dead shall not have
died in vain; that this nation, under God, shall have a new
birth of freedom; and that government of the people, by the
people, for the people, shall not perish from the earth."

Gettysburg's immortality was forever consecrated in these
simple words spoken by a war-weary President. As Lincoln
arose to speak his few humble sentences he must have seemed
a lean, unhappy, self-conscious man to those who remembered
that his presence at this dedication of Gettysburg Cemetery
as a national shrine had been an afterthought. But throughout his life Lincoln possessed a genius for epic visions, and
he could see one now: In Little Round Top and Big Round
Top, in Devil's Den, in the Peach Orchard and the Wheatfield,
in Cemetery Ridge and the Bloody Angle, in the whole expanse of rolling country where the men of South Carolina
had died beside the men of Massachusetts, and the men of
Virginia and Texas had died beside the men of Maine and
Vermont. In death there was no longer Rebellion; on fields
where the red-cedar canteens of an agricultural South lay
beside the tin canteens of an industrial North there remained
only the promise that "another spring shall green these
trampled slopes, and flowers, planted by unseen hands, shall
bloom upon these graves."

This book is designed to re-create the story of Gettysburg
in terms of the men and women who lived through the anxiety
of the invasion and the battle. From diaries, letters, yellowing
manuscripts, regimental histories, and the memoirs of generals
and soldiers the editors have sought to reconstruct the emerging narrative of those decisive days. There appeared no need
to offer the reader simply another military history of Gettysburg, for that task has been well performed at least a score
of times. Instead the editors have concerned themselves with
the human document of Gettysburg: Why these men of the

North and South fought and died here, what mean or noble thoughts motivated their acts, what passions and compassions stirred their hearts. To the testimony of generals and their lieutenants the editors have given patient attention, but no more so than to the testimony of the foot soldier or the cannoneer, the housewife or the farm boy.

Since all history is lived in half truth, the reader who follows this unfolding of the story of Gettysburg will not be dismayed by the contradictions that are sometimes apparent in the recollections of various participants. The impression of facts rather than the facts themselves motivate the events of history, and that is why history as written after years of research and reflection is often more truthful than the actual experience of history. The professional historian, gathering all the evidence around him, deals with reality after it has emerged and thus is enabled to speculate upon what might have been. In this respect the historian cannot dispute that he plays a game of detection and inductive reasoning denied to the housewife who hears with dread the rumors of a hostile invasion or to the exhausted foot soldier who watches the enemy advance across a field and believes as he clutches his rifle that he and his company are hopelessly outnumbered.

The essential differenec between this narrative and the more formal work of history is in the fact that by presenting the story of Gettysburg through one hundred excerpts from the testimony of forty-five witnesses the reader is not deprived of sharing in the historian's adventure of evaluating how much is truth and how much is impression. If any word of caution is necessary it is merely that the reader must learn to judge individual selections by their internal evidence, giving one value to those which were written within a matter of hours or days after the events they describe, and another value to those that were recorded years afterward when memory may have become dimmed or when later knowledge may have colored the recollection of events. It seems safe to assume that every reader will quickly understand and thus forgive the personal bias and the human tendency toward self-vindication that sometimes creep into such sources of history.

But aside from these simple cautions, the editors have no

hesitancy in inviting the reader to find in this book both the story of Gettysburg and the adventure of discovering at least in part the historical truth behind the events that took place there. The quest in the end will become a search for those human elements that make the unpredictable believable, and even the unbelievable comprehensible.

The substance of this book, if not its form, was suggested by Douglas Southall Freeman, who graciously examined the list of sources from which the final selections were made. Paul M. Angle, Director of the Chicago Historical Society, read the manuscript in its entirety and gave it not only the critical scrutiny of the professional historian but also the incisively candid analysis of a good editor. To Mark Kiley, Librarian of the New York University Club, must go special expression of gratitude for direction to sources relatively unknown, even to specialists in the field; and the editors are similarly indebted to Frederick Tilberg, Historian of the Library of the Gettysburg National Military Park, and to the library staffs at Rutgers University, Columbia University, Princeton University, and the New York and Newark Public Libraries. In the end, however, this book could never have existed without the faithful guardianship of Miss Alva E. Flood, who lived with it for more than two years, typing and retyping the manuscript, collating sources, and tracking down correct spellings until both she and I were on the verge of tears. For the most part the research that has gone into this work was performed by Richard A. Brown; the editorial work was performed by the undersigned, who must bear the entire responsibility for its shortcomings.

The sources from which all selections in this book have been taken are listed under *References* at the end of the text. The listing, which follows the same order in which the selections appear, is by short title only. Full titles, with other bibliographical information, will be found in the *Bibliography*.

EARL SCHENCK MIERS

Edison, New Jersey
January 3, 1948

Gettysburg

Chapter 1

"Our Town Had a Great Fright"

IN JUNE in Pennsylvania the young green stalks of corn stand straight and firm. In the meadows where violets and daisies mingle with the sweet, rich grasses and clovers the grazing cattle are fat and sleek. Above the meadows roll prosperous farm lands that from one generation to the next produce bountiful harvests of vegetables and fruit, of tobacco and grain.

That spring of 1863 when Robert E. Lee ordered the Army of Northern Virginia to move across the Rappahannock, conjecture could supply many reasons why Lee found appeal in an invasion of Pennsylvania. To feed an army on an enemy's ripening harvests is any general's legitimate objective. Doubtless Lee also gave weight to the fact that the Army of the Potomac too long had lingered along the Rappahannock, for Virginia tempers would be the quicker improved, Virginian appetites the sooner whetted, if the Federals could be lured elsewhere. Moreover, both north and south it was possible to find those who calculated Lee's movements in terms of Washington and Baltimore and Philadelphia—of a shorter war and a more certain victory if these three cities could be closed off and if the Confederate States of America could receive from England and France recognition as a nation and loans urgently needed to bolster her wavering economy.

Lee, ready to gamble an invasion of Pennsylvania, drew his plans carefully. Under the command of Richard S. Ewell, who stomped around on a wooden leg and was known as "Old Bald Head," the Second Corps set the pace. Ewell's orders were to collect horses, cattle, and flour, but Lee also had said: "If Harrisburg comes within your reach, capture it," and Ewell set his heart on snatching that plum as well. Crossing the Potomac, the Second Corps moved ahead in three lines of advance along routes that touched Hagerstown, Greencastle, Chambersburg, Shippensburg, and Carlisle on the west, and Frederick, Emmitsburg, Gettysburg, and York on the east.

To James Longstreet, commander of the First Corps, Lee gave orders to march behind Ewell's troops. At Williamsport, Longstreet watched his men cross the Potomac in some confusion, for as they were wading the river without their trousers they came upon a carriage-load of young Maryland ladies traveling to Virginia on an excursion. Longstreet, however, surveyed the scene with the complete equanimity and dignity that became one who held unofficial rank as first among Lee's lieutenant generals since the death of Stonewall Jackson. With the the same equipoise Longstreet, alone of all these lieutenants, could stand beside his commander at the War's end and say: "General, unless he [Grant] offers us honorable terms, come back and let us fight it out!"

The Third Corps under A. P. Hill was assigned the duty of watching the enemy's army, and, if necessary, of keeping it occupied while the First and Second Corps advanced into Pennsylvania. If Hill chafed at the delay it was small wonder, for he already had been disconcerted by his wife's imprudence in lingering too long at the front. With one eye on the Army of the Potomac and the other on Mrs. Hill to see that she reached home safely, Hill learned by mid-June that the Federals had quit the line of the Rappahannock so that they could stand between Lee and Washington. Free at last of both vigils, Hill quickly led the Third Corps into Pennsylvania along a line of advance that carried his men through Greencastle, Chambersburg, and Fayetteville.

Notes of exultancy, of unwavering confidence, of light-hearted hopefulness ran through the reports that were sent home as all three corps of Lee's men pentrated into Pennsylvania. Old Bald Head Ewell, astonished at the abundance of the country, said joyfully, "It's like a hole full of blubber to a Greenlander!" And to Lizzie Ewell he wrote: "It is wonderful how well our hungry, foot-sore, ragged men behave in this land of plenty—better than at home." Dorsey Pender, of Hill's Corps, confided in a letter to his wife: "We

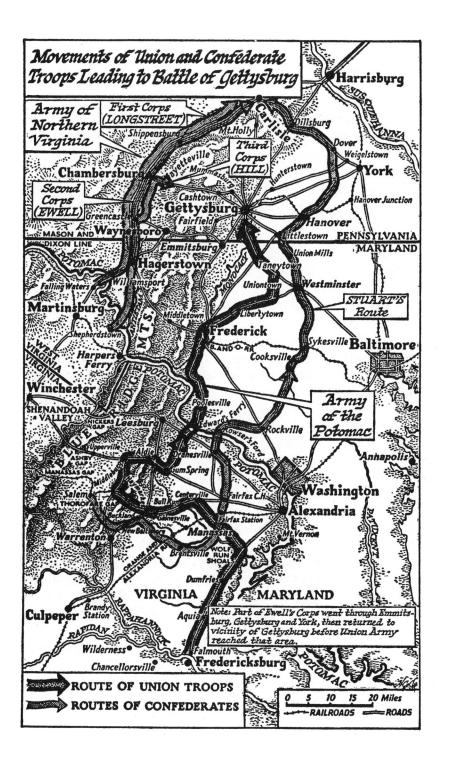

Movements of Union and Confederate Troops Leading to Battle of Gettysburg

Army of Northern Virginia

First Corps (LONGSTREET)

Third Corps (HILL)

Second Corps (EWELL)

STUART'S Route

Army of the Potomac

Harrisburg

Carlisle

Mt. Holly

Dillsburg

Shippensburg

Dover

Weigelstown

York

Chambersburg

Fayetteville

Mummasburg

Hunterstown

Hanover Junction

Cashtown

Gettysburg

Fairfield

Greencastle

Hanover

Littlestown

PENNSYLVANIA

MARYLAND

MASON AND DIXON LINE

Waynesboro

Emmitsburg

Union Mills

Taneytown

Hagerstown

Uniontown

Westminster

Falling Waters

Williamsport

Middletown

Libertytown

Martinsburg

Shepherdstown

Frederick

Sykesville

Baltimore

Cooksville

B. AND O. R.R.

Harpers Ferry

Winchester

Poolesville

Edward's Ferry

Rockville

Annapolis

SHENANDOAH VALLEY

SNICKERS GAP

Leesburg

Bowser's Ford

ASHBY GAP

Upperville

Aldie

Dranesville

MANASSAS GAP

Gum Spring

Washington

Salem

THOROUGHFARE GAP

Centerville

Fairfax C.H.

Alexandria

Bull Run

Buckland

Gainesville

Fairfax Station

Mt. Vernon

Warrenton

New Baltimore

Manassas

ORANGE AND ALEXANDRIA R.R.

Brentsville

WOLF RUN SHOALS

Dumfries

VIRGINIA

MARYLAND

Culpeper

Brandy Station

Aquia

RAPPAHANNOCK

RAPIDAN

Wilderness

Chancellorsville

Falmouth

Fredericksburg

POTOMAC

Note: Part of Ewell's Corps went through Emmitsburg, Gettysburg and York, then returned to vicinity of Gettysburg before Union Army reached that area.

ROUTE OF UNION TROOPS

ROUTES OF CONFEDERATES

0   5   10   15   20 Miles

RAILROADS   ROADS

might get to Philadelphia without a fight, I believe, if we should desire to go."

As the days of late June vanished and as letters from one occupied town after another relayed the news of how twenty-five barrels of sauerkraut had been requisitioned from this place, or how the sour looks of the natives had all but turned the drinking water into vinegar, or how the ironworks of Thaddeus Stevens had been burned to the ground, the invasion of Pennsylvania seemed at times more lark than war.

1

But the coming of the Confederates to Pennsylvania aroused dread in the breasts of thousands of people, among them Sallie Robbins Broadhead. A schoolteacher who had married an engineer, Sallie lived on the Chambersburg Pike near the center of the sleepy little town of Gettysburg. Day by day as the rumors grew into reality and Lee's troops, crossing the Potomac, swung northward, Sallie kept a diary—"with no other thought," she confessed, "than to aid in whiling away time filled up with anxiety, apprehension, and danger."

June 15. Today we heard that the Rebels were crossing the river in heavy force, and advancing on to this state. No alarm was felt until Governor Curtin sent a telegram directing the people to move their stores as quickly as possible. This made us begin to realize the fact that we were in some danger from the enemy, and some persons, thinking the Rebels were near, became very much frightened, though the report was a mistake.

June 16. Our town had a great fright last night between twelve and one o'clock. I had retired, and was soundly asleep, when my child cried for a drink of water. When I got up to get it, I heard so great a noise in the street that I went to the window, and the first thing I saw was a large fire, seemingly not far off, and the people were hallooing, "The Rebels are coming and burning as they go." Many left town, but, having waited for the fire to go down a little, I returned to bed and slept till morning. Then I learned that the fire was in Emmitsburg, ten miles from here, just over the Maryland line, and that the buildings were fired by one of her townsmen. Twenty-seven houses were burned, and thirty-six families made homeless, all efforts to stop the flames being useless, as owing to everything being so dry, they spread with great rapidity.

June 19. Another excitement today. The eighty-seventh Pennsylvania Volunteers is composed of men from this and adjacent counties, one company from our town being of the number.

Word came that the captain, both lieutenants, and nearly all the officers and men had been killed or captured. Such a time as we had with those having friends in the regiment! At ten o'clock it was rumored that some of the men were coming in on the Chambersburg Pike, and not long after about one dozen of those who lived in town came in, and their report and presence relieved some and agonized others.

Those whose friends were not of the party were in a heart-rending plight, for those returned ones could not tell of the others; some would say, "This one was killed or taken prisoner," and others, "We saw him at such a place, and the Rebels may have taken him," and so they were kept in suspense.

June 20. The report of today is that the Rebels are at Chambersburg and are advancing on here, and refugees begin to come in by scores.

Some say the Rebels number from twenty to thirty thousand, others that Lee's whole army is advancing this way.

All day we have been much excited.

June 21. Great excitement prevails and there is no reliable intelligence from abroad.

One report declares that the enemy are at Waynesboro, twenty miles off; another that Harrisburg is the point.

June 22. Sunday. The report now is that a large force is in the mountains about eighteen miles away, and a call is made for a party of men to go out and cut down trees to obstruct the passages of the mountains.

About fifty, among them my husband, started.

I was very uneasy lest they might be captured, but they

had not gone halfway when the discovery was made that it was too late; that the Rebels were on this side of the mountain, and coming this way. Our men turned back, uninjured, though their advance, composed of a few men, was fired upon. About seventy of the Rebels came within eight miles, and then returned by another road to their main force.

They stole all the horses and cattle they could find, and drove them back to their encampment.

We did not know but that the whole body would be down upon us, until eleven o'clock, when a man came in and said that he had seen them, and that they had recrossed. I shall now retire, and sleep much better than I had expected an hour since.

June 24. As I expected, the Rebels have several times been within two or three miles, but they have not yet reached here.

Two cavalry companies are on scouting duty here, but they can be of little use, as they have never seen service. Deserters come in every little while, who report the enemy near in large forces. This morning early a dispatch was received, saying that a regiment of infantry was coming from Harrisburg.

We do not feel much safer, for they are only raw militia. The train bringing them came within ten miles, when it ran over a cow which threw the cars off the track. No one was hurt, and they are now encamped near the place of the accident. The town is a little quieter than on yesterday. We are getting used to excitement, and many think the enemy, having been so long in the vicinity without visiting us, will not favor us with their presence.

They have carried off many horses. Some who had taken their stock away returned, supposing the Rebels had left the neighborhood, and lost their teams.

June 25. Today passed much as yesterday. Everyone is asking, "Where is our army, that they let the enemy scour the country and do as they please?" It is reported that Lee's whole army is this side of the river, and marching on Harrisburg; also that a large force is coming on here to destroy the railroad between there and Baltimore. Our militia did not come to town, but remained where they were yesterday.

2

With the division of George Edward Pickett as it advanced into Pennsylvania marched John Dooley. He was just twenty-one, a handsome boy, tall and lithe and proud, and his background as a member of the Virginian aristocracy had been so deeply impressed upon him that one day—long youthful years ago now—he could remember dashing home with the greatest scandal of his life: "Ma, 'Liza Plumes mother *works!*" But war became a mellowing experience for John Dooley; and the tenderness developing in him came out in the pages of his war journal as he trudged the weary miles toward Gettysburg.

Our division is the rearmost, and we are left in the vicinity of Chambersburg to cover the march of the main body advancing on Gettysburg, to protect the convoys of horses, cattle, etc., the spoils of our invasion, which with very frail guards were being constantly sent across the Potomac; and to be ready at a moment's warning to join the main army whenever the enemy might be found, for as yet we were ignorant of his position.

In and around the town of Chambersburg we found the people very sullen and maliciously disposed, and not a few maledictions were hurled at us from garret windows by croaking crones; and many young but frowning brows and pouting lips we saw in doorways and even on the sidewalks. But our boys laughed cheerfully, and when contempt and scorn where shown them answered by jests and witticisms.

I was not a little surprised to see on the muddy road a nicely dressed young girl without shoes or stockings on her feet; and her companion, evidently a menial, likewise barefoot, being distinguished however from her young mistress by the size and uncleanliness of her feet. Here anywhere may be seen young ladies in silks padding along the pavement without *shoes or stockings.* Such sights are worthy of note as manifesting one of the peculiar customs of this *race of people,* if indeed it be not a peculiarity arising from the war.

A girl came to the ambulance where Lieutenant Blair and others were, and told them with tears streaming down her cheeks that her brother had been killed in the second battle of Manassas. And this poor creature had no idea of how many sorrowing and breaking hearts there were in the South.

We know how straight into the very jaws of destruction and death leads this road of Gettysburg; and none of us are yet aware that a battle is before us; still there pervades our ranks a solemn feeling, as if some unforeseen danger was ever dropping darksome shadows over the road we unshrinkingly tread.

For myself, I must confess that the terrors of the battlefield grew not less as we advanced in the war, for I felt far less fear in the second battle of Manassas than at South Mountain or even at Fredericksburg; and I believe that soldiers generally do not fear death less because of their repeated escape from its jaws. For in every battle they see so many new forms of death, see so many frightful and novel kinds of mutilation, see such varying fortunes in the tide of strife, and appreciate so highly their deliverance from destruction, that their dread of incurring the like fearful perils unnerves them for each succeeding conflict, quite as much as their confidence in their oft tried courage sustains them and stimulates them to gain new laurels at the cannon's mouth.

Unpleasantly for myself, I am today in command of the rear guard, whose duty it is to urge forward stragglers and to keep up in fact all who desert their ranks under any pretense whatever. This is at times a painful duty, for frequently it happens—especially when the division is moving rapidly, as today—that many soldiers leave their ranks through necessity, and, weakened by diarrhoea, can scarcely with all their efforts rejoin the ranks. Others fall by the roadside either deadly sick or pretending to be so (and who can be sure that they are only pretending?); others are barefoot, and although they may have thrown away their shoes purposely so as to have an excuse for desertion and straggling, still their feet are bruised and even bleeding, and it is a hard thing to keep these men upon the move.

3

John Dooley, the foot soldier, loved Uncle Robert, the general. Although Dooley's contacts with his commander-in-chief were few, he cherished each; and from these rich memories, while marching toward Gettysburg, he could construct a portrait of Lee as he was known to the men who fought for the Army of Northern Virginia.

[*A morning after a battle*]: We have now settled down for a good rest and indeed we need it. General Lee, great, noble, kindhearted General Lee, has cheered us much. He set forth in feeling words his admiration of our heroism and endurance . . . . without the slightest exaggeration made every man of us a hero, adorned us with the laurels of victory, and filled our hearts with exuberant joy to think and to know that we have fulfilled the highest expectations and met with the highest approbation of our beloved leader. For who does not love General Lee, who would not barter life for his smile? And now that he speaks in words of love and admiration to his wearied troops, who does not feel every syllable burning in his very heart's core?

*

[*Lee on horseback*]: He is riding, perhaps, with a few aides, dressed in a neat gray uniform, mounted upon a gently moving charger. By the plain gray uniform you would simply recognize him as a general. His hair and beard turning gray; his mildly beaming face, large black eyes recognizing all around him; his mouth firmly but pleasingly set, and his whole figure expressing gentleness, dignity, and command. As he passes the admiring throngs they doff their warworn hats and greet his presence with reiterated shouts. . . . He answers each burst with a placid smile and with a dignified but most courteous bend of his noble head.

*

[*Lee crossing the Potomac*]: We crossed. . . . with General

Lee close to the riverbank, mounted and motionless as the night itself. Few reflect upon the anxiety which fills the breast of such a man upon an occasion when the lives and safety of so many depend on his will and direction.

*

[*Now, marching on Gettysburg*]: The wheat fields are everywhere nearly ripe for harvesting, and all around plenty appears to bless the fertile land. We destroy nothing uselessly, but in self-defense (on account of the roads) are obliged to cut a passage through these rich fields of wheat, which however is no larger than necessary; for our generals are even more careful of the property of these thrifty German farmers than they were of the lands and houses of their own soil. And General Lee was so solicitous for the safety of the fences that he dismounted this morning (so we are told) and on the muddy roadside made some of his staff officers assist him in putting up the portion of a rail fence which had been through negligence left down. We are further informed that several of the soldiers in the van of the army have already been shot by their general for plundering the houses of these peace-loving German Yankees.

4

As the days ran out toward the fateful first of July, concerns graver than rail fences began to weigh heavily on Lee's mind. During those uncertain days perhaps nothing was more constant in Lee's thoughts than the image of Jeb Stuart—lovable, dashing, showoffish Jeb, a man to swear by or to swear at, according to one's taste. The Union General Sedgwick had summed up the accepted opinion when he said: "Stuart is the best cavalryman ever foaled in North America." The entire Army of Northern Virginia depended on Stuart, and the events of the next few days were to be determined in large measure as much by Stuart's personality as by his military skill. In this sketch Colonel John Esten Cooke, who had served on Stuart's staff, reveals the nature of the commander he loved.

There was about the man a perennial interest as vivid with

those who saw him, hour by hour, as with strangers glancing at him in his splendid uniform at the head of his column, or leading a charge. The ardor, mirth, and romance of the man in his public phase were all natural, and as characteristic of him in private with friends and staff officers as on the field before the eyes of the world. He had an immensely strong physique, and unfailing animal spirits—loved song, laughter, jesting, rough practical jokes, and all the virile divertissements of camp. His surroundings were all in unison with his youthful love of movement, incident, and adventure. He rarely settled down, unless compelled to do so, in any formal headquarters. Thus his quarters were, except in winter, the most impromptu affairs. A canvas "fly" stretched over a pole, the horses affixed to the boughs of the forest near, saddled and champing their bits, the red battle flag rippling in the brilliant sunshine, couriers going and coming, the staff grouped around waiting, booted and spurred, for the order to mount, which they knew might come at any moment, and from the canvas tent the song or laughter of Stuart busy at his desk, from which he would rise from time to time to come to the opening, yawn, throw a jest at some one, and then return to his work—such, in brief outline, were these first bivouacs of Stuart, who always moved in "light marching order," that is to say, with his blanket behind his saddle, and his hat, gloves, and sabre beside him; a true cavalier, ready at all moments to be up and away.

With a very warm and kind heart, he had little of the softness of disposition which induces reluctance to punish neglect of duty. This latter trait is said to have, in some measure, characterized General Lee. It did not characterize Stuart. He was a very stern man where he had convinced himself that there was willful opposition to his orders, or even a failure, from negligence, to comply with them. From this resulted a very excellent state of discipline generally, and a wholesome indisposition to act in opposition to his known wishes or brave his displeasure. . . .

His quarters near Fredericksburg in the winter of 1862 he humorously styled "Camp No Camp." Here, with his tent pitched under shelter of a pine thicket, and his horses picketed near—for he believed that exposure hardened them—with a slender little Whitworth gun posted like a graceful watchdog in front, and surrounded by his mirthful young staff officers, Stuart passed the long months of the winter succeeding the hard battle. . . . At "Camp No Camp" the days and nights were full of song and laughter. Stuart's delight was to have his banjo-player, Sweeney, in his tent; and even while busily engaged in his official correspondence, he loved to hear the gay rattle of the instrument, and the voice of Sweeney singing "J'ine the Cavalry," "Sweet Eveline," or some other favorite ditty. From time to time he would lay down his pen, throw one knee over the arm of his chair, and call his two dogs—two handsome young setters, which he had brought across the Rappahannock—or falling back, utter some jest at the expense of his staff. As frequently he would join in the song, or volunteer one of his own—his favorites being "The Bugles Sang Truce," "The Dew is on the Blossom," and some comic ballads, of which the one beginning "My Wife's in Castle Thunder" was a fair specimen. These he roared out with immense glee, rising and gesticulating, slapping his staff officers on the back, and throwing back his head while he sang, and almost always ending in a burst of laughter.

5

In the Spring of 1863 as Lee prepared to move the Army of Northern Virginia toward the Potomac, Jeb Stuart had lost face in the affair at Brandy Station. Here the Union cavalry under Alfred Pleasonton had crossed the Rappahannock in the cool dawn haze of June 9. Heavily engaged in the front, then caught in the rear by another blue-coated detachment that had slipped across the river four miles below him, Stuart found himself in a trap. That after several hours of bitter struggle Stuart repulsed the Federals could neither explain why he had not known of the enemy's presence nor why the blunder had been worth 523 Confederate casualties. All Virginia flamed with indignation at the surprise attack, and doubtless even the young ladies who had come down to Culpeper a few nights before to dance with Stuart and his men were inclined to agree with the editorial in the *Richmond Examiner* for June 12: "If the war was a tournament, invented and supported for the pleasure of a few vain and weakheaded officers, these disasters might be dismissed with compassion." Infuriated, Stuart carried out his part of the beginning of the invasion—the screening of Hill and Longstreet as they advanced toward the Potomac. Then Lee sent Stuart orders to cross into Maryland and move northward into Pennsylvania. Stuart knew that he was not supposed to delay in joining his troops with Ewell's, but Maryland suddenly offered a rich prize that he could not resist. An unidentified newspaperman found himself caught in the path of Stuart's foray into Maryland.

Yesterday morning [June 28], at about half-past nine o'clock, I started from Washington in company with three officers of the topographical engineers. It was our intention to ride through to Frederick, stopping at Rockville for the purpose of taking dinner, but we all knew the liability of well-laid schemes, whether bi- or quadrupedal, to go wrong. By the time we reached our first post of cavalry pickets we came up with the rear of a long wagon train, comprising one hundred and fifty vehicles, each drawn by six mules, driven by a very black and picturesque Negro. This train must have been at least two miles long, for by the time we had reached the other end, riding leisurely, we were within a mile or two of Rockville. Here, just as we had passed the last wagon, an excited horseman, coming from the direction of Rockville, halted our party, and in a somewhat confused voice gave us the pleasing intelligence that about four hundred rebel cavalry were close at his heels. A short consultation of war resulted in our making up our minds to retreat. This conclusion was scarcely arrived at when two more men came full tilt past us, shouting that the rebels had fired on them and were close behind. Then came a cavalry soldier, one of the six who formed our paltry guard, leading a riderless horse, whose master (another of our guard) had just been shot. Then came thundering along a second trooper, much excited, and evidently charged with some important mission. He immediately halted all the mule teams, ordering them to turn back.

And now commenced a scene of excitement and confusion which none but a maniac could properly describe. Wagons upset by their drivers in abortive attempts to turn them round, others locked together, mule teams inextricably snarled up, and through this jam and mess some twenty or thirty horsemen (your correspondent among the number) galloping like mad. Had the devil been behind us, it would have been impossible to go faster; as fast as the frightened horses could lay their legs to the ground they went, kicking up stones and earth with their heels in the most exciting manner. Two scared farmers led the retreat on powerful horses, and so long as they galloped it was impossible to stop any of the other horses. At last we got sufficiently far from the train to deem ourselves safe, and as the farmers had got out of reach, we pulled up and reconnoiterd. Away far back on the road we could distinguish smoke from the burning teams. They were doubtless all destroyed. All the mules were captured, and two ambulances containing officers were likewise gobbled up.

At about four o'clock we, the fortunate ones, reached the city, [Washington] after a six hours' ride of nearly thirty miles, very sore and very tired.

6

W. W. Blackford, riding with Stuart, quickly found thrills and dangers intermingled—first in Rockville, then later on turning back into Pennsylvania.

Galloping full tilt into the head of the train, we captured a small guard and a lot of gayly dressed quartermasters, and over half the wagons, before they could turn round; but then those beyond took the alarm, turned and fled as fast as their splendid mule teams could go. After them we flew, popping away with our pistols at such drivers as did not pull up, but the more we popped the faster those in front plied the whip;

finally, coming to a sharp turn in the road, one upset and a dozen or two others piled up on top of it, until you could see nothing but the long ears and kicking legs of the mules sticking above bags of oats emptied from the wagons upon them. All behind this blockade were effectually stopped, but half a dozen wagons had made the turn before this happened and after them two or three of us dashed. It was as exciting as a fox chase for several miles, until when the last was taken I found myself on a hill in full view of Washington. One hundred and twenty-five uninjured wagons were taken and safely brought into our lines, together with the animals of the others. Here was a godsend to our poor horses, for every wagon was loaded with oats for Meade's army and it did one's heart good to see the way the poor brutes got on the outside of those oats. After giving my horses all they could eat I slung half a bag, saddle-bag fashion, across my saddle for future use, and my horse seemed to know what this additional load was, for he occasionally turned an affectionate glance back toward it. . . .

With the exception of a squadron of the enemy, encountered at Winchester, we met no opposition until Hanover was reached about noon on the thirtieth. It seems remarkable that the enemy should not have used more enterprise than this, for we were destroying his communications as we advanced. At Hanover, however, we met Kilpatrick's Division of cavalry and had a hot affair with them. We were just opposite Gettysburg and if we could have made our way direct, the fifteen miles of distance to that place would have passed that day, and we would have effected a junction with General Lee the day before the battle began. It was here the wagon train began to interfere with our movements, and if General Stuart could only have known what we do now it would have been burned; but he knew nothing of the concentration which accidental circumstances were to bring about at Gettsyburg in the next two days, and as he expected to meet Early at York very soon, he held on to them.

The Second North Carolina Regiment made the first charge through the town, driving the enemy out, but receiving strong reinforcements they rallied and drove the North Carolinians back in their turn in great confusion. As General Stuart saw them rushing out of the place, he started down the road to meet them, calling me to follow him. We tried to rally them, but the long charge *in* and the repulse *out* and the hot skirmish fire opened upon them from the windows on the street by citizens had thrown them into utter confusion, and in spite of all we could do they got by us, and before we were aware of it we found ourselves at the head of the enemy's charging column.

The road was lined on each side by an ill-kept hedge grown up high, but at some places, fortunately for us, there were gaps of lower growth. Stuart pulled up and, waving his sabre with a merry laugh, shouted to me, "Rally them, Blackford!" and then lifted his mare, Virginia, over the hedge into the field. I knew that he only said what he did to let me know that he was off, so I followed him. I had only that morning, fortunately, mounted Magic, having had her led previously, and Stuart had done the same with Virginia, so they were fresh. As we alighted in the field, we found ourselves within ten paces of the front of a flanking party of twenty-five or thirty men which was accompanying the charging regiment, and they called to us to halt; but as we let our two thoroughbreds out, they followed in hot pursuit, firing as fast as they could cock their pistols. The field was in tall timothy grass and we did not see, nor did our horses until close to it, a huge gully fifteen feet wide and as many deep stretched across our path. There were only a couple of strides of distance for our horses to regulate their step, and Magic had to rise at least six feet from the brink. Stuart and myself were riding side by side and as soon as Magic rose I turned my head to see how Virginia had done it, and I shall never forget the glimpse I then saw of this beautiful animal away up in mid-air over the chasm and Stuart's fine figure sitting erect and firm in the saddle. Magic, seeing the size of the place and having received a very unusual sharp application of my spurs, had put out her strength to its full in this leap and she landed six or seven feet beyond the further bank, making a stride of certainly twenty-seven feet. The moment our horses rose, our pursuers saw that there was something there, and it was with difficulty they could pull up in time to avoid plunging headlong into it, and their firing was of course arrested.

7

As Jeb Stuart rampaged through Maryland, capturing a Federal wagon train and tearing up the tracks of the B. & O., he was having the time of his life, but he wasn't helping Lee. John Dooley's war journal revealed that even the foot soldier felt uneasy because of Stuart: "There are also from seven to ten thousand cavalry who should be with us· but who, under the command of their dashing general, are far away toward Washington City, leaving our infantry and artillery unguarded in flank and rear, and stripping our cautious Lee of sufficient force to explore the exact position of the enemy." But these were worries to fill the minds of soldiers and generals; for thirteen-year-old Billy Bayly the coming of war into Pennsylvania posed other problems.

One day late in June, 1863, we had been busy haying until noon, when a rain set in and drove us to the shelter of the house. All sorts of rumors were flying as to the approach of the enemy and there was consequent anxiety and apprehension on the part of the elders in my family, the farm hands and neighbors who came and went during the forenoon. "The Rebels are coming this time!" and "The advance has crossed the mountain foothills only eight miles west," was the word passed during the morning. After the noon meal I found a cool spot in the darkened room in the house and went to sleep, only to be wakened with the rude intelligence that the "Rebs were coming" and that father wanted me at the barn at once. I stood not on the order of my going, but ran to the barn barefooted and coatless, where father had two of the best horses saddled, and I was tossed on the back of "Nellie," a beautiful chestnut mare, and told to follow. Passing the house, my mother ran out with coat and shoes for me, which, however, I did not then take time to put on.

Along the wood-bordered ridge which constituted the west boundary of the farm we could see soldiers moving at a rapid pace in an easterly direction—the general direction in which we were going. The afternoon being cloudy and dark, with rain still falling, made it impossible for us to distinguish uniforms, and we knew not whether the soldiers were friends or foes. But we took no chance and rode off at a John Gilpin rate, I using my coat and shoes forcibly to urge "Nellie" to more rapid motion. One of my uncles living in the vicinity and other neighbors had ridden up to the barn while father was saddling the horses, but seeing the "Rebs," as they supposed, only a quarter of a mile distant, hastily fled leaving us to follow. As we were well mounted, we soon overtook the party and remained with them three or four days.

Our first purpose was to go toward Harrisburg, but fearing that the enemy had cut us off in that direction, we turned toward Hanover.

On crossing one of the roads radiating from Gettysburg, I noticed a horseman coming over the hill toward us and being anxious for information about the enemy, I hung back and let my party go on, having every confidence in the fleetness of my mount. The horseman, covered with a rubber poncho splashed with mud, rode up to where my horse was standing, and I recognized him as a recruit in Bell's Cavalry whom I knew, so I said, "Hello, Bill! What's up?"

Bill replied, "If you don't get out of here pretty quick you'll find out what's up. The Rebel Cavalry chased me out of town about fifteen minutes ago, and must now be close on my heels."

My desire for information not being satisfied however, I said, "But where is the rest of your company?"

"Oh hell," said the trooper, "I don't know; they ran long before I did. But you git or you'll be got." And away he rode toward Harrisburg and I after my party.

Our riding party continued for about fifteen miles, and darkness approaching, concluded that the Rebels would not overtake us that night so we put up with a farmer who fed us abundantly, and I was tired enough to sleep soundly regardless of what the morrow might bring forth.

We rode away in the morning leaving one of my cousins who was older than I to follow later and overtake us at another farmhouse. We received our first shock and surprise by the sudden appearance of four Confederate cavalrymen. To say that we were bait in a trap caught by our own stupidity about describes the situation. The barn on this place was unusually large even for a country noted for commodious barns. There were about twenty horses stabled in it, including ours, and we all thought what a fine haul they would get.

While some of the men got into a heated argument with the soldiers over the war, my father, uncle and the other boy and I worked our way quietly to the barn, the farmhouse shielding us from view. We contrived to get our horses, mounted in hot haste, and, jumping over the barnyard fence into the meadow, cut for the timber about a quarter of a mile distant. . . . After a run of several miles we came to a halt in a heavily wooded section in York County, where we concealed our horses and were given personal accommodations in a near-by farmhouse. Hay and corn and water were carried to the horses for two days, the Confederate cavalry in the meantime having passed us by the main roads on their way to York and the Susquehanna River. Learning this, we left our place of concealment and rode back the thirty-odd miles to our respective homes.

When we arrived at my home I well remember the warm welcome of my mother, who reported, however, that no damage had been done by the troops. She had in some manner (by serving a good meal is my recollection) secured the goodwill of an officer who placed a guard on the premises. No Confederate soldiers were in evidence when we returned home, and not until two days later did we have our introduction to a part of General Lee's army.

Chapter 2

"No Band of Schoolgirls"

WHENEVER THE Army of the Potomac moved it was as though a city like Albany or Columbus or Indianapolis had arisen one morning and walked away complete in every detail—clothing, food, medicine, ammunition, horses, wagons, people. Seldom did this great army of the North move with less than one hundred thousand men, and at times its strength was as large as one hundred and twenty-five thousand. The pride and the confidence of a nation in so great an army should have been unshakable, the morale of its soldiers above reproach, and yet as Lee invaded Pennsylvania and the North looked to the Army of the Potomac to drive out the Rebel hordes neither of these conditions was precisely true. That the foot soldier in the Army of the Potomac received forty cents a day for his services and then was paid off in greenbacks barely worthy fifty cents on the dollar was a source of grumbling, but not of despair; the weakness of the army was two years of bungling, inept generalship.

In those sultry summer days of 1863 as the Army of the Potomac drew back from the Rappahannock and wheeled around to chase Lee into Pennsylvania two grim memories haunted its movements—Fredericksburg and Chancellorsville. At Fredericksburg its commander had been Ambrose E. Burnside, who liked to sit erect on his dark-brown bobtail horse reviewing his troops, but as his men marched by, turning their heads sharply right, the impression they carried of their leader was not entirely complimentary—a portly and handsome man, side whiskers, mustache, beautiful white teeth, but no dash or rousing expression in his face. It was Burnside, the bungler, who allowed Lee to entrench his troops on Marye's Hill at Fredericksburg and then six times ordered the Union forces to charge—to charge into the fire of a hundred cannon, into a live volcano of hell that left 1,180 of his men killed on the field, another 9,028 wounded, and 2,145 taken prisoner.

At Chancellorsville the Army of the Potomac fought under a new commander in Joseph Hooker—"Fighting Joe," his men called him, and as they scanned his steel-blue eyes, his sandy hair, and clear-cut features they remembered that Hooker personally had tried to dissuade Burnside from the second mad charge at Marye's Hill. With the Virginia dogwoods all in bloom, the Army of the Potomac—in good trim and heart—marched down to Chancellorsville to even scores with "the Confederate gamecock." But again Lee won, not by numbers but by superior generalship, and Hooker's strongest excuse for his failure was the fact that in the very pinch of the battle, while standing on the porch of the Chancellor House, a Confederate cannon ball struck a pillar of the porch against which he was leaning, and the pillar in falling knocked him senseless. With Hooker dazed, half paralyzed, helpless for several hours, the Army of the Potomac suffered at Chancellorsville not only for the want of a commander, but also for want of a commanding staff. The battle was fought piecemeal—not more than half of the Union troops were put into action—and a victory that had seemed certain turned into another costly and melancholy defeat.

Hooker still commanded the Army of the Potomac in June, 1863, as the focal point of the war swung from the South to the North. Despite the smarting setback at Chancellorsville— if there had been any Northern gain at all in that engagement it could be reckoned only in the fact that, both figuratively and literally, Lee had lost the right arm of his command through the death of Stonewall Jackson—Hooker was content in the belief that since then he had acquitted himself with distinction by checkmating every move Lee had made in Virginia, and he was confident that if given another chance he could whip the Army of Northern Virginia. But three important men failed to share this belief with Hooker. The first was Edwin M. Stanton, Secretary of War; the second, Henry W. Halleck, Chief of Staff; the third, Abraham Lincoln.

1

With the Army of the Potomac during those days of decision rode Frank Arteas Haskell. Born in Vermont, educated at Dartmouth, afterward a lawyer in Madison, Wisconsin, Haskell served with the famous Iron Brigade as aide-de-camp to General Gibbon. Thirteen days after the battle of Gettysburg, Haskell wrote a letter to his brother that must rank among classic American historical documents. In descriptive phrases that many times are masterful, with an understanding of the signifiance of events that often would have done credit to an historian generations later, Haskell recorded what he saw and heard and felt. Less than a year after Gettysburg he was dead, killed on the battlefield at Cold Harbor. But in the passage that follows—and in other passages that will appear frequently in the pages of this book—the genius of Frank Arteas Haskell is entirely alive. The reader will understand the simple precaution that, when reading some of the severe reflections the author casts upon certain officers and soldiers of the Union army, it is wise to remember that Haskell never intended these remarks for publication.

The great battle of Gettysburg . . . did not so "cast its shadow before," as to moderate the hot sunshine that streamed upon our preceding march, or to relieve our minds of all apprehension of the result of the second great Rebel invasion of the soil North of the Potomac.

No, not many days since, at times we were filled with fears and forebodings. The people of the country, I suppose, shared the anxieties of the Army, somewhat in common with us, but they could not have felt them as keenly as we did. We were upon the immediate theatre of events, as they occurred from day to day, and were of them. We were the Army whose province it should be to meet this invasion and repel it; on us was the immediate responsibility for results, most momentous for good or ill, as yet in the future. And so in addition to the solicitude of all good patriots, we felt that our own honor as men and as an army, as well as the safety of the Capitol and the country, were at stake.

And what if that invasion should be successful, and in the coming battle the Army of the Potomac should be overpowered? Would it not be? When our Army was much larger than at present—had rested all winter—and nearly perfect in all its departments and arrangements, was the most splendid army this continent ever saw, only a part of the Rebel force, which it now had to contend with, had defeated it—its leader, rather—at Chancellorsville! Now the Rebel had his whole force assembled, he was flushed with recent victory, was arrogant in his career of unopposed invasion, at a favorable season of the year. His daring plans, made by no unskilled head, to transfer the war from his own to his enemies' ground, were being successful. He had gone a day's march from his front before Hooker moved, or was aware of his departure. Then, I believe, the army in general, both officers and men, had no confidence in Hooker, in either his honesty or ability.

Did they not charge him, personally, with the defeat at Chancellorsville? Were they not still burning with indignation against him for that disgrace? And now, again under his leadership, they were marching against the enemy! And they knew of nothing, short of the providence of God, that could, or would, remove him. For many reasons during the marches prior to the battle, we were anxious, and at times heavy at heart.

But the Army of the Potomac was no band of schoolgirls. They were not the men likely to be crushed or utterly discouraged by any new circumstances in which they might find themselves placed. They had lost some battles, they had gained some. They knew what defeat was, and what was victory. But here is the greatest praise that I can bestow upon them, or upon any army: With the elation of victory, or the depression of defeat, amidst the hardest toils of the campaign, under unwelcome leadership, at all times, and under all circumstances, they were a reliable army still. The Army of the Potomac would do as it was told, always.

Well clothed and well fed—there never could be any ground for complaint on these heads—but a mighty work was before them. Onward they moved—night and day were blended—over many a weary mile, through dust, through mud, in the broiling sunshine, in the flooding rain, over steeps, through defiles, across rivers, over last year's battlefields where the skeletons of our dead brethren by hundreds lay bare and bleaching, weary, without sleep for days, tormented with the newspapers and their rumors that the enemy was in Philadelphia, in Baltimore, in all places where he was not, yet these men could still be relied upon, I believe, when the day of conflict should come. *"Haec olim meninisse juvabit."* We did not then know this. I mention them now, that you may see that in those times we had several matters to think about, and to do, that were not as pleasant as sleeping upon a bank of violets in the shade.

In moving from near Falmouth, Virginia, the Army was formed in several columns, and took several roads. The Second Corps, the rear of the whole, was the last to move, and left Falmouth at daybreak on the fifteenth of June, and pursued its march through Aquia, Dumfries, Wolf Run Shoals, Centerville, Gainsville, Thoroughfare Gap—this last we left on the twenty-fifth, marching back to Haymarket, where we had a skirmish with the cavalry and horse artillery of the enemy—Gum Spring, crossing the Potomac at Edward's Ferry, thence through Poolesville, Frederick, Liberty, and Union Town. We marched from near Frederick to Union Town, a distance of thirty-two miles, from eight o'clock A.M. to nine P.M., on the twenty-eighth, and I think this is the longest march, accomplished in so short a time, by a corps during the war. On the twenty-eighth, while we were near this latter place, we breathed a full breath of joy and of hope. The providence of God had been with us—we ought not to have doubted it—General Meade commanded the Army of the Potomac.

2

Whitelaw Reid, brilliant young correspondent for the *Cincinnati Gazette,* pictured the shock this announcement produced in the nation's capital.

Washington was all a-buzz with the removal. A few idol-worshippers hissed their exultation at the constructive disgrace; but for the most part, there was astonishment at the unprecedented act and indignation at the one cause to which all attributed it—Halleck. How the cause worked, how they quarrelled about holding Harper's Ferry, how Hooker was relieved in consequence, and how, within an hour afterward, Halleck stultified himself by telling Hooker's successor [Meade] to do as he pleased concerning this very point, all this will be in print long before this letter can get west.

For once, Washington forgot its blasé air, and, through a few hours, there was a genuine, old-fashioned excitement. The two or three Congressmen who happened to be in town were indignant, and scarcely tried to conceal it; the crowds talked over the strange affair in all its phases; a thousand false stories were put in circulation, the basest of which, perhaps, was that Hooker had been relieved for a fortnight's continuous drunkenness; rumors of other changes, as usual, came darkening the very air.

Never before, in the history of modern warfare, had there been such a case. A General had brought his army by brilliant forced marches face to face with the enemy. They were at the very crisis of the campaign; a great battle, perhaps the battle of the war, was daily if not hourly impending. No fault of generalship was alleged, but it happened that a parlor chieftain [Halleck], in his quiet study, three score miles from the hourly-changing field, differed in judgment on a single point from the General at the head of the troops. The latter carefully examined anew the point in issue, again satisfied himself, and insisted on his conviction, or on his relief from responsibility for a course he felt assured was utterly wrong. For this he was relieved—and within five hours was vindicated by his own successor.

But a good, perhaps a better general was put in his place— except for the unfortunate timing of the change, we had good reason to hope it would work at least no harm. There was little regret for Hooker personally; it was only the national sense of fair play that was outraged.

3

Haskell rejoiced in the transfer of command.

Not a favorable time, one would be apt to suppose, to change the general of a large army on the eve of battle, the result of which might be to destroy the government and country! But it should have been done long before. At all

events, any change could not have been for the worse, and
the administration, therefore, hazarded little in making it now.
From this moment my own mind was easy concerning results. I now felt that we had a clear-headed, honest soldier
to command the Army, who would do his best always—that
there would be no repetition of Chancellorsville. Meade was
not as much known in the Army as many of the other corps
commanders, but the officers who knew, all thought highly
of him, a man of great modesty, with none of those qualities
which are noisy and assuming, and hankering for cheap newspaper fame, not at all of the *"gallant"* Sickles stamp. I happened to know much of General Meade—he and General
Gibbon had always been very intimate, and I had seen much
of him—I think my own notions concerning General Meade
at this time were shared quite generally by the Army; at all
events, all who knew him shared them.

By this time, by reports that were not mere rumors, we
began to hear frequently of the enemy and of his proximity.
His cavalry was all about us, making little raids here and
there, capturing now and then a few of our wagons, and
stealing a good many horses, but doing us really the least
amount possible of harm, for we were not by these means
impeded at all; and his cavalry gave no information at all to
Lee that he could rely upon of the movements of the Army
of the Potomac. The infantry of the enemy was at this time
in the neighborhood of Hagerstown, Chambersburg, and some
had been at Gettysburg, possibly were there now. Gettysburg
was a point of strategic importance, a great many roads, some
ten or twelve at least concentrating there, so the Army could
easily converge to, or, should a further march be necessary,
diverge from this point. General Meade, therefore, resolved to
try to seize Gettysburg, and accordingly gave the necessary
orders for the concentration of his different columns there.
Under the new auspices the Army brightened, and moved on
with a more elastic step toward the yet undefined field of
conflict.

4

Haskell's castigation of Hooker is needlessly harsh, and it

would have sufficed to say that whereas at Chancellorsville his strategy may have been good, his tactics failed. For "Fighting Joe" had his friends as well as his enemies within the Army of the Potomac—friends who would have pointed out how he had set up brigade bakeries and brought fresh bread in place of hardtack to his soldiers, and how after the Proclamation of Emancipation he had dealt severely with the deserters who declared that "they did not enlist to fight for the Niggers." When on June 28—the day that Jeb Stuart was spying out the Federal wagon train at Rockville—Lincoln appointed George G. Meade commander of the Army, Hooker packed up his personal effects and left without any effort to disguise his bitter disappointment. And Meade, taking over the command, chose to address his Army:

By direction of the President of the United States, I hereby assume command of the Army of the Potomac. As a soldier, in obeying this order—an order totally unexpected and unsolicited—I have no promises or pledges to make. The country looks to this Army to relieve it from the devastation and disgrace of a hostile invasion. Whatever fatigues and sacrifices we may be called upon to undergo, let us have in view constantly the magnitude of the interests involved, and let each man determine to do his duty, leaving to an all-controlling Providence the decision of the contest. It is with just diffidence that I relieve in the command of this Army an eminent and accomplished soldier, whose name must ever appear conspicuous in the history of its achievements; but I rely upon the hearty support of my companions in arms to assist me in the discharge of the important trust which has been confided to me.

5

A graduate of West Point, a native Pennsylvanian, Meade was quickly popular with his men despite the fact that his sudden elevation from commander of the Fifth Corps to general of the army came as a surprise—to no one so much as to Meade himself. Hooker had been a brilliant conversationalist, the *beau ideal* of the army; Meade was simply a

quiet man who worked with his head and his heart. James
F. Rusling, brigadier general by brevet with the Army of the
Potomac, pictures Meade in camp.

I saw much of General Meade during this period, and came
to have a high appreciation of his mind and character. I
found him to be a conscientious and hard worker; as a rule,
rising early and retiring late. He did not seem to care much
for "Reviews," but believed greatly in reports and inspections,
and by means of these and his own keen observations kept
himself well informed as to the character and condition of
all parts of the Army. He was not social—had few, indeed,
of the popular arts that Hooker possessed—was habitually
grave and reticent. But he was accessible for all needed purposes, and constantly grew in the estimation of capable and
worthy officers.

Of course, we lived in tents, and as the autumn came on
our huge headquarter campfire became a point of reunion
for all headquarter officers, especially after nightfall. Here
every evening you would find Meade, with his hands clasped
behind him and his head bent forward, with his fatigue cap or
old slouch hat well down over his eyes, chatting gravely with
Humphrey, his chief of staff, or Seth Williams, his adjutant
general, or Ingalls, his chief quartermaster, or Hunt, his
chief of artillery, or Warren, his chief engineer, or other general officers that happened along, and midnight often found
his solitary candle still burning in his tent and the commander
in chief hard at work there.

As a rule, he was a better listener than talker. Ingalls and
Hunt were the great talkers there, and they both talked ex-
ceedingly well, and Warren, too, was keen and bright. What
campaigns they planned and unplanned! How they outwitted
Lee and ended the rebellion again and again! What camp
stories they told! What old soldier "yarns" they spun! Meade's
sense of humor was not large, but he was keen and intelli-
gent, his mind worked broadly and comprehensively, his
patriotism was perfect, his sense of duty intense; and he would
willingly have laid down his life at any time had our cause

required it. In manner he was often sharp and peremptory, but this was because of his utter absorption in great affairs.

6

Reid, catching up with the Army of the Potomac, also was impressed by Meade.

In a plain little wall-tent, just like the rest, pen in hand, seated on a camp-stool and bending over a map, is the new "General commanding" for the Army of the Potomac. Tall, slender, not ungainly, but certainly not handsome or graceful, thin-faced with grizzled beard and moustache, a broad and high but retreating forehead, from each corner of which the slightly-curling hair recedes, as if giving premonition of baldness—apparently between forty-five and fifty years of age—altogether a man who impresses you rather as a thoughtful student than as a dashing soldier—so General Meade looks in his tent.

"I tell you, I think a great deal of that fine fellow Meade," I chanced to hear the President say, a few days after Chancellorsville. Here was the result of that good opinion. There is every reason to hope that the events of the next few days will justify it.

7

—And so the Army of the Potomac marched on Gettysburg with a new commander. Lee already had set up his headquarters at Cashtown, only eight miles away from where Sallie Robbins Broadhead sensed that irresistible forces had been released.

June 26. Our militia passed through town this morning about ten o'clock, and encamped about three miles to the west.

Before they had unpacked their baggage, a scout came in with a report, which proved true, that the enemy was quite near.

Our men then had to retreat and get off the best way they could. About two hundred were captured. The town was quiet after our men retreated, until about two o'clock P.M., when a report spread that the Rebels were only two miles from town.

No one believed this, for they had so often been reported as just coming, and had as often failed to appear, and little attention was now paid to the rumor.

When, however, the wagons of the militia came thundering through the streets, and the guard stated that they had been chased back, we began to realize that the report was a fact. In about half an hour the entrance of Jenkins' Rebel cavalry began, and they came with such horrid yells that it was enough to frighten us all to death. They came in on three roads, and we soon were surrounded by them.

We all stood in the doors whilst the cavalry passed, but when the infantry came we closed them for fear they would run into our houses and carry off everything we had, and went up stairs and looked out of the windows.

They went along very orderly, only asking every now and then how many Yankee soldiers we had in town. I answered one that I did not know. He replied: "You are a funny woman; if I lived in town I would know that much." The last regiment stacked arms on both sides of the street in front of our door, and remained for an hour. They were a miserable-looking set. They wore all kinds of hats and caps, even to heavy fur ones, and some were barefooted. The Rebel band was playing Southern tunes in the Diamond. I cannot tell how bad I felt to hear them, and to see the traitors' flag floating overhead.

My humiliation was complete when I saw our men marching behind them surrounded by a guard. Last of all came an officer, and behind him a Negro on as fine a horse as I ever saw. One, looking up, and noticing my admiration of the animal, said: "We captured this horse from General Milroy, and do you see the wagons up there? We captured them, too. How we did whip the Yankees and we intend to do it again soon." I hope they may not.

June 27. I passed the most uncomfortable night of my life. My husband had gone in the cars to Hanover Junction, not thinking the Rebels were so near, or that there was much danger of their coming to town, and I was left entirely alone, surrounded by thousands of ugly, rude, hostile soldiers, from whom violence might be expected. Even if the neighbors were at hand, it was not pleasant, and I feared my husband would be taken prisoner before he could return, or whilst trying to reach me. I was not disturbed, however, by anything except my fears, and this morning when I got up I found that the Rebels had departed, having, on the night of the twenty-seventh, burned the railroad bridge over Rock Creek, just outside of the town and the cars that had brought up the militia, and had torn up the track and done other mischief. I became more uneasy about my husband, and I went to see some of the railroad hands to find out what I could relating to him. They told me that he had been captured and paroled, and that he had gone to Harrisburg; so I feel easier, and hope to rest tonight. Three of our scouts came in this morning just after the Rebels left, and report a large force of our soldiers near, making all feel much safer.

June 28. Sunday. About ten o'clock a large body of our cavalry began to pass through town, and we were all busy feeding them as they passed along. It seemed to me that the long line would never get through.

I hope they may catch the Rebels and give them a sound thrashing. Some say we may look for a battle here in a few days, and others say it will be fought near Harrisburg. There is no telling where it will be.

June 29. Quiet has prevailed all day. Our cavalry came up with the Rebels at Hanover, fourteen miles from here, and had quite a spirited fight, driving them through the town. Their infantry had reached York and had taken possession, as they did here, and demanded goods, stores, and money; threatening, if the demand was not complied with, to burn the town. Dunce-like the people paid them $28,000 which they pocketed, and passed on to Wrightsville. A company of our militia guarded the approach of the Rebels, and fired the bridge, which was entirely consumed, preventing the enemy from setting foot on the east bank, and ending their offensive movements for a time.

June 30. My husband came home last night at one o'clock,

having walked from Harrisburg, thirty-six miles, since nine o'clock of yesterday morning.

His return has put me in good spirits. I wonder that he escaped the Rebels, who are scouring the country between here and there.

Fatigue is all the ill that befell him. This morning the Rebels came to the top of the hill overlooking the town on the Chambersburg Pike, and looked over at our place.

We had a good view of them from our house, and every moment we expected to hear the booming of cannon, and thought they might shell the town. As it turned out, they were only reconnoitering the town preparatory to an advance if no force opposed them. We were told that a heavy force of our soldiers was within five miles, and the Rebels, learning that a body of cavalry was quite near, retraced their steps and encamped some distance from town.

It begins to look as though we will have a battle soon, and we are in great fear.

Chapter 3

"I Had Just Put My Bread in the Pans"

WHEN CONFEDERATE General Henry Heth awoke on the morning of July 1 it was not yet five o'clock, and the sun, stealing quietly over the Pennsylvania hills, gave promise of another hot, sultry day. Commander of a division in A. P. Hill's Third Corps, a Virginian well respected throughout the Army of Northern Virginia for his quick mind and social graciousness, Heth had still to become used to his new rank of major general won at Chancellorsville.

But this morning Heth was less concerned with rank than with shoes. Yesterday Johnston Pettigrew, another of Hill's division generals, had set off for Gettysburg to secure shoes for the bare-footed men of the Third Corps, but near Gettysburg Pettigrew had encountered a Union cavalry outpost and had returned to Cashtown empty-handed. Heth wanted those shoes. Now as he arose, splashing water into his sleepy eyes, he recalled a conversation of the previous evening with Hill.

"The only force at Gettysburg is cavalry, probably a detachment of observation," Hill had said with confidence.

"If there is no objection," Heth had replied, "I will take my division and go to Gettysburg tomorrow and get those shoes."

Hill had assented.

Once Heth could shake the sleep out of his eyes that morning he moved quickly, and by five o'clock he was ready to start for Gettysburg. He traveled in force, taking with him Archer's experienced brigade, Joe Davis's brigade, Pettigrew's North Carolinians, Field's Virginians, Pegram's battalion of artillery. And Hill, never forgetful that this was enemy country, decided to have the division under Dorsey Pender follow immediately behind—not that there would be any real danger, but war was unpredictable.

51

1

Perhaps a mile and a half from Gettysburg along the Chambersburg Pike is Willoughby Run. Here Heth, watchful and uncertain, stopped to observe the terrain, his thoughts going back a mile and a half to where blue vedettes had been encountered but had promptly withdrawn. To his right, as Heth looked down on Willoughby Run, there was a cover of woods. Union troops could be hidden there. Playing every step safe now, Heth ordered the woods shelled and waited. Nothing happened. Deploying Archer's Brigade on the left and Davis's on the right, Heth advanced. And from the other side of Willoughby Run Lieutenant Colonel H. E. Dana watched the Confederates coming down the road and recorded the scene as the opening shot at Gettysburg was fired.

About daylight on the first of July the report came in from Lieutenant Jones in charge of the pickets that the enemy were in sight; and a short time afterwards, perhaps fifteen minutes, while on my way out with the reserve, the report met me that the enemy was moving toward us. When I reached the outposts, about sunrise, I could see the enemy's skirmish line advancing slowly and reaching from right to left across the Cashtown Road, as we thought, for a distance of a mile and a half, concealed at intervals by timber, but evidently a continuous line formed for advancing a short distance in the rear of this skirmish line. In the open road, in our front, were lines of infantry deploying in the woods, evidently forming their line of battle.

I immediately forwarded a report of my observations to headquarters, then dismounting my entire company and sending the horses to the rear, called in the pickets and formed the first line of twenty men including myself. This line was formed a few hundred yards in the rear of the picket line held during the night, the position being more favorable for observation— it ran across the pike and railroad bed—Lieutenant Marcellus E. Jones, Eighth Illinois Cavalry, *firing the first shot* a little after sunrise before leaving the outposts. The enemy advanced steadily, though slow and cautiously. Our first position proved to be well taken—in front there was a large open field. Scat-

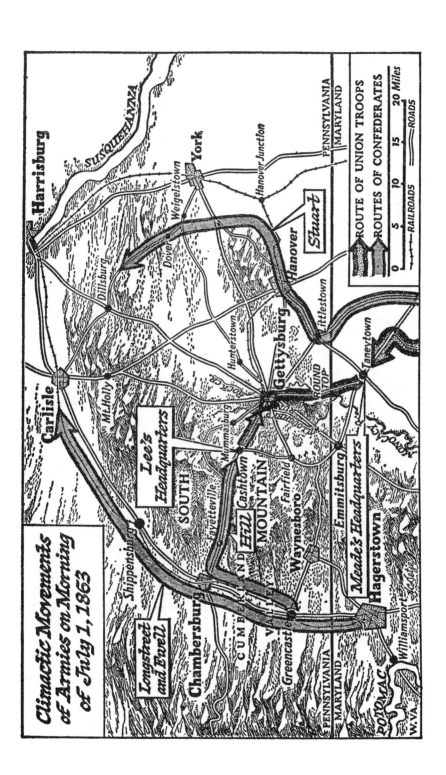

Climactic Movements of Armies on Morning of July 1, 1863

SUSQUEHANNA

Harrisburg

York

Weigelstown

Dover

Hanover Junction

PENNSYLVANIA
MARYLAND

Stuart

Dillsburg

Hanover

Carlisle

Mt.Holly

Huntterstown

Littlestown

Lee's Headquarters

ROCK CR

Gettysburg

ROUND TOP

Taneytown

SOUTH

Mummasburg

Cashtown

Longstreet and Ewell

Shippensburg

Fayetteville

AND HILL MOUNTAIN

Fairfield

Emmitsburg

MONOCACY

Meade's Headquarters

CUMBERLAND

Waynesboro

Chambersburg

Greencastle

PENNSYLVANIA
MARYLAND

Hagerstown

POTOMAC

Williamsport

W. VA.

ROUTE OF UNION TROOPS
ROUTES OF CONFEDERATES
RAILROADS
ROADS

0 5 10 15 20 Miles

tering my men to the right and left at intervals of thirty feet, and behind posts and rail fences, I directed them to throw up their carbine sights for eight hundred yards, then taking rest on the top rail, we gave the enemy the benefit of long-range practice from a long, much attenuated line. The firing was rapid from our carbines, and, at the time, induced the belief of four times the number of men actually present, as we learned from prisoners taken soon afterward.

2

For Billy Bayly the battle of Gettysburg began under somewhat different circumstances.

My father, unsuspectingly, started with a horse and buggy to town on some errand, and we did not see him until the next afternoon. Mother also had left the house, having been called to a sick neighbor's. I, with a boy's restlessness, concluded to go somewhere too, and in company with several boys my own age, walked to Gettysburg. The exact hour I cannot recall, but think it must have been about nine o'clock, for I know we found the first evidence of the arrival of the Army of the Potomac as we pattered in our bare feet up the main street of the town.

We did not stay long, exciting and glorious as it was to see troops swing into town, deploy pickets, and rest on their arms awaiting events and orders.

Perhaps someone told us we had better go home. I do not remember; however, we did not linger, but started as fast as we could go back over the three miles we had just covered a half hour before, passing our picket outposts on the way back.

Arriving on the top of the ridge (the extension of Seminary Ridge) on the Newville Road, we stopped for breath and to survey the situation. Several farmers whom we knew were standing at a blacksmith's shop by the roadside but no troops were in sight, Blue or Gray, and only a solitary Union picket a quarter of a mile off standing on the road we had just traversed.

This was too dull after what we had just left in town.

"What's the use going home, boys? Let's go back along the ridge and pick berries. There's lots of ripe raspberries."

This motion did not carry unanimously, but two boys and myself went along the ridge and, in the absorbing interest of filling our stomachs with berries, forgot all about war and rumors of war for the time being until startled by the discharge of a cannon, the sharp impact of which made us jump, as it seemed to be just beyond the bushes concealing us. This was instantly followed by a rapid succession of discharges, and we three boys broke for the open and back to the blacksmith's shop.

But to me as a boy it was glorious! Here were my aspirations for months being gratified. Had I not tramped fifteen miles the year before with a Philadelphia regiment of new recruits in the expectation of seeing a battle, but here it was right at home and evidently going to be a bang-up fight at that.

The blacksmith's shop was deserted by all but its owner; his anvil was silent and the forge dead.

Realizing that the cannon balls were not coming in our direction, and that to run down the hill to my home would simply mean getting under cover where I could not see the battle, one of my brothers about nine years old, a cousin of my own age, and I were all that were left of our party, so we perched ourselves on the topmost rail of the road fence and drank in the melody of the battle.

But our gallery seats, although good for the whole show, began to have features of disomfort when we noticed up the road, coming over the nearest hill, great masses of troops and clouds of dust; how the first wave swelled into successive waves, gray masses with the glint of steel as the sun struck the gun barrels, filling the highway, spreading out into the fields, and still coming on and on, wave after wave, billow after billow. We waited not until we could "see the whites of their eyes" but until there were but a few hundred yards between us and the advance column, and then we departed for home, not riotously or in confusion, but decorously and in order as became boys who had pre-empted seats to see a battle but found conditions too hot for comfort.

There was suspicion in my mind that mother might possibly be worrying about us. But she was not—not in the way we expected, at least—for she was not at home, and the remaining members of a large family—aunts, cousins, and also some of our neighbors—were extremely apprehensive and wanted to know where my father and mother were—and oh! was it not terrifying, this incessant roar of artillery and rattle of musketry—"this awful shooting!" I think was the expression used—and I, the oldest responsible male member of our family at home, must see that the horses were concealed, the cows driven to shelter, and the feminine portion of the family protected.

But the question was, how could I look after a number of hysterical women and at the same time feel the joy that warriors feel, and see that the fight was properly conducted?

However, the noise kept up and, in fact, gathered in force and volume as the soldiers whom I had seen marching down the road went into action immediately south of us, between our home and the town of Gettysburg. I had sacrificed my point of advantage when I left the hill, which, by the way, commanded an unobstructed view of the whole amphitheater of the battlefield, and sought safety under cover of the hillside —our house being located near the foot of this ridge.

Mother returned shortly after I arrived there, and had to pass through the ranks of the Confederate Army just as it was passing over the last hill and forming into line of battle on the plains below.

That we were glad to see mother goes without saying. And just about this time we began to realize that we were having plenty of strangers for company—men who wore gray uniforms and who passed in military formation, cavalry or infantry, in squads or small troops, or as individuals. Some would stop for a drink of water or a bite to eat and, enjoying the shade of an old apple tree, forget to keep up with their commands. In fact, as we had the same callers for a couple of days, particularly about mealtime, we concluded that these fellows were not the kind that won battles, and if by feeding them we could reduce the ranks of the enemy, we were doing a patriotic duty.

3

For Sallie Robbins Broadhead the battle began under still other circumstances.

I got up early this morning to get my baking done before any battle would begin. I had just put my bread in the pans when the cannons began to fire, and true enough the fighting had begun in earnest.

What to do or where to go, I did not know. People were running here and there, screaming that the town would be shelled.

My husband advised remaining where we were, but all said we ought not to remain in our exposed position, and that it would be better to go to some part of the town farther away from the scene of the conflict. As our neighbors had all gone away, I would not remain, but my husband said he would stay at home.

About ten o'clock the shells began to "fly around quite thick," and I took my child and went to the house of a friend up town. As we passed up the street we met wounded men coming in from the field. When we saw them, we, for the first time, began to realize our fearful situation, and anxiously to ask, "Will our army be whipped?" Some said there was no danger of that yet, and pointed to Confederate prisoners who began to be sent through our streets to the rear.

Such a dirty, filthy set, no one ever saw. They were dressed in all kinds of clothes, of all kinds and no kind of cuts. Some were barefooted and a few wounded. Though enemies, I pitied them. I, with others, was sitting at the doorstep bathing the wounds of some of our brave soldiers, and became so much excited as the artillery galloped through the town, and the infantry hurried out to reinforce those fighting, that for a time we forgot our fears and our danger.

4

The Union forces at Gettysburg as the battle opened were

the First Corps under Pennsylvania-born General John F. Reynolds and a cavalry brigade under the command of Brigadier General John Buford. Reynolds was a seasoned fighter—a graduate of the Point who had served under Zachary Taylor in the defense of Fort Brown and in the battles of Monterey and Buena Vista, and who had fought Indians in Oregon and helped suppress the Mormon uprising in Utah. Kentucky-born, Buford likewise was a West Pointer and a veteran of Indian fighting and of the Utah expedition. Earlier in the war between the Union and the Confederacy Buford served with Pope in the Virginia campaign of 1862, and his pursuit of Stonewall Jackson through Madison Courthouse, Kelley Ford, and Thoroughfare Gap (August, 1862) must rank—in Union eyes at least—among the famous exploits of the conflict. With Reynolds and Buford was General Abner Doubleday, who, if he was not the father of baseball, at least aided in drawing up the game's first rules. Doubleday gives himself credit for having fired the first shot in reply to the attack on Fort Sumter, and with the Army of the Potomac fought in the Shenandoah Valley, at the Rappahannock, at Sharp Mountain, and at Antietam, Fredericksburg, and Chancellorsville. His account of the opening skirmishes at Gettysburg is among the best that have been preserved.

Reynolds sent for me about six o'clock, read me the various dispatches he had received from Meade and Buford, and told me he should go forward at once with the nearest division—that of Wadsworth—to aid the cavalry. He then ordered me to draw in my pickets, assemble the artillery and the remainder of the corps, and join him as soon as possible. Having given these orders he rode off, at the head of the column, and I never saw him again. . . .

As the Rebels had had several encounters with militia, who were easily dispersed, they did not expect to meet any serious resistance at this time, and advanced confidently and carelessly. Buford gave way slowly, taking advantage of every accident of ground to protract the struggle. After an hour's fighting he felt anxious and went up into the steeple of the Theological Seminary, from which a wide view could be ob-

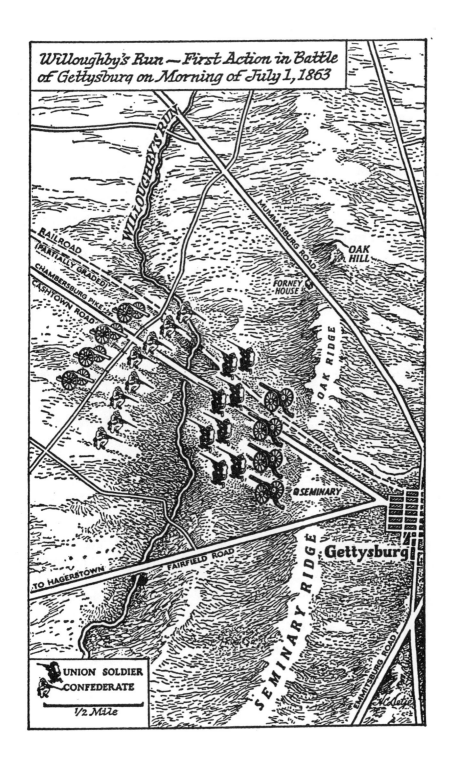

Willoughby's Run — First Action in Battle of Gettysburg on Morning of July 1, 1863

WILLOUGHBY'S RUN

RAILROAD (PARTIALLY GRADED)

CHAMBERSBURG PIKE

CASHTOWN ROAD

MUMMASBURG ROAD

OAK HILL

FORNEY HOUSE

OAK RIDGE

SEMINARY

SEMINARY RIDGE

Gettysburg

FAIRFIELD ROAD

TO HAGERSTOWN

EMMITSBURG ROAD

UNION SOLDIER
CONFEDERATE

1/2 Mile

tained, to see if the First Corps was in sight. One division of it was close at hand, and Reynolds, who had preceded it, climbed up into the belfry to confer with him, and there examined the country around. Although there is no positive evidence to that effect, his attention was doubtless attracted to Cemetery Ridge in his rear, as it was one of the most prominent features in the landscape. An aide of General Howard—presumably Major Hall—soon after he had descended from the belfry, came up to ask if he had any instructions with regard to the Eleventh Corps. Reynolds, in reply, directed that General Howard bring his corps forward at once and form on *Cemetery Hill* as a reserve. General Howard has no recollection of receiving any such orders, but as he did get orders to come forward, and his corps was to occupy *some place* in the rear, as a support to the First Corps, nothing is more probable than that General Reynolds directed him to go there, for its military advantages were obvious to any experienced commander. . . .

Buford, being aware that Ewell's Corps would soon be on its way from Heidlersburg to the field of battle, was obliged to form facing north with Deven's Brigade and leave Gamble's Brigade to keep back the overpowering weight of Hill's corps advancing from the west.

While this fight was going on, and Reynolds and Wadsworth were pressing to the front, I was engaged in withdrawing the pickets, and assembling the other two divisions together with the corps artillery. As soon as I saw that my orders were in the process of execution, I galloped to the front, leaving the troops to follow, and caught up with Meredith's brigade of Wadsworth's division, commonly called The Iron Brigade, just as it was going into action. . . .

As Davis' rebel brigade of Heth's Division facing Wadsworth was hidden behind an intervening ridge, Wadsworth did not see them at first, but formed his three regiments perpendicularly to the road, with a reconnaissance. The right flank of this line, unable to defend itself, was forced back and directed by Wadsworth to take post in a piece of woods in the rear of Seminary Ridge. The two regiments on the right accordingly withdrew, but the One Hundred and Forty-seventh New York, next to the road, did not receive the order as their colonel was shot down before he could deliver it. They were at once surrounded and very much cut up before they could be rescued from this perilous position.

* * *

There was a piece of woods between the two roads [Fairfield Road and Chambersburg Pike], with open ground on each side. It seemed to me this was the key of the position, for if the woods were held, the enemy could not pass on either road without being taken in flank by infantry and in front by the cavalry. I therefore urged the men as they filed past me to hold it at all hazards. Full of enthusiasm and the memories of their past achievements they said to me proudly, "If we can't hold it, where will you find the men who can?" . . .

Both parties were now trying to obtain possession of the woods. Archer's rebel brigade, preceded by a skirmish line, was crossing Willoughby's Run to enter them on one side as the Iron Brigade went in on the other. General Reynolds was on horseback in the edge of the woods, surrounded by his staff. He felt some anxiety as to the results and turned his head frequently to see if our troops would be up in time. While looking back in this way, a rebel sharpshooter shot him through the back of the head, the bullet coming out near the eye. He fell dead in an instant without a word[1]. . . .

The situation was very peculiar. The rebel left under Davis had driven in Cutler's Brigade, and our left, under Morrow, charged into the woods, preceded by the Second Wisconsin, under Colonel Fitzgerald, swept suddenly and unexpectedly around the right flank of Archer's Brigade capturing a large

[1] Readers of the *New York World* learned of Reynold's death from the account of a war correspondent who signed himself "Bonaparte": ". . . a bullet struck General Reynolds in the neck, wounding him mortally. Crying out with a voice that thrilled the hearts of his soldiers, 'Forward, for God's sake, forward,' he turned an instant, beheld the order obeyed by a line of shooting infantry, and falling into the arms of Captain Wilcox, his aide, who rode beside him, his life went out with the words, 'Good God, Wilcox, I am killed.' "

part of it, including Archer himself . . . . the rebels were careless and underrated us, thinking . . . . they had only militia to contend with. The Iron Brigade had a different headgear from the rest of the army and were recognized by their old antagonists. Some of the latter were heard to exclaim, "There are those d——d black-hatted fellows again. 'Taint no militia. It's the Army of the Potomac." . . . .

The disaster on the right required immediate attention, for the enemy, with loud yells, were pursuing Cutler's Brigade toward the town. . . . Fortunately, Fowler's two regiments came on to join Dawes [whom Doubleday had been keeping in reserve] who went forward with great spirit but who was altogether too weak to assail so large a force. As he approached, the rebels ceased to pursue Cutler, and rushed into the railroad cut to obtain the shelter of the grading. They made a fierce and obstinate resistance, but, while Fowler confronted them above, Dawes brought a gun to enfilade their position, and formed his men across the cut, by Fowler's order, to fire through it. The rebels could not resist this; the greater number gave themselves up as prisoners, and the others scattered over the country and escaped. . . .

It was a hot place for troops, for the whole position was alive with bursting shells, but the men went forward in fine spirits. Under the impression that the place was to be held at all hazards, they cried out, "We have come to stay!" The battle afterward became so severe that the greater portion of them did stay, laying down their lives for the cause they loved so well.

5

The capture of Maryland-born James J. Archer was a blow to Southern pride, for Archer became the first general officer of the Army of Northern Virginia to be captured since Lee had taken command. Major E. P. Halstead, adjutant to Doubleday, supplies an interesting footnote to history.

A guard brought him back to General Doubleday, who, in a very courteous manner—they had been cadets at West

Point together—said, "Good morning, Archer. How are you? I am glad to see you!"

General Archer replied, "Well, I am not glad to see you by a——sight!"

6

While Reynold's stubborn troops and Buford's cavalry threw back the Confederates at Willoughby Run, the Eleventh Corps under General Oliver Otis Howard was moving up to Gettysburg along the Emmitsburg Road. Howard was an unpopular man, filled with many prejudices and intolerances, disliked by the men in his own corps whom in turn he disliked because they were largely foreign-born Germans. Some felt that Howard's severely religious background in Leeds, Maine, had affected his personality, and they remembered him as seeming "queer" even during his student days at Bowdoin College and West Point. This antipathy between Howard and his men reached its height at Chancellorsville where he was openly accused of negligence. But Howard bore himself as he lived—and even as he wrote—primly.

With my staff and small escort of horsemen I set out, as the march began, toward Gettysburg, taking the fields and woods in order to avoid the trains and columns which occupied the road. Many officers remember the rapidity of that ride. By ten-thirty A.M., by my own time, I was in sight of the village of Gettysburg, when the staff officer which Reynolds had dispatched met me. . . .

A battle was evidently in progress, judging by the sound of the cannon and small arms and the rising smoke a mile and a half to my left. I could then see the divisions of Doubleday moving northwesterly across the open fields toward the seminary. My previous orders were to keep within supporting distance. When neither corps was in action this was interpreted to be a distance of four or five miles, but the aide who met me said: "Come quite up to Gettysburg." I remember distinctly, as if it were but yesterday, asking him where the general desired to place me and the aide replied: "Stop anywhere about here, according to your judgment at present." The spot where this remark was made was on the Emmitsburg Road, near Sherfy's peach orchard. The aide left and the firing continued. I sent Captain Daniel Hall to find Reynolds and bring me word that I might go to him.

Then with my staff, as was my habit when coming to a new field, I began to examine the position with the view to obtaining the best location in that vicinity for our troops. I rode from place to place, first visiting a high portion of a cross-ridge to my left, near the Emmitsburg Road. Not finding a point from which I could get an extended view, and noticing higher ground eastward, I turned and rode to the highest point on Cemetery Ridge. Here was a broad view which embraced the town, the seminary, the college and all the undulating valley of open country spread out between the ridges. There was a beautiful break in the ridge to the north of me where Culp's Hill abuts against the cemetery, and touches the creek below. It struck me that here one could make a strong right flank. . . .

Mounting to the top, [of Fahnstock's "observatory" in the village][2] I was delighted with the open view. With maps and field glasses, we examined the battlefield. Wadsworth's infantry, Buford's cavalry and one or two batteries were nearest, and their fighting was manifest. Confederate prisoners were just then being sent to the rear in large groups from the Seminary Ridge down the street past my post of observation.

We were noting the numerous roads which emerge from Gettysburg and from our charts comparing the locations and names, when a young soldier riding up the street below stopped, and, looking up, saluted me and said: "General Reynolds is wounded, sir." And I replied to him: "I am very sorry. I hope he will be able to keep the field."

It was not many minutes afterward that an officer (I believe it was Captain Hall) stood in the same street and,

---

[2] The reference is vague. Fahnstock's "observatory" probably was merely a residence (perhaps with a small store or shop attached) standing either in Middle Street or in one of the side streets leading off Baltimore Street.

looking up, sadly said: "General Reynolds is dead, and you are the senior officer in the field." This, of course, put me in the commander's place. . . .

Under my order Osborn's batteries were placed on Cemetery Ridge and some of them covered by small epaulments. General Steinwehr's division I put on the same heights near the Baltimore Pike. Dilger's Ohio Battery preceded the corps, and soon after Wheeler's, the two pacing through the town at a trot, to take their places on the right of the First Corps. Schurz ordered General Schimmelfennig (who had Schurz's division now) to advance briskly through Gettysburg and form on the right of the First Corps in two lines. Shortly after that the first division under Barlow arrived by the Emmitsburg Road proper, and advanced through the town on the right of the third division. I rode with Barlow through the city and out to what is now Barlow Hill.

The firing at the front was now severe and an occasional shell burst over our heads or among the houses. When I think of this day, I shall always recall one incident which still cheers my heart: it was that a young lady, after all other persons had disappeared for safety, remained behind on her porch and waved her handkerchief at the soldiers as they passed. Our living comrades who were there will not forget this episode, nor the greeting which her heroism awakened as they were going to battle. How heartily they cheered her!

7

In his official report Henry Heth wrote laconically: "The enemy had now been felt and found to be in heavy force in and around Gettysburg" but this was rare restraint. Archer had been captured and his brigade wrecked, two regiments of Joe Davis's brigade had surrendered—the skirmish at Willoughby Run was far from being a Confederate victory! On the other hand, the position of the Union forces was none too happy, and John Buford was busy writing a note to Meade: "General Reynolds was killed this morning. In my opinion there seems to be no directing person." But at

Taneytown where Meade had set up his headquarters Reynold's death already was known. Haskell recreates the moment as the dispatches came in.

At eleven o'clock A.M., on that day, the Second Corps was halted at Taneytown, which is thirteen miles from Gettysburg, south, and there awaiting orders, the men were allowed to make coffee and rest. At between one and two o'clock in the afternoon, a message was brought to General Gibbon, requiring his immediate presence at the headquarters of General Hancock, who commanded the Corps. I went with General Gibbon, and we rode at a rapid gallop, to General Hancock.

At General Hancock's headquarters the following was learned: The First Corps had met the enemy at Gettysburg, and had possession of the town. General Reynolds was badly, it was feared mortally, wounded; the fight of the First Corps still continued. By General Meade's order, General Hancock was to hurry forward and take command upon the field, of all troops there, or which should arrive there. The Eleventh Corps was near Gettysburg when the messenger who told of the fight left there, and the Third Corps was marching up, by order, on the Emmitsburg Road. General Gibbon—he was not the ranking officer of the Second Corps after Hancock —was ordered to assume the command of the Second Corps.

All this was sudden, and for that reason at least, exciting; but there were other elements in this information, that aroused our profoundest interest. The great battle that we had so anxiously looked for during so many days, had at length opened, and it was a relief, in some sense, to have these accidents of time and place established. What would be the result? Might not the enemy fall upon and destroy the First Corps before succor could arrive?

General Hancock, with his personal staff, at about two o'clock P.M., galloped off toward Gettysburg; General Gibbon took his place in command of the Corps, appointing me his acting Assistant Adjutant General. The Second Corps took arms at once, and moved rapidly toward the field. It was not long before we began to hear the dull booming of the

guns, and as we advanced, from many an eminence or opening among the trees, we could look out upon the white
battery smoke, puffing up from the distant field of blood, and
drifting up to the clouds. At these sights and sounds, the men
looked more serious than before and were more silent, but
they marched faster, and straggled less. At about five o'clock
P.M., as we were riding along at the head of the column, we
met an ambulance, accompanied by two or three mounted
officers—we knew them to be staff officers of General
Reynolds—their faces told plainly enough what load the
vehicle carried—it was the dead body of General Reynolds.
. . . His death at this time affected us much, for he was one
of the *soldier* generals of the army, a man whose soul was
in his country's work, which he did with a soldier's high honor
and fidelity.

I remember seeing him often at the first battle of Fredericksburg—he then commanded the First Corps—and while
Meade's and Gibbon's divisions were assaulting the enemy's
works, he was the very *beau ideal* of the gallant general.
Mounted upon a superb black horse, with his head thrown
back and his great black eyes flashing fire, he was everywhere
upon the field, seeing all things and giving commands in
person. He died as many a friend, and many a foe to the
country have died in this war. . . .

As we came near the field, from some slightly wounded
men we met, and occasional stragglers from the scene of
operations in front, we got many rumors, and much disjointed information of battle, of lakes of blood, of rout and
panic and undescribable disaster, from all of which the
narrators were just fortunate enough to have barely escaped,
the sole survivors. These stragglers are always terrible
liars! . . . .

While I was yet engaged in showing the troops their positions, I met General Hancock. . . . Upon horseback I think
he was the most magnificent looking general in the whole
Army of the Potomac at that time. With a large, well-shaped
person, always dressed with elegance, even upon that field
of confusion, he would look as if he was "monarch of all

he surveyed," and few of his subjects would dare to question his right to command, or do aught else but to obey. His quick eye, in a flash, saw what was to be done, and his voice and his royal right hand at once commenced to do it.

8

Winfield Scott Hancock graduated from West Point in the same class with Ulysses S. Grant and George Edward Pickett. His military record, beginning in the Mexican War, had been a creditable one. At Fredericksburg he had led his division in a fateful charge up Marye's Heights and at Chancellorsville it was said that Hancock's steadfastness and ability saved the Union forces from complete rout. He arrived at Gettysburg on July 1 more than a veteran fighter and an experienced commander; like Meade, he was a native Pennsylvanian defending his home soil. But he was Howard's junior, and Howard already had assumed command. There is contradictory evidence in those first few brittle moments after Hancock's arrival as to whether Howard refused to submit to Hancock's orders; Doubleday and Halstead tell one story, Howard in his official report another.

[*Doubleday*]: Howard refused to submit to Hancock's assumption of authority, and quite a scene occurred. He said, "Why, Hancock, you can't give any orders here. I am in command and I rank you!" Hancock said he was sent by orders of General Meade, but Howard said he refused to acknowledge his authority. Hancock then said he would go back to headquarters and report, but Howard asked him to remain and help him organize the troops. Hancock then rode over to me, a little doubtful as to whether I would join Howard in not recognizing his right to command—as he ranked me, and I had the greatest confidence in his abilities, I was happy to serve under him. . . .

[*Howard*]: General Hancock came to me about this time four-thirty P.M. and said General Meade had sent him on hearing of the state of affairs; that he had given him his instructions while under the impression that he was my senior.

We agreed at once that that was no time for talking and that General Hancock should further arrange the troops and place the batteries on the left of the Baltimore Pike, while I should take the right of the same.[3]

[*Halstead*]: I returned to where General Howard sat, just as General Hancock approached at a swinging gallop. When near General Howard, who was then alone, he saluted, and with great animation, as if there was no time for ceremony, said General Meade had sent him to take command of the three corps. General Howard replied that he was the senior. General Hancock said, "I am aware of that, General, but I have written orders in my pocket from General Meade which I will show you if you wish to see them." General Howard said, "No, I don't doubt your word, General Hancock, but you can give no orders here while I am here." General Hancock replied, "Very well, General Howard, I will second any orders you have to give, but General Meade also directed me to select a field on which to fight this battle in the rear of Pipe Creek." Then casting one glance from Culp's Hill to Round Top, he continued, "But I think this the strongest position by nature upon which to fight a battle that I ever saw, and if it meets [with] your approbation, I will select this as the battlefield." General Howard responded, "I think it a very strong position, General Hancock: a very strong position!"

---

[3] In his autobiography General Howard prefers to recall the scene as follows: ". . . General Hancock joined me near the Baltimore pike; he said that General Meade had sent him to represent him on the field. I answered as the bullets rent the air: 'All right, Hancock, you take the left of the Baltimore pike and I will take the right, and we will put these troops in line.'"

Chapter 4

"A Brisk Little Scurry"

WHEN LATE IN THE morning of July 1 Henry Heth had reformed his battered brigades at Willoughby Run, the status
of the battle had been accurately described in the dispatch
that War Reporter Charles Coffin sent to the *Boston Journal:*
"Thus far success had attended the Union arms. A large
number of prisoners had been taken, and the troops were
holding their own against a superior force."

But the afternoon brought a change. In his headquarters
at Cashtown, Lee had heard the sound of battle and had
hurried forward to Gettysburg. Heth supplied his commander-
in-chief with a full report on the morning's fighting, and Lee
appeared satisfied with the action to that point; but, Lee said,
a major battle should be avoided until all the Southern
columns had converged, and on that order depended in large
measure many of the tumultuous events of the next twenty-
four hours.

Meanwhile A. P. Hill had succeeded in contacting Ewell,
who was marching his Second Corps from Fayetteville to
Cashtown. In effect, Hill's message said come to Gettysburg
at once, and Ewell, whirling his troops around almost as
sharply as though he were taking a spin on his own wooden
leg, pressed his men forward through the broiling summer
heat. First of Ewell's corps to sight the Federals was the
division under Robert Emmett Rodes, who brought with him
some of the finest fighters in the Army of Northern Virginia—
the troops of Doles and Ramseur, O'Neal and Iverson. Junius
Daniel, whose brigade supported Iverson, alone had been
untested in the fighting in Virginia that had begun with
Chancellorsville.

1

Rodes, whose name was to belong to history that after-

70

noon, describes in his official report the situation he found on approaching Gettysburg.

When within four miles of the town, to my surprise, the presence of the enemy was announced by the sound of a sharp cannonade, and instant preparations for battle were made. On arriving on the field, I found that by keeping along the wooded [Seminary] ridge on the left side of which the town of Gettysburg is situated, I could strike the force of the enemy with which General Hill's troops were engaged upon the flank, and that, beside moving undercover, whenever we struck the enemy, we could engage him with advantage in ground. The division was therefore moved along the ridge with only one brigade deployed at first, and finally— as the enemy's cavalry had discovered us, and the ground was of such a character as to admit of cover for a large opposing force—with three brigades deployed; Doles on the left, "Rodes' old brigade," Colonel O'Neal commanding, in the center, and Iverson on the right. The artillery and two other brigades moved up closely to the line of battle.

The division moved nearly a mile before coming in view of the enemy's forces, except a few mounted men, and finally arrived at a point, a prominent hill on the ridge, whence a whole of that portion of the force opposing General Hill's troops could be seen. To get at these troops properly, which were still over half a mile from us, it was necessary to move the whole of my command by the right flank, and to change direction to the right. Whilst this was being done, Carter's battalion was ordered forward, and soon opened fire upon the enemy, who at this moment, as far as I could see, had no troops facing me at all. He had apparently been surprised —only a desultory fire of artillery was going on between his troops and General Hill's—but before my dispositions were made, the enemy began to show large bodies of troops in front of the town, most of which were directed upon the position which I held, and almost at the same time a portion of the force opposed to General Hill changed poistion so as to oc-cupy the summit of the ridge I occupied (I refer to the forest touching the railroad, and extending along the summit of the ridge at the base of the hill I held).

Either these last troops, or others which had hitherto been unobserved behind the same body of woods, soon made their appearance directly opposite my center. Being thus threatened from two directions, I determined to attack with my center and right, holding at bay still another force, then emerging from the town apparently with the intention of turning my left, with Doles' brigade, which was moved somewhat to the left for this purpose, and trusting to this gallant brigade thus holding them until General Early's division arrived, which I knew would be soon, and which could strike this portion of the enemy's force on the flank before it could overpower Doles. . . .

Finding the enemy rash enough to come out of the woods to attack me, I determined to meet him when he got to the foot of the hill I occupied, and as he did so, I caused Iverson's brigade to advance, and at the same moment gave in person the order to O'Neal to attack, indicating to him precisely the point to which he was to direct the left of the four regiments then under his orders; the Fifth Alabama, which formed the extreme left of this brigade, being held in reserve under my immediate command to defend the gap between O'Neal and Doles.

2

The stilted language of an official report fails to convey adequately the delicate situation in which the Union forces now found themselves. Actually the potential power of the Federal troops had been split almost in two, with Hill's division occupying Doubleday's First Corps along Willoughby Run and Rodes engaging the two divisions of Howard's Eleventh Corps along Seminary Ridge. These divisions of the Eleventh Corps under Schurz and Barlow were seasoned veterans of Chancellorsville, and in meeting Rodes they were opposing an old foe with whom they were determined to settle a score. That they gave him moments of discomfiture even Rodes' official report cannot conceal.

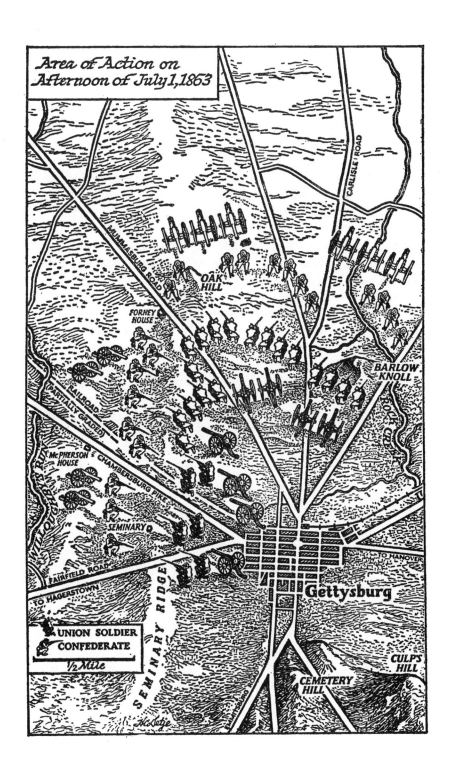

Area of Action on Afternoon of July 1, 1863

CARLISLE ROAD

MUMMASBURG ROAD

OAK HILL

FORNEY HOUSE

BARLOW KNOLL

ROCK CREEK

RAILROAD (PARTIALLY GRADED)

WILLOUGHBY RUN

McPHERSON HOUSE

CHAMBERSBURG PIKE

SEMINARY

TO HANOVER

FAIRFIELD ROAD

TO HAGERSTOWN

SEMINARY RIDGE

Gettysburg

UNION SOLDIER
CONFEDERATE
½ Mile

CULP'S HILL

CEMETERY HILL

Iverson's brigade attacked handsomely, but suffered very heavily from the enemy's musketry fire from behind a stone wall along the crest of the ridge. The Alabama brigade went into action in some confusion, and with only three of its regiments, the Sixth, Twelfth and Twenty-sixth, the Fifth having been retained by my order and . . . . the Third having been permitted . . . . to move with Daniel's brigade. The three first-mentioned regiments moved with alacrity (but not in accordance with my orders as to direction) and in confusion into the action. It was soon apparent that we were making no impression upon the enemy, and hence I ordered the Fifth Alabama to their support but, to my surprise, in giving this command to its colonel, Hall, I found that Colonel O'Neal, instead of personally superintending the movements of his brigade, had chosen to remain with the reserve regiment. The result was that the whole brigade, with the exception of the Third Alabama . . . . was repulsed quickly and with loss. . . .

Iverson's left being exposed thus, heavy losses were inflicted on his brigade. His men fought and died like heroes. His dead lay in a distinctly marked line of battle. His left was overpowered, and many of his men, being surrounded, were captured.

3

Here, indeed, is the rare restraint that only the literary shortcomings of an official report can achieve, for to quote Douglas Southall Freeman, "Word was brought to Rodes from the frantic Iverson that one of his regiments had raised the white flag and had gone over to the enemy! Such a thing had never happened on any field where the Army of Northern Virginia had fought; it was inconceivable now, but Iverson affirmed it. For a few minutes there was chaos. Rodes' plan seemed to be ruined. He had to fight with his left destroyed and, for all he knew, employed against him. Soon the ghastly truth was discovered: In Iverson's advance, his line of battle had come under a decimating fire from Federals who were concealed behind a low stone wall. The North Carolinians had fallen by scores, almost as if they had been halted and had been ordered to lie down. Still fighting, the left units of Iverson were exposed when O'Neal was repulsed. Some of Iverson's men, realizing they were about to be surrounded and slaughtered, waved their handkerchiefs in surrender. Iverson saw this and thought the dead men in the line were alive and were yielding. So unnerved was Iverson . . . . that his assistant adjutant general . . . . had to rally the men and assume command."[1] But Rodes, writing his official report when he had become composed, continues his dispassionate account.

General Daniel's gallant brigade, by a slight change in the direction of Iverson's attack, had been left too far to his right to assist him directly, and had already become engaged. The right of this brigade coming upon the enemy strongly posted in a railroad cut, was, under its able commander's orders, thrown back skillfully, and the position of the whole brigade was altered so as to enfilade it, and attack to advantage. After this change came General Daniel's most desperate, gallant and entirely successful charge upon the enemy, driving him at all points, but suffering terribly. The conduct of General Daniel and his brigade in this most desperate engagement elicited the admiration and praise of all who witnessed it.

4

Again Rodes achieves a masterpiece of understatement! As Daniel pressed boldly on the railroad cut, supported by a reserve brigade under Ramseur, his intention was to get astride the cut and sweep it clear of the enemy. Now, perhaps, the fighting of the afternoon flamed to its greatest height, and there is no lackluster quality to the highly fictionalized description of it supplied by Augustus Buell who claimed to have been a Union cannoneer that day.

First we could see the tips of their colorstaffs coming up over the little ridge, then the points of their bayonets, and then the Johnnies themselves, coming on with a steady tramp, tramp, and with loud yells. It was now apparent that the old battery's turn had come again, and the embattled boys who

[1] Freeman, Douglas Southall. *Lee's Lieutenants.* Vol. III, p. 86.

stood so grimly at their posts felt that another page must be added to the record of Buena Vista and Antietam. As the day was very hot, many of the boys had their jackets off, and they exchanged little words of cheer with one another as the gray line came on. In quick, sharp tones, like successive reports of a repeating rifle, came Davidson's orders: "Load—Canister—Double!" There was a hustling of cannoneers, a few thumps of the rammer heads, and then "Ready—By piece —Fire!"

Then for seven or eight minutes ensued probably the most desperate fight ever waged between artillery and infantry at close range without a particle of cover on either side. They gave us volley after volley in front and flank, and we gave them double canister as fast as we could load. The Sixth Wisconsin and Eleventh Pennsylvania men crawled up over the bank of the cut and joined their musketry to our canister in one solid streak.

Twenty-six years have but softened in memory the picture of the burly corporal, bareheaded, his hair matted with blood from a scalp wound, and wiping the crimson fluid out of his eyes to sight the gun; of the steady orderly sergeant, moving calmly from gun to gun, now and then changing men about as one after another was hit and fell, stooping over a wounded man to help him up, or aiding another to stagger to the rear; of the dauntless Davidson on foot among the guns, cheering the men, praising this one and that one, and ever and anon profanely exhorting to us to "feed it to 'em, God damn 'em! Feed it to 'em!"

The very guns became things of life—not implements, but comrades. Every man was doing the work of two or three. At our gun at the finish there were only the corporal and two drivers fetching ammunition. The water in the bucket was like ink. Up and down the line men reeling and falling; splinters flying from wheels and axles where bullets hit; in rear, horses tearing and plunging, mad with wounds or terror; drivers yelling, shells bursting, shot shrieking overhead, howling about our ears or throwing up great clouds of dust where they struck; the musketry crashing on three sides of us; bullets hissing, humming and whistling everywhere; cannon roaring; all crash on crash and peal on peal, smoke, dust, splinters, blood, wreck and carnage indescribable; but the brass guns of Old B still bellowed and not a man or boy flinched or faltered.

For a few moments the whole Rebel line, clear down to the Fairfield Road, seemed to waver, and we thought that maybe we could repulse them, single-handed. But their second line came steadily on. The ordnance sergeant gave the order to limber to the rear, the Sixth Wisconsin and the Eleventh Pennsylvania behind us having begun to fall back down the railroad track toward the town, turning about and firing as they retreated.

5

Moments before, again to quote Freeman, it had seemed as though "Robert Rodes might be headed for a humiliating defeat"; now in the railroad cut Daniel had driven deep and the issue turned. No one understood the change that had come better than Prussian-born Carl Schurz as he fought with the Eleventh Corps and his report to Howard upon the action minced few words.

The firing on my extreme left appeared to increase in volume, and on leaving the point I had selected for myself and staff on the Mummasburg Road, I rode over to the left, to see what was going on. The right of the First Corps appeared to be engaged in a very severe struggle. The enemy was evidently pressing hard upon that point. At the same time signs were apparent of an advance of the enemy upon my line, especially the right. The enemy was apparently stronger than he was at the commencement of the battle, and the probability was that reinforcements were still arriving. Feeling much anxiety about my right, which was liable to be turned if any of the enemy's forces were advancing by the Heidlersburg Road, I dispatched one of my aides . . . with the request to have one brigade of the Second Division placed on the north side of the town, near the railroad as an *échelon* to the First

Division. My intention was to have that brigade ready to charge any force the enemy might move around my right.

After making the necessary observations on my extreme left, I returned to the Mummasburg Road, where I discovered that General Barlow had moved forward his whole line, thus losing on his left the connection with the Third Division; moreover the Second Brigade of the First Division had been taken out of its position *en échelon* behind the right of the First Brigade. I immediately gave orders to re-establish the connection by advancing the right wing of the Third Division and hurried off aide after aide to look after the brigade of the Second Division which I had requested you to send me to protect my right and rear, but it had not yet arrived.

Suddenly the enemy opened upon the First Division from two batteries placed near the Harrisburg Road, completely enfilading General Barlow's line. This fire, replied to by our batteries, had but little effect upon our men. Soon afterward, however, about 3 o'clock, before the forward movement of the First Division could be arrested by my orders, the enemy appeared in our front with heavy masses of infantry, extending far beyond our right. It was now clear that the two small divisions under my command, hardly numbering 6,000 effective men when going into battle, had a whole corps of the Rebel army to contend against. . . .

While I was doing my utmost, assisted by the officers of my staff, to rally what was in my reach of the First Division, in order to check the enemy's advance upon my right, and to hold the entrance of the town, the First Brigade of the Second Division under Colonel Coster at last made its appearance. I led it out of town and ordered it to deploy on the right of the junction of the roads near the railroad depot, which the enemy was fast approaching. It was now too late for executing the offensive movement upon the enemy's left flank, which I had originally contemplated and which might have been made to great advantage ten minutes before, but the brigade, assisted by a battery, succeeded, at all events, in checking the enemy long enough to permit the First Division to enter the town without being seriously molested on its retreat. The Third Division had meanwhile to sustain a furious attack.

According to orders, it fell back on the town in good order, contesting the ground step by step with the greatest firmness.

6

The full extent of the Union collapse was even more sharply revealed to Abner Doubleday, who was with the First Corps on the left. Gordon's brigade of Early's division, just arriving on the field, was rushed into action. Then, with a nod from Lee, Hill threw the divisions of Heth and Pender against the First Corps. Doubleday sees clearly that the end is near.

The Confederate Forces made their final advance in double lines, backed by strong reserves, and it was impossible for the few men left in the First Corps to keep them back, especially as Pender's large division overlapped ours for a quarter of a mile; Robinson's right was turned, and General Paul was shot through both eyes in an effort to stem the tide. They could not contend with Ramseur in front, and O'Neal on the flank at the same time.

Under these circumstances, it became a very serious question how to extricate the First Corps and save its artillery before it was entirely surrounded and captured. . . .

What was left of the First Corps after all this slaughter rallied on Seminary Ridge. Many of the men entered a semicircular rail entrenchment that I had caused to be thrown up earlier in the day, and held that for a time by lying down and firing over a pile of rails. The enemy were now closing in on us from south, west, and north, and still no orders came to retreat.

The first long line that came from the west was swept away by our artillery which was most effective, [and which] beat back and almost destroyed the first line of Scales's brigade, wounding both Scales and Pender. . . . My Adjutant Generals, Baird and Halstead, and my aides, Lee Marten, Jones and Lambdin, had hot work carrying out orders at this time and it is a marvel that any of them survived the storm of bullets that swept the field.

Robinson was forced back toward the Seminary, but halted,

notwithstanding the pressure upon him and formed line to save Stewart's battery north of the railroad cut, which had remained too long in danger of being captured.

Cutler's brigade in the meantime had formed behind the railroad grading to face the men who were pursuing the Eleventh Corps. This show of force had a happy effect on the skirmish line, and the delay enabled the artillery soon after to pass through the interval between Cutler on the north, and Buford's cavalry in the south. . . .

It became necessary, however, to abandon one gun of Captain Reynold's battery, as several of the horses were shot and there was no time to disengage them from the piece. Three broken and damaged caisson bodies were left behind. The danger this time came principally from Hoke's and Hayes's brigades, who were making their way into the town on the eastern side threatening to cut us off from Cemetery Hill. The troops in front of the Seminary were stayed by the firm attitude of Buford's cavalry, and made a bend in their line, apparently with a view to form squares.

I waited until the artillery had gone then rode back to the town with my staff. As we passed through the streets, pale and frightened, two men came out and offered us coffee and food and implored us not to abandon them. . . .

On the way I met an aide that Howard says he sent to me with orders to retreat, but I do not remember receiving a message of any kind. . . .

They [the First Corps] walked leisurely from the Seminary to the town and did not run. I remember seeing Hall's battery and the Sixth Wisconsin halt from time to time, to face the enemy and fire down the streets. . . .

We lay on our arms that night, among the tombs of the cemetery, so suggestive of the shortness of life and the nothingness of fame. But the men were little disposed to moralize on themes like these and were too much exhausted to think of anything but much-needed rest.

7

Even though Doubleday, surrounded by gravestones, could

forget the afternoon's disasters in sleep, Sallie Robbins Broadhead could not.

All was bustle and confusion. No one can imagine in what extreme fright we were when our men began to retreat. A citizen galloped up to the door in which we were sitting and called out, "For God's sake, go into the house! The Rebels are in the other end of town, and all will be killed!"

We quickly ran in, and the cannonading coming nearer and becoming heavier, we went to the cellar, and in a few minutes the town was full of the filthy Rebels.

They did not get farther, for our soldiers having possession of the hills just beyond, shelled them so that they were glad to give over the pursuit, and the fighting for the day was ended. We remained in the cellar until the firing ceased, and then feared to come out, not knowing what the Rebels might do.

How changed the town looked when we came to the light. The streets were strewn over with clothes, blankets, knapsacks, cartridge boxes, dead horses, and the bodies of a few men, but not so many of these last as I expected to see. "Can we go out?" was asked of the Rebels. "Certainly," was the answer; they would not hurt us. We started home, and found things all right.

As I write all is quiet, but O! how I dread tomorrow.

8

Haskell records an incident of the retreat.

I saw John Burns, the only citizen of Gettysburg who fought in the battle, and I asked him what troops he fought with.

He said: "O, I pitched in with them Wisconsin fellers."

I asked what sort of men they were, and he answered: "They fit terribly. The Rebs couldn't make anything of them fellers."

9

Tillie Alleman, a young girl who easily could have been

one of Sallie Broadhead's students in more peaceful days, shuddered at the dreadful aftermath of a battle.

The first wounded soldier whom I met had his thumb tied up. This I thought was dreadful, and told him so.

"Oh," said he, "this is nothing; you'll see worse than this before long."

Soon two officers carrying their arms in slings made their appearance, and I more fully began to realize that something terrible had taken place.

Now the wounded began to come in greater numbers. Some limping, some ·with their heads and arms in bandages, some crawling, others carried on stretchers or brought in ambulances. Suffering, cast down and dejected, it was a truly pitiable gathering. Before night the barn was filled with shattered and dying heroes of this day's struggle.

That evening Beckie Weikert and I went out to the barn to see what was transpiring there. Nothing before in my experience had ever paralleled the sight we then and there beheld. There were the groaning and the crying, the struggling and dying crowded side by side, while attendants sought to aid and relieve them as best they could.

We were so overcome by the sad and awful spectacle that we hastened back to the house weeping bitterly.

As we entered the basement or cellar-kitchen of the house, we found many nurses making beef tea for the wounded. Seeing that we were crying . . . they at once endeavored to cheer us by telling funny stories and ridiculing our tears. They soon dispelled our terror and caused us to laugh so much that many times when we should have been sober minded we were not, the reactions having been too sudden for our overstrung nerves.

10

The Confederates were jubilant. Gettysburg had become another Chancellorsville: the enemy was in rout! The spirit of rejoicing reached far behind the lines to where Longstreet was still bringing up his First Corps. Marching toward Gettysburg with Longstreet while the first day's fighting was going

on was Sir Arthur James Lyon-Fremantle. As the British
Government favored the Confederate cause it was not diffi-
cult for Fremantle, a lieutenant colonel in Her Majesty's
Coldstream Guards, to be accredited to and accepted by the
Confederacy as a military observer.

We did not leave our camp till noon, as nearly all General
Hill's corps had to pass our quarters on its march toward
Gettysburg. One division of Ewell's had to join a little beyond
Greenwood, and Longstreet's corps had to bring up the rear.
During the morning I met Colonel Walton, who used to command the well-known Washington Artillery, but is now chief
of artillery to Longstreet's *corps d'armée.* He is a big man,
ci-devant auctioneer in New Orleans, and I understand he
pines to return to his hammer.

Soon after starting we got into a pass in South Mountain,
a continuation, I believe, of the Blue Ridge range, which is
broken at the Potomac by Harper's Ferry. The scenery
through the pass is very fine. The first troops, alongside of
whom we rode, belonged to Johnson's division of Ewell's
corps. Among them I saw, for the first time, the famous
"Stonewall" brigade, formerly commanded by Jackson. In
appearance the men differed little from other Confederate
soldiers, except, perhaps, the brigade contains more elderly
men and fewer boys. All (except, I think, one regiment) are
Virginians. As they nearly always have been on detached
duty, few of them knew General Longstreet, except by reputa-
tion. Numbers of them asked me whether the general in front
was Longstreet; and when I answered in the affirmative, many
would run a hundred yards in order to take a good look at
him. This I take to be an immense compliment from any
soldier on a long march. . . .

At three P.M. we began to meet wounded men coming to
the rear, and the number of these soon increased most rapidly,
some hobbling alone, others on stretchers carried by the
ambulance corps, and others in ambulance wagons. Many of
the latter were stripped nearly naked, and displayed very bad
wounds. This spectacle, so revolting to a person unaccustomed
to such sights, produced no impression whatever upon the ad-

vancing troops who certainly go under fire with perfect nonchalance. They show no enthusiasm or excitement, but the most complete indifference. This is the effect of two years' almost uninterrupted fighting.

We now began to meet Yankee prisoners coming to the rear in considerable numbers. Many of them were wounded, but they seemd already to be on excellent terms with their captors, with whom they had commenced swapping canteens, tobacco, etc. Among them was a Pennsylvania colonel, a miserable object from a wound on his face. In answer to a question I heard one of them remark, with a laugh, "We're pretty nigh whipped already." . . . .

At four-thirty P.M. we came in sight of Gettysburg, and joined General Lee and General Hill, who were on the top of one of the ridges which form the peculiar feature of the country round Gettysburg. We could see the enemy retreating up the side of one of the opposite ridges, pursued by the Confederates, with loud yells. The position into which the enemy had been driven was evidently a strong one. His right appeared to rest on a cemetery, on the top of a high ridge to the right of Gettysburg, as we looked at it.

General Hill now came up and told me he had been very unwell all day, and in fact he looks very delicate. He said he had two of his divisions engaged, and had driven the enemy four miles into his present position, capturing a great many prisoners, some cannon, and some colors. He said, however, that the Yankees had fought with a determination unusual to them. He pointed out a railway cutting, in which they had made a good stand; also a field in the center of which he had seen a man plant the regimental color, round which the regiment had fought for some time with much obstinacy, and when at last it was obliged to retreat, the color-bearer retreated last of all, turning round every now and then to shake his fist at the advancing Rebels. General Hill said he felt quite sorry when he saw this gallant Yankee meet his doom. . . .

The town of Gettysburg was now occupied by Ewell, and was full of Yankee dead and wounded. I climbed up a tree in the most commanding place I could find and could form a pretty good general idea of the enemy's position, although the tops of the ridges being covered with pinewoods, it was difficult to see anything of the troops concealed within them. The firing ceased about dark at which time I rode back with General Longstreet and his staff to his headquarters at Cashtown, a little village eight miles from Gettysburg. At that time troops were pouring along the road, and were being marched toward the position they are to occupy tomorrow.

In the fight today nearly 6,000 prisoners have been taken, and ten guns. About 20,000 men must have been on the field, on the Confederate side. The enemy had two *corps d'armée* engaged. All the prisoners belong, I think, to the first and eleventh corps. This day's work is called a "brisk little scurry" and all anticipate a "big battle" tomorrow. . . .

At supper this evening General Longstreet spoke of the enemy's position as being "very formidable." He said that they would doubtlessly entrench themselves strongly during the night. The staff officers spoke of the battle as a certainty, and the universal feeling in the army was one of profound contempt for an enemy they had beaten so constantly, and under so many disadvantages.

11

For Billy Bayly, living on his farm three miles behind the Confederate lines, the afternoon was passed contending with an army foraging as it fought.

The call for chicken soup and bread—as long as the chickens lasted—was constant, and flour by the barrel was baked into bread. My services were required to catch or help catch chickens but I developed serious foot trouble, and was told that I did not amount to a hurrah as a chicken catcher. But the guns and pistols of our "company" were brought into use and all of our poultry vanished from the face of the earth.

These soldiers from the South had discovered that cherry pie was a very seductive pastry, and as the land back of the barn was bordered with cherry trees that were laden with fruit, it fell to my lot to pick cherries for the use of the family and, incidentally, for our guests. Those who cared to tarry long enough to get a pie did so. The others had to be content with branches broken off and thrown to them when passing, and I remember trying to supply one company of cavalry that passed underneath the overhanging boughs, much to the disfigurement of the tree after the limbs within reach had been broken off. But what a base use for the martial spirit that longed to see more, if not to see less, of the circumstance of war!

But there on the hillside were the sheep, a flock of about one hundred rushing wildly from one end of the field to the other, and their number growing constantly less as the Southerners, who loved mutton, banged away, hit or miss, and carried away either the whole carcass or as much as suited their convenience and appetite. . . .

Sometime after midnight we were awakened by a knocking at the kitchen door, and mother told me to follow her down stairs. At the door we found a little fellow in a gray uniform, hardly taller than I and only a couple of years older, who said he had been through the battle of the day before, that his company had been cut to pieces, that he was from North Carolina, was tired of fighting and never wanted to see another battle—would not mother conceal him somewhere until the battle was over? He was given a suit of clothes and sent to the garret where the feather beds were stored for the summer and several bedsteads not in use, told to find a bed and in the morning change his gray uniform for the civilian attire.

Chapter 5

"The World is Most Unchristian Yet!"

OLD BALD HEAD Ewell was satisfied with the victory the Confederates had won. As he rode through the town exchanging pleasantries with his exuberant soldiers, now declining the offer of a bottle of wine pilfered from a Gettysburg cellar, he ignored the grumbling of his younger officers. Let them argue that this was the moment to pursue the fleeing blue-coats into the heights beyond the town, let them grouse because he refused to entrench a division—or even a brigade—on Culp's Hill before the Federals could seize that commanding position, he knew his orders.

But the younger officers persisted: Strike the enemy now! Complete the rout! Ewell set his jaw, stubborn and angry. Lee's orders to Heth that a general engagement must be avoided until all the corps of the army had converged remained unchanged in Ewell's mind, and Ewell would be damned if he'd be stampeded by a handful of headstrong young hellions—or a handful of old ones, either—who couldn't wait for another day to get their bellies full of fighting.

There were those riding in their saddles behind Ewell who wished fervently that Stonewall Jackson were still alive. With a chance to trounce the Yankees while their blue coattails were whipping between their legs, Jackson never would have hesitated! "Our Corps commander," wrote Captain James Power Smith of one of the Louisiana brigades, "was simply waiting orders, when every moment of time could not be balanced with gold."

Why did Ewell hesitate? Was it true, as Freeman believes, that he had become sick in mind and spirit? And if Lee, as the adjutant general of the army testifies, recognized the instant he saw "the enemy retreating without organization and

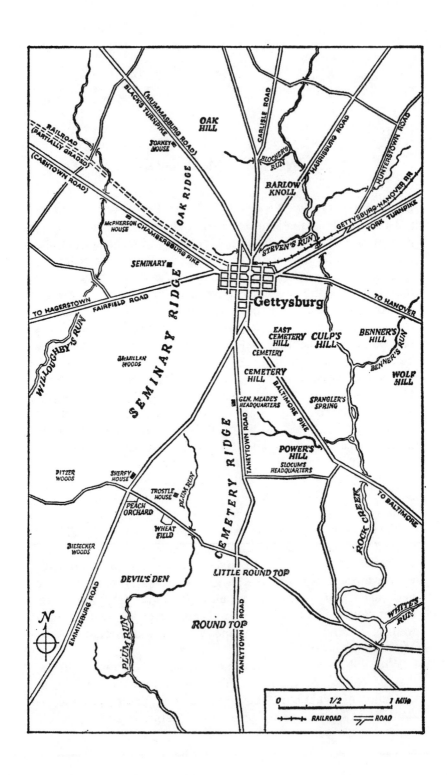

OAK HILL

CARLISLE ROAD

(MUMMASBURG ROAD)

BLACK'S TURNPIKE

RAILROAD (PARTIALLY GRADED)

(CASHTOWN ROAD)

FORNEY HOUSE

BLOCHER'S RUN

HARRISBURG ROAD

HUNTERSTOWN ROAD

BARLOW KNOLL

OAK RIDGE

GETTYSBURG-HANOVER RR

McPHERSON HOUSE

CHAMBERSBURG PIKE

STEVEN'S RUN

YORK TURNPIKE

SEMINARY

TO HAGERSTOWN

FAIRFIELD ROAD

WILLOUGHBY'S RUN

Gettysburg

TO HANOVER

EAST CEMETERY HILL

CULP'S HILL

BENNER'S HILL

SEMINARY RIDGE

McMILLAN WOODS

CEMETERY

BENNER'S RUN

CEMETERY HILL

WOLF HILL

GEN. MEADE'S HEADQUARTERS

SPANGLER'S SPRING

BALTIMORE PIKE

TANEYTOWN ROAD

POWER'S HILL

SLOCUM'S HEADQUARTERS

PITZER WOODS

SHERFY HOUSE

PLUM RUN

CEMETERY RIDGE

TROSTLE HOUSE

PEACH ORCHARD

TO BALTIMORE

WHEAT FIELD

ROCK CREEK

BIESECKER WOODS

DEVIL'S DEN

LITTLE ROUND TOP

EMMITSBURG ROAD

TANEYTOWN ROAD

WHITE'S RUN

N

PLUM RUN

ROUND TOP

0   1/2   1 Mile

RAILROAD   ROAD

in great confusion" that it was necessary "only to press 'those people' in order to secure possession of Cemetery Heights," why didn't he insist that Ewell move? Was it because Lee accorded his lieutenants too much leeway in exercising their own discretion in such matters? These are questions that have been debated for almost a century; they remain now, as they remained after the first day of fighting at Gettysburg, in large part unanswered and perhaps unanswerable.

1

But because Ewell did hesitate the Army of the Potomac gained its second wind. Brevet Captain Edward N. Whittier gives a vivid impression of the emotions that stirred the Union soldiers as they escaped into the heights beyond Gettysburg.

Barely twenty-four hundred fighting men of the corps[1] found their way up the slopes of Cemetery Hill, and formed lines anew in this position at the close of that first day's desperate struggle. No sight more welcome ever strengthened the hearts of soldiers than that which burst upon our longing eyes when, escaping capture in the streets and lanes of Gettysburg, we gained the plateau of East Cemetery Hill. From this high ground which dominated the town and the fields, in all directions save one there was an unobstructed view of rolling country open and accessible to the fire of our guns. To the north and northeast, the town and the scattered buildings along its edge; to the right and east, a great expanse of farming country bisected by Rock Creek, which, flowing in a southeasterly direction, ran nearly parallel to that portion of our front; in the southeast and at a distance of about seven hundred yards, Culp's Hill, bold, rough, and densely wooded, rising from the bed of the stream whose tortuous channel skirted its eastern base for nearly three-quarters of a mile until its southern slopes merged in the swamp, rocky and almost impassable, separating Culp's from Wolf's Hill bristling with the welcome bayonets of the Twelfth Corps. Following a

[1] The returns of the First Corps for the previous day listed 708 officers and 9,314 enlisted men.

course almost southerly, the Baltimore Pike reached nearly to the horizon, covered with fugitives, or masked by the dust of columns hurrying to the front. To the southwest the Round Tops, and in the west the splendid spectacle of Buford's cavalry in lines of battalions *en masse*, standing steady as if on parade, unshaken and undaunted in face of the advancing victorious Confederate infantry.

But more than this, and of deepest significance to all who saw it, in the center of the plateau was a group of generals with staff officers and orderlies. It was a scene of the utmost activity, yet there was no confusion. The condition was changed from that described by General Buford in the morning when he informed General Pleasonton of the sad tidings of Reynold's death, adding, "in my opinion there seems to be no directing person," for in the center of the group, on horseback, unmoved by all the confusion among the retreating soldiers, sat a man born to command, competent to evolve order out of the chaos, the master of the first position that day found for successful resistance. I shall never forget (for I reported to him for orders) the inspiration of his commanding, controlling presence, and the fresh courage he imparted. I recall even his linen, clean and white, his collar open at the neck, and his broad wristbands rolled back from his firm, finely molded hand. This was General Hancock.

2

Meanwhile, at Taneytown, Meade waited impatiently for word from Hancock. Darkness had fallen and still the commanding general of the Army of the Potomac paced the floor of his headquarters, uncertain of the day's results at Gettysburg. The members of Meade's personal staff had packed their belongings and were ready to move—if the news from thirteen miles away proved encouraging. The tension broke with the sound of a galloping horse, and the courier who appeared in the headquarters doorway handed Meade the dispatch from Hancock: "We can fight here, as the ground appears not unfavorable, with good troops." Sometime after midnight on July 2 Meade reached Gettysburg. Frank Arteas

Haskell describes the events of those darkened hours and supplies a word picture of the positions which the Union forces
held as dawn broke.

The night before a great pitched battle would not ordinarily,
I suppose, be a time for much sleep for generals and their staff
officers. We needed it enough, but there was work to be done.
This war makes strange confusion of night and day! I did not
sleep at all that night. It would, perhaps, be expected on the
eve of such great events that one should have some peculiar
sort of feeling, something extraordinary, some great arousing
and excitement of the sensibilities and faculties, commensurate
with the event itself; this certainly would be very poetical and
pretty, but so far as I was concerned, and I think I can speak
for the Army in this matter, there was nothing of the kind.
Men who had volunteered to fight the battles of the country,
had met the enemy in many battles, and had been constantly
before them as had the Army of the Potomac, were too old
soldiers, and long ago too well had weighed chances and
probabilities, to be so disturbed now. No, I believe the Army
slept soundly that night, and well, and I am glad the men
did, for they needed it.

At midnight General Meade and staff rode by General
Gibbon's headquarters on their way to the field; and in conversation with General Gibbon, General Meade announced
that he had decided to assemble the whole Army before
Gettysburg and offer the enemy battle there. The Second Corps
would move at the earliest daylight to take up its position.

At three o'clock A.M. of the second of July, the sleepy
soldiers of the Corps were aroused; before six the Corps was
up to the field, and halted temporarily by the side of the
Taneytown Road, upon which it had marched, while some
movements of the other troops were being made to enable it
to take position in the order of battle. The morning was
thick and sultry, the sky overcast with low, vapory clouds.
As we approached all was astir upon the crests near the
Cemetery, and the work of preparation was speedily going on.
Men looked like giants there in the mist, and the guns of

the frowning batteries so big that it was a relief to know that they were our friends.

Without a topographical map, some description of the ground and location is necessary to a clear understanding of the battle. . . . The line of battle as it was established on the evening of the first, and morning of the second of July, was in the form of the letter "U," the troops facing outward and the Cemetery, which is at the point of the sharpest curvature of the line, being due south of the town of Gettysburg. Round Top, the extreme left of the line, is a small, woody, rocky elevation, a very little west of south of the town, and nearly two miles from it.

The sides of this are in places very steep, and its rocky summit is almost inaccessible. A short distance north . . . is a smaller elevation called Little Round Top. . . . Near the right of the line is a small, woody eminence, named Culp's Hill. Three roads come up to the town from the south, which near the town are quite straight, and at the town the external ones unite, forming an angle of about sixty or more degrees. Of these, the farthest to the east is the Baltimore Pike, which passes by the east entrance to the Cemetery; the farthest to the west is the Emmitsburg Road, which is wholly outside our line of battle, but near the Cemetery is within a hundred yards of it; the Taneytown Road is between these, running nearly due north and south, by the eastern base of Round Top, by the western side of the Cemetery, and uniting with the Emmitsburg Road between the Cemetery and the town. High ground near the Cemetery is named Cemetery Ridge. . . .

The dispositions were all made early, I think before eight o'clock in the morning. Skirmishers were posted well out all around the line, and all put in readiness for battle. The enemy did not yet demonstrate himself. With a look at the ground now, I think you may understand the movements of the battle. From Round Top, by the line of battle, round to the extreme right, I suppose is about three miles. From this same eminence to the Cemetery extends a long ridge or hill— more resembling a great wave than a hill, however—with its crest, which was the line of battle, quite direct between the points mentioned. To the west of this, that is toward the enemy, the ground falls away by a very gradual descent across the Emmitsburg Road, and then rises again, forming another ridge [Seminary Ridge], nearly parallel to the first, but inferior in altitude, and something over a thousand yards away. A belt of woods extends partly along this second ridge, and partly farther to the west, at distances of from one thousand to thirteen hundred yards away from our line. Between these ridges, and along their slopes, that is, in front of the Second and Third Corps, the ground is cultivated, and is covered with fields of wheat, now nearly ripe, with grass and pastures, with some peach orchards, with fields of waving corn, and some farm houses and their outbuildings along the Emmitsburg Road. There are very few places within the limits mentioned where troops and guns could move concealed. There are some oaks of considerable growth along the position of the right of the Second Corps, a group of small trees, sassafras and oak, in front of the right of the Second Division of this Corps also; and considerable woods immediately in front of the left of the Third Corps, and also to the west of and near Round Top. At the Cemetery, where is Cemetery Ridge, to which the line of the Eleventh Corps conforms, is the highest point in our line except Round Top. From this the ground falls quite abruptly to the town, the nearest point of which is some five hundred yards away from the line, and is cultivated and checkered with stone fences.

The same is the character of the ground occupied by, and in front of the left of the First Corps, which is also on a part of Cemetery Ridge. The right of this corps, and the whole of the Twelfth, are along Culp's Hill, and in woods, and the ground is very rocky and in places in front precipitous— a most admirable position for defense from an attack in front, where, on account of the woods, no artillery could be used with effect by the enemy. Then these last three mentioned corps had, by taking rails, by appropriating stone fences, by felling trees, and digging the earth during the night of the first of July, made for themselves excellent breastworks, which were a very good thing indeed.

The position of the First and Twelfth Corps was admirably stong, therefore. Within the line of battle is an irregular basin,

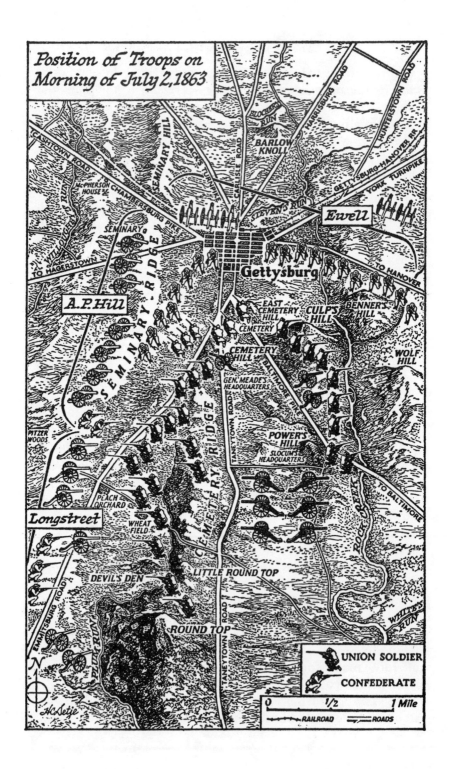

Position of Troops on Morning of July 2, 1863

somewhat woody and rocky in places, but presenting few obstacles to the moving of troops and guns from place to place along the lines, and also affording the advantage that all such movements, by reason of the surrounding crests, were out of view of the enemy. On the whole this was an admirable position to fight a defensive battle; good enough, I thought, when I saw it first, and better I believe than could be found elsewhere in a circle of many miles. Evils, sometimes at least, are blessings in disguise, for the repulse of our forces, and the death of Reynolds, on the first of July, with the opportune arrival of Hancock to arrest the tide of fugitives and fix it on these heights, gave us this position. . . .

On arriving upon the field, General Meade established his headquarters at a shabby little farmhouse on the left of the Taneytown Road, the house nearest the line, and a little more than five hundred yards in the rear of what became the center of the position of the Second Corps, a point where he could communicate readily and rapidly with all parts of the army. The advantages of the position, briefly, were these: the flanks were quite well protected by the natural defenses there, Round Top up the left, and a rocky, steep, untraversable ground up the right. Our line was more elevated than that of the enemy, consequently our artillery had a greater range and power than theirs. On account of the convexity of our line, every part of the line could be reinforced by troops having to move a shorter distance than if the line were straight; further, for the same reason, the line of the enemy must be concave, and consequently longer, and with an equal force, thinner and so weaker than ours. Upon those parts of our line which were wooded, neither we nor the enemy could use artillery; but they were so strong by nature, aided by art, as to be readily defended by a small against a very large body of infantry. When the line was open, it had the advantage of having open country in front; consequently, the enemy here could not surprise, as we were on a crest, which besides the other advantages that I have mentioned, had this: the enemy must advance to the attack up an ascent, and must therefore move slower, and be, before coming upon us, longer under our fire, as well as more exhausted. These, and some other things, rendered out position admirable—for a defensive battle.

3

James Longstreet worried over the strength of the position the Federal forces now held. There was a tenacious streak in Longstreet; he could hold to a point. At Fredericksburg as Longstreet stood among the cannons roaring on Marye's Hill and saw Burnside's men falling almost in even rows, he had become converted to the gospel of a tactical defensive—to force the enemy to attack an entrenched position. If Ewell's hesitancy made him the controversial figure of the first day's fighting, certainly Longstreet was without rival for that honor on the second. He had no taste for the battle that was taking shape—any fool could see that Gettysburg had become Fredericksburg in reverse! But Lee also had his tenacious streak; Longstreet's reminiscences clearly indicate the difference that developed between them as early as July 1.

When I overtook General Lee at five o'clock that afternoon, he said, to my surprise, that he thought of attacking General Meade upon the heights the next day. I suggested that this course seemed to be at variance with the plan of the campaign that had been agreed upon before leaving Fredericksburg.

He said: "If the enemy is there tomorrow, we must attack him."

I replied: "If he is there, it will be because he is anxious that we should attack him—a good reason, in my judgment, for not doing so."

I urged that we should move around by our right to the left of Meade, and put our army between him and Washington, threatening his left and rear, and thus force him to attack us in such position as we might select. I said that it seemed to me that if, during our council at Fredericksburg, we had described the position in which we desired to get the two armies, we could not have expected to get the enemy in a better position for us than that he then occupied; that [now] he was in strong position and would be awaiting us, which was evidence that he desired that we should attack him. I said, further, that his weak point seemed to be his left; hence, I thought that we should move around to his left, that we might threaten it if we intended to maneuver, or attack it if we determined upon a battle. I called his attention to the fact that the country was admirably adapted for a defensive battle, and that we should surely repulse Meade with crushing loss if we would take position so as to force him to attack us, and suggested that, even if we carried the heights in front of us and drove Meade out, we should be so badly crippled that we could not reap the fruits of victory; and that the heights of Gettysburg were in themselves of no more importance to us than the ground we then occupied, and that the mere possession of the ground was not worth a hundred men to us. Meade's army, not its position, was our objective.

General Lee was impressed with the idea that by attacking the Federals he could whip them in detail. I reminded him that if the Federals were there in the morning, it would be proof that they had their forces well in hand, and that with Pickett in Chambersburg and Stuart out of reach we should be somewhat in detail. He, however, did not seem to abandon the idea of attack on the next day. He seemed under a subdued excitement, which occasionally took possession of him when "the hunt was up," and threatened his superb equipoise. The sharp battle fought by Hill and Ewell on that day had given him a taste of victory. . . .

When I left General Lee on the night of the first, I believed that he had made up his mind to attack, but was confident that he had not yet determined as to when the attack should be made. The assertion first made by General Pendleton, and echoed by his confederates, that I was ordered to open the attack at sunrise is totally false. . . . General Lee never in his life gave me orders to open an attack at a specific hour. He was perfectly satisfied that when I had my troops in position, and was ordered to attack, no time was ever lost. On the night of the first, I left him without any orders at all. On the morning of the second, I went to General Lee's headquarters at daylight, and renewed my views against making an attack. He seemed resolved, however, and we discussed the probable results. We observed the position of the Federals and got a general idea of the nature of the ground. About sunrise General Lee sent Colonel Venable, of his staff, to General Ewell's headquarters, ordering him to make a reconnaissance of the ground in his front with a view of making the main attack on his left. A short time afterward he followed Colonel Venable in person. He returned at about nine o'clock and informed me that it would not do to have Ewell open the attack. He finally determined that I should make the main attack on the extreme right. It was fully eleven o'clock when General Lee arrived at this conclusion and ordered the movement.

4

The day wore on, Haskell reports, the weather still sultry, and the sky overcast, with a mizzling effort at rain. In Gettysburg, Sallie Robbins Broadhead awoke reluctantly to her second day of the battle.

Of course we had no rest last night. Part of the time we watched the Rebels rob the house opposite. The family had left sometime during the day, and the robbers must have gotten all they left in the house.

They went from the garret to the cellar, and loading up the plunder in a large four-horse wagon, drove it off.

I expected every minute that they would burst in our door, but they did not come near us. It was a beautiful moonlight night, and we could see all they did.

The cannonading commenced about ten o'clock, and we went to the cellar and remained until it ceased. When the noise subsided, we came to the light again, and tried to get something to eat. My husband went to the garden and picked a mess of beans, though stray firing was going on all the time and bullets from sharpshooters or others whizzed about his head in a way I would not have liked.

He persevered until he had picked all, for he declared the Rebels should not have one. I baked a pan of shortcake and boiled a piece of ham, the last we had in the house, and some neighbors coming in joined us, and we had the first quiet meal since the contest began.

I enjoyed it very much. It seemed so nice after so much confusion to have a little quiet once more. We had not felt like eating before, being worried by danger and excitement.

5

For Billy Bayly the morning tested his inward courage—that his mother would be safe, that his father would come home, that the cause in which he so desperately believed had not been lost.

Mother, accompanied by her niece, took bandages and hospital supplies during the forenoon to the scene of the first day's battle, where she remained for several hours looking after the wounded.

During her absence father returned and reported that the morning previous he had run into the cavalry coming back from its raid upon York (the same we had fled from the week before), and he was not permitted to turn around and return home; that he kept moving until he had passed through the entire body of troops, then made a detour and arrived in Gettysburg just about the time that the battle opened. Finding his way home cut off by the two armies fighting north of the town and the battle so hot, he stabled his horse and soon sought shelter in the house of a friend. This house was taken during the day, after the Union forces were driven back, and the forenoon of the second day father succeeded in passing through the Confederate lines to his home. I saw him coming up the lane and ran to meet him, glad to grasp his hand again and feel the security that its pressure brought. . . .

"How is your mother?" was, of course, the first question asked. I told him "all right when she left home" some hours earlier; that she had taken supplies to the wounded near town and had not yet returned. This news worried father very much not knowing then that he had passed within calling distance of where she was dressing wounds of Union soldiers on his way home. So not knowing where to find mother, we had to wait as patiently as possible for her return, which, I believe, was about three o'clock that afternoon.

The result of the first day's battle had been the forcing of the Union Army to the hills south of the town, and the troops of Lee's army were jubilant that morning and all of that second day. Some of our visitors of the day before were back for more bread and "black spread," as they called the apple-butter, and we had to hear the "I told you so," "Didn't I tell you that we would whip the Yanks," sung to us in all its keys during that day. And the evidence was against us, for the fighting had moved further away. However, we kept up our courage and voiced the conviction that the battle was not over, that our men still hold the heights and you cannot dislodge them.

Some of our soldiers were without shoes, but most of them were well shod. As a rule they were good-natured and courteous, just such men as I as a farmer's boy met in my daily life; in fact, those with whom we had the best opportunity to become acquainted were not the ones who were doing the fighting, hence deductions as to character and disposition can only be very general and of no special value.

Among the first things insisted upon by father when he found that a deserter was concealed in the house was to direct him to come out and take his chances with the family, which he did, passing as one of the boys of the household. He was added to the cherry picking brigade and broke off branches and threw them to his late comrades in arms, who of course, had no suspicions of the boy's recent connection with the Confederate army as they passed beneath the trees.

In the meantime eight large stall-fed steers of father's had been driven off and doubtless were soon converted into juicy steaks and roasts by the "Johnnies," although we did not see the animals slaughtered.

During the afternoon mother called me into the house and asked me to go into the sitting room for her recipe book and write out for a neighbor woman who had dropped in to see how we were getting along, a recipe for chopped pickle, which I did, carelessly leaving the desk open, not noticing that a worthless loafer in a corner of the partially darkened room had been watching me. The result was that a $20.00 greenback note disappeared from the desk—as did the loafer soon afterwards. Another item to be added to the losses of the occasion.

6

As Sallie enjoyed her shortcake and ham and Billy mourned the theft of the greenback, Haskell wondered with the passing of the forenoon if there would be a battle. He watched the action behind the lines with mingled emotions.

All was put in the last state of readiness for battle. Surgeons were busy riding about selecting eligible places for hospitals, and hunting streams and springs and wells. Ambulances and ambulance men were brought up near the lines, and stretchers gotten ready for use. Who of us could tell but that he would be the first to need them? The provost guards were busy driving up all stragglers, and causing them to join their regiments. Ammunition wagons were driven to suitable places, and pack mules bearing boxes of cartridges; and the commands were informed where they might be found. Officers were sent to see that the men had each his hundred rounds of ammunition. Generals and their staffs were riding here and there among their commands to see that all was right. A staff officer or an orderly might be seen galloping furiously in the transmission of some order or message. All, all was ready—and yet the sound of no gun had disturbed the air or ear today.

And so the men stacked their arms—in long bristling rows they stood along the crests—and were at ease. Some men of the Second and Third Corps pulled down the rail fences near and piled them up for breastworks in their front. Some loitered, some went to sleep upon the ground, some, a single man, carrying twenty canteens slung over his shoulder, went for water. Some made them a fire and boiled a dipper of coffee. Some with knees cocked up enjoyed the soldier's peculiar solace, a pipe of tobacco. Some were mirthful and chatty, and some were serious and silent. . . .

During all the morning—and of the night, too—the skirmishers, of the enemy had been confronting those of the

Eleventh, First, and Twelfth Corps. At the time of the fight of the First, he was seen in heavy force north of the town—he was believed to be now in the same neighborhood in full force. But from the woody character of the country, and thereby the careful concealment of troops, which the Rebel is always sure to effect, during the early part of the morning almost nothing was actually seen by us of the invaders of the north. About nine o'clock in the morning, I should think, our glasses began to reveal them at the west and northwest of the town, a mile and a half away from our lines. They were moving toward our left, but the woods of Seminary Ridge so concealed them that we could not make out much of their movements. About this time some rifled guns in the Cemetery, at the left of the Eleventh Corps, opened fire—almost the first shots of any kind this morning—and when it was found they were firing at a Rebel line of skirmishers merely, that were advancing upon the left of that, and the right of the Second Corps, the officer in charge of the guns was ordered to cease firing, and was rebuked for having fired at all. These skirmishers soon engaged those at the right of the Second Corps, who stood their ground and were reinforced to make the line entirely secure. The Rebel skirmish line kept extending further and further to their right—toward our left. They would dash up close upon ours and sometimes drive them back a short distance, in turn to be repulsed themselves —and so they continued to do until their right was opposite the extreme left of the Third Corps. By these means they had ascertained the position and extent of our lines—but their own masses were still out of view. From the time that the firing commenced, as I have mentioned, it was kept up among the skirmishers until quite noon, often briskly; but with no definite results further than those mentioned, and with no considerable show of infantry on the part of the enemy to support.

There was a farmhouse and outbuildings in front of the Third Division of the Second Corps at which the skirmishers of the enemy had made a dash, and dislodged ours posted there, and from there their sharpshooters began to annoy our line of skirmishers and even the main line with their long range rifles. I was up to the line, and a bullet from one of the rascals hid there hissed by my cheek so close that I felt the movement of the air distinctly. And so I was not at all displeased when I saw one of our regiments go down and attack and capture the house and buildings and several prisoners, after a spirited little fight, and, by General Hays' order, burn the buildings to the ground.

About noon the Signal Corps, from the top of Little Round Top, . . . and the cavalry at the extreme left, began to report the enemy in heavy force, making disposition of battle to the west of Round Top and opposite to the left of the Third Corps. Some few prisoners had been captured, some deserters from the enemy had come in, and from all sources by this time we had much important and reliable information of the enemy—of his disposition and apparent purposes. The Rebel infantry consisted of three army corps, each consisting of three divisions. Longstreet, Ewell—the same whose leg Gibbon's shell knocked off at Gainesville on the 28th of August last year—and A. P. Hill, each in the Rebel service having the rank of Lieutenant General, were the commanders of these corps. Longstreet's division commanders were Hood, McLaws, and Pickett; Ewell's were Rodes, Early, and Johnson; and Hill's were Pender, Heth, and Anderson. Stuart and and Fitzhugh Lee commanded divisions of the Rebel cavalry.

The Rebels had about as much artillery as we did; but we never have thought much of this arm in the hands of our adversaries. They have courage enough, but not the skill to handle it well. They generally fire far too high, and the ammunition is usually of a very inferior quality. And, of late, we have begun to despise the enemies' cavalry too. It used to have enterprise and dash, but in the late cavalry contests ours have always been victor; and so now we think about all this *chivalry* is fit for is to steal a few of our mules occasionally and their Negro drivers.

This army of the Rebel infantry, however, is good—to deny this is useless. I never had any desire to—and if one should count up, it would possibly be found that they have gained more victories over us than we have over them, and they will now, doubtless, fight well, even desperately. And it is not

horses or cannon that will determine the result of this confronting of the two armies, but the men with the muskets
must do it—the infantry must do the sharp work.

So we watched all this posting of forces as closely as
possible, for it was a matter of vital interest to us, and all
information relating to it was hurried to the commander of
the Army. The Rebel line of battle was concave, bending
around our own, with the extremities of the wings opposite
to, or a little outside of ours. Longstreet's corps was upon
their right; Hill's in the center. These two Rebel corps occupied the second or inferior ridge to the west of our position, as I have mentioned, with Hill's left bending toward,
and resting near the town, and Ewell's was upon their left,
his troops being in and to the east of the town. This last corps
confronted our Twelfth, First, and the right of the Eleventh
Corps. When I have said that ours was a good *defensive* position, this is equivalent to saying that that of the enemy was
not a good *offensive* one; for these are relative terms, and
cannot be both predicated of the same respective positions
of the two armies at the same time. The reasons that this
was not a good offensive position are the same already stated
in favor of ours for defense. Excepting occasionally for a
brief time during some movement of troops, as when advancing to attack, their men and guns were kept constantly
and carefully, by woods and inequalities of ground, out of
our view.

Noon is past, one o'clock is past, and, save the skirmishing
that I have mentioned and an occasional shot from our guns
at something or other, the nature of which the ones who fired
it were ignorant, there was no fight yet. Our arms were still
stacked, and the men were at ease. As I looked upon those
interminable rows of muskets along the crests, and saw how
cool and good-spirited the men were who were lounging about
on the ground among them, I could not, and did not, have
any fears as to the result of the battle. The storm was near,
and we all knew it well enough by this time, which was to
rain death upon these crests and down their slopes, and yet
the men who could not, and would not escape it, were as
calm and cheerful, generally, as if nothing unusual were about

to happen. You see, these men were veterans, and had been in such places so often that they were accustomed to them. But I was well pleased with the tone of the men today— I could almost see the foreshadowing of victory upon their faces, I thought. And I thought, too, as I had seen the mighty preparations go on to completion for this great conflict— the marshaling of these two hundred thousand men and the guns of the hosts, that now but a narrow valley divided, that to have been in such a battle, and to survive on the side of the victors, would be glorious. Oh, the world is most unchristian yet!

7

To Longstreet the delay in the start of battle was entirely understandable.

By General Lee's authority, Law's Brigade, which had been put upon picket duty, was ordered to rejoin my command, and upon my suggestion that it would be better to await its arrival General Lee assented. We waited about forty minutes for these troops and then moved forward. A delay of several hours occurred in the march of the troops. The cause of this delay was that we had been ordered by General Lee to proceed cautiously upon the forward movement so as to avoid being seen by the enemy. General Lee ordered Colonel Johnston, of his engineer corps, to lead and conduct the head of the column. My troops, therefore, moved forward under guidance of a special officer of General Lee and with instructions to follow his directions. I left General Lee only after the line had stretched out on the march, and rode along with Hood's Division, which was in the rear.

The march was necessarily slow, the conductor frequently encountering points that exposed the troops to the view of the signal station on Round Top. At length the column halted. After waiting some time, supposing that it would soon move forward, I sent to the front to inquire the occasion of the delay. It was reported that the column was awaiting the movements of Colonel Johnston, who was trying to lead it by some route by which it could pursue its march without falling under

view of the Federal signal station. Looking up toward Round
Top, I saw that the signal station was in full view; and, as we
could plainly see this station, it was apparent that our heavy
columns were seen from their position and that further efforts
to conceal ourselves would be a waste of time.

I became very impatient at this delay and determined to
take upon myself the responsibility of hurrying the troops forward. I did not order General McLaws forward, because, as
the head of the column, he had direct orders from General
Lee to follow the conduct of Colonel Johnston. Therefore, I
sent orders to Hood, who was in the rear and not encumbered
by these instructions, to push his division forward by the
most direct route so as to take position on my right. He did
so, and thus broke up the delay. The troops were rapidly
thrown into position, and preparations were made for the
attack.

It may be proper just here to consider the relative strength
and position of the two armies. Our army was fifty-two thousand infantry; Meade's was ninety-five thousand. These are
our highest figures and the enemy's lowest. We had learned
on the night of the first, from some prisoners captured near
Seminary Ridge, that the First, Eleventh, and Third Corps
had arrived by the Emmitsburg Road and had taken position
on the heights in front of us, and that reinforcements had
been seen coming by the Baltimore Road just after the fight
of the first. From an intercepted dispatch we learned that
another corps was in camp, about four miles from the field.
We had every reason, therefore, to believe that the Federals
were prepared to renew the battle. Our army was stretched
in an elliptical curve, reaching from the front of Round Top
around Seminary Ridge, and enveloping Cemetery Heights on
the left; thus covering a space of four or five miles. The enemy
occupied the high ground in front of us, being massed within
a curve of about two miles nearly concentric with the curve
described by our forces. His line was about one thousand four
hundred yards from ours. Anyone will see that the proposition
for this inferior force to assault and drive out the masses of
troops upon the heights was a very problematical one. My
orders from General Lee were "to envelop the enemy's left,

and begin the attack there, following up, as near as possible, the direction of the Emmitsburg Road."

My corps occupied our right, with Hood on the extreme right, and McLaws next. Hill's corps was next to mine, in front of the Federal center, and Ewell was on our extreme left. My corps, with Pickett's division absent, numbered hardly thirteen thousand men. I realized that the fight was to be a fearful one; but being assured that my flank would be protected by the brigades of Wilcox, Perry, Wright, Posey, and Mahone moving *en échelon,* and that Ewell was to co-operate by a direct attack on the enemy's right, and Hill to threaten his center and attack if opportunity offered and thus prevent reinforcements from being launched either against myself or Ewell, it seemed possible that we might dislodge the great army in front of us. At half-past three o'clock the order was given General Hood to advance upon the enemy, and, hurrying to the head of McLaw's division, I moved with his line.

8

If earlier in the morning Longstreet could question Lee's general plan, now John B. Hood, brigadier general of the fighting Texas Brigade, could question Longstreet's execution of it. Born in Kentucky, a graduate of West Point, Hood's qualties as a military leader were well respected; his service with the Army of Northern Virginia had begun on the Peninsula as a captain of cavalry, and in time he was to command the Army of Tennessee. With the bluntness of a Texan-by-adoption, his report to Longstreet revealed their dispute.

General Lee was, seemingly, anxious you should attack that morning. He remarked to me, "The enemy is here, and if we do not whip him, he will whip us." You thought it better to await the arrival of Pickett's division—at that time still in the rear—in order to make the attack; and you said to me, subsequently, whilst we were seated together near the trunk of a tree: "The General is a little nervous this morning; he wishes me to attack; I do not wish to do so without Pickett. I never like to go into battle with one boot off."

Thus passed the forenoon of that eventful day; then in the

afternoon—about three o'clock—it was decided to await no longer Pickett's division, but to proceed to our extreme right and attack up the Emmitsburg Road. McLaws moved off, and I followed with my division. In a short time I was ordered to quicken the march of my troops and to pass to the front of McLaws.

This movement was accomplished by throwing out an advanced force to tear down fences and clear the way. The instructions I received were to place my division across the Emmitsburg Road, form line of battle, and attack. Before reaching this road, however, I had sent forward some of my picked Texas scouts to ascertain the position of the enemy's extreme left flank. They soon reported to me that it rested upon Round Top Mountain [Little Round Top]; that the country was open, and that I could march through an open woodland pasture around Round Top [Great Round Top], and assault the enemy in flank and rear; that their wagon trains were parked in rear of their lines and were badly exposed to our attack in that direction. As soon as I arrived upon the Emmitsburg Road I placed one or two batteries in position and opened fire. A reply from the enemy's guns soon developed his lines. His left rested on, or near, Round Top [Little Round Top], with line bending back and again forward, forming, as it were, a concave line as approached by the Emmitsburg Road. A considerable body of troops was posted in front of their main line between the Emmitsburg Road and Round Top Mountain. This force was in line of battle upon an eminence near a peach orchard. . . .

I found that in making the attack according to orders, viz., up the Emmitsburg Road, I should have first to encounter and drive off this advanced line of battle; secondly, at the base and along the slope of the mountain, to confront immense boulders of stone, so massed together as to form narrow openings, which would break our ranks and cause the men to scatter whilst climbing up the rocky precipice. I found, moreover, that my division would be exposed to a heavy fire from the main line of the enemy in position on the crest of the high range, of which Round Top was the extreme left, and, by reason of the concavity of the enemy's line, that we would be subject to a destructive fire in flank and rear as well as in front; and deemed it almost an impossibility to clamber along the boulders up this steep and rugged mountain, and, under this number of cross fires, put the enemy to flight. I knew that if the feat was accomplished, it must be at a most fearful sacrifice of as brave and gallant soldiers as ever engaged in battle.

The reconnaissance of my Texas scouts and the development of the Federal lines were effected in a very short space of time; in truth, shorter than I have taken to recall and jot down these facts, although the scenes and events of that day are as clear to my mind as if the great battle had been fought yesterday. I was in possession of these important facts shortly after reaching the Emmitsburg Road as ordered, and urged that you allow me to turn Round Top and attack the enemy in flank and rear. Accordingly I dispatched a staff officer, bearing to you my request to be allowed to make the proposed movement. . . . Your reply was quickly received: "General Lee's orders are to attack up the Emmitsburg Road." I sent another officer saying I feared nothing could be accomplished by such an attack, and renewed my request to turn Round Top. Again your answer was, "General Lee's orders are to attack up the Emmitsburg Road." During this interim I had continued the use of the batteries upon the enemy, and had become more and more convinced that the Federal line extended to Round Top, and that I could not reasonably hope to accomplish much by the attack as ordered. In fact, it seemed to me that the enemy occupied a position by nature so strong—I may say impregnable—that, independently of their flank fire, they could easily repel our attack by merely throwing and rolling stones down the mountain side as we approached.

A third time I dispatched one of my staff to explain fully in regard to the situation and suggest that you had better come and look for yourself. I selected, in this instance, my adjutant general, Colonel Harry Sellers, whom you know to be not only an officer of great courage, but also of marked ability. Colonel Sellers returned with the same message: "General Lee's orders are to attack up the Emmitsburg Road." Almost simultaneously Colonel Fairfax, of your staff, rode up and repeated the above orders.

After this urgent protest against entering the battle at Gettysburg, according to instructions—which protest is the first and only one I ever made during my entire military career —I ordered my line to advance and make the assault.

As my troops were moving forward, you rode up in person; a brief conversation passed between us, during which I again expressed the fears above mentioned, and regret at not being allowed to attack in flank around Round Top. You answered to this effect: "We must obey the orders of General Lee." I then rode forward with my line under a heavy fire. In about twenty minutes, after reaching the peach orchard, I was severely wounded in the arm and borne from the field.

With this wound terminated my participation in this great battle. As I was borne off on a litter to the rear, I could but experience deep distress of mind and heart at the thought of the inevitable fate of my brave fellow-soldiers, who formed one of the grandest divisions of that world-renowned army; and I shall ever believe had I been permitted to turn Round Top Mountain, we would not only have gained that position but have been able finally to route the enemy.

9

With Longstreet rode Fremantle, whose day already had been long and tiring.

Colonel Sorrell, the Austrian, and I arrived at 5 A.M. at the same commanding position we were on yesterday and I climbed up a tree in company with Captain Schreibert of the Prussian Army. Just below us were seated Generals Lee, Hill, in consultation—the two latter assisting their deliberations by the truly American custom of *whittling* sticks. General Heth was also present; he was wounded in the head yesterday, and although not allowed to command his brigade, he insisted on coming to the field. . . .

As the whole morning was to be occupied in disposing the troops for the attack, I rode to the extreme right with Colonel Manning and Major Walton, where we ate quantities of cherries and got a feed of corn for our horses. We also bathed in a small stream, but not without some trepidation on our part, for we were almost beyond the lines, and were exposed to the enemy's cavalry.

At one P.M. I met a quantity of Yankee prisoners who had been picked up straggling. They told me they belonged to Sickles's corps (Third, I think), and had arrived from Emmitsburg during the night. At this time skirmishing began along part of the line, but not heavily.

At two P.M. General Longstreet advised me if I wished to have a good view of the battle to return to my tree of yesterday. I did so, and remained there with Lawly and Captain Schreibert during the rest of the afternoon. But until four forty-five P.M. all was profoundly still and we began to doubt whether a fight was coming off today at all. At that time, however, Longstreet suddenly commenced a heavy cannonade on the right. Ewell immediately took it up on the left. The enemy replied with at least equal fury and in a few moments the firing along the whole line was as heavy as it is possible to conceive. A dense smoke arose for six miles; there was little wind to drive it away, and the air seemed full of shells—each of which appeared to have a different style of going, and to make a different noise than the others. The ordnance on both sides is of a very varied description. Every now and then a caisson would blow up—if a Federal one, a Confederate yell would immediately follow. The Southern troops, when charging or to express their delight, always yell in a manner peculiar to themselves. The Yankee cheer is much more like ours; but the Confederate officers declare that the Rebel yell has a peculiar merit and always produces a salutary and useful effect upon their adversaries. A corps is sometimes spoken of as a "good yelling regiment."

So soon as the firing began, General Lee joined Hill just below our tree, and he remained there nearly all the time looking through his field glasses—sometimes talking to Hill and sometimes to Colonel Long of his staff. But generally he sat quite alone on the stump of a tree. What I remarked especially was that during the whole time the firing continued he only sent one message and only received one report. It is evidently his system to arrange the plan thoroughly with the three corps commanders, and then leave to them the duty of modifying and carrying it out to the best of their abilities.

When the cannonade was at its height, a Confederate band of music, between the cemetery and ourselves, began to play polkas and waltzes, which sounded very curious accompanied by the hissing and bursting of shells.

10

So from his seat in a tree, while the cannons roared and the Confederate band played polkas and waltzes, Fremantle watched the progress of a battle that was to leave as shrines in the pages of American history the Peach Orchard and the Wheatfield, Little Round Top and Devil's Den. And to Haskell, also watching and waiting, the action turned on the blunder of a Union general.

Somewhat after one o'clock P.M.—the skirmish firing had nearly ceased now—a movement of the Third Corps occurred, which I shall describe. . . . From the position of the Third Corps, as I have mentioned, to the second ridge west, the distance is about a thousand yards, and there the Emmitsburg Road runs near the crest of the ridge. General Sickles commenced to advance his whole corps from the general line straight to the front with a view to occupy this second ridge along and near the road. What his purpose could have been is past conjecture. It was not ordered by General Meade, as I heard him say, and he disapproved of it as soon as it was made known to him. Generals Hancock and Gibbon, as they saw the move in progress, criticized its propriety sharply, as I know, and foretold quite accurately what would be the result.

I suppose the truth probably is that General Sickles supposed he was doing for the best; but he was neither born nor bred a soldier. But one can scarcely tell what may have been the motives of such a man—a politician, and some other things, exclusive of the *Barton Key* affair[2]—a man after show

[2] Sickles discovered that "a guilty intimacy" had developed between his wife and Philip Barton Key, U. S. Attorney for the

and notoriety and newspaper fame and the adulation of the mob! O, there is a grave responsibility on those in whose hands are the lives of ten thousand men; and on those who put stars upon men's shoulders, too! Bah! I kindle when I see some things that I have to see. But this move of the Third Corps was an important one—it developed the battle—the results of the move to the corps itself we shall see. O, if this corps had kept its strong position upon the crest, and supported by the rest of the army, had waited for the attack of the enemy![3]

It was magnificent to see those ten or twelve thousand men —they were good men—with their batteries, and some squadrons of cavalry upon the left flank, all in battle order, in several lines, with flags streaming, sweep steadily down the slope, across the valley, and up the next ascent toward their destined position! From our position we could see it all. In advance Sickles pushed forward his heavy line of skirmishers, who drove back those of the enemy across the Emmitsburg Road, and thus cleared the way for the main body. The Third Corps now became the absorbing object of interest of all eyes. The Second Corps took arms, and the 1st Division of this corps was ordered to be in readiness to support the Third Corps should circumstances render support necessary. As the Third Corp was the extreme left of our line as it advanced, if the enemy was assembling to the west of Round Top with a

---

District of Columbia, and on February 27, 1859, he shot and killed Key. Indicted for murder, Sickles was acquitted after a trial of twenty days at which, for the first time, the defense pleaded "temporary aberration of the mind."

[3] Meade, in his official report, expressed the opinion that Sickles had simply misunderstood orders, and was stung when later the *New York Herald* published an article, signed by "Historicus," that reflected severely on Meade's military judgment while elevating Sickles to the stature of Napoleon. Insofar as Meade believed that Sickles was "Historicus," his resentment was not surprising; Halleck likewise was sure that Sickles was the culprit behind this bit of self-glorification at Meade's expense, and was not especially surprised at the New Yorker's underhandedness. *Official Records*, Ser. 1, XXVII, Pt. 1, 128-37.

view to turn our left as we had heard, there would be nothing
between the left flank of the corps and the enemy; and the
enemy would be square upon its flank by the time it had attained the road. So when this advance line came near the
Emmitsburg Road, and we saw the squadrons of cavalry mentioned come dashing back from their position as flankers, and
the smoke of some guns, and we heard the reports away to
Sickles's left, anxiety became an element in our interest in
these movements. The enemy opened slowly at first, and from
long range; but he was square upon Sickles's left flank.
General Caldwell was ordered at once to put his division—
the 1st of the Second Corps, as mentioned—in motion, and
to take post in the woods at the left slope of Round Top, in
such a manner as to resist the enemy should he attempt to
come around Sickles's left and gain his rear. The division
moved as ordered, and disappeared from view in the woods
toward the point indicated at between two and three o'clock
P.M., and the reserve brigade—the First, Colonel Heath temporarily commanding—of the Second Division, was therefore
moved up and occupied the position vacated by the Third
Division. About the same time the Fifth Corps could be seen
marching by the flank from its position on the Baltimore
Pike, and in the opening of the woods heading for the same
locality where the First Division of the Second Corps had
gone. The Sixth Corps had now come up and was halted upon
the Baltimore Pike.

As the enemy opened upon Sickles with his batteries, some
five or six in all, I suppose, firing slowly, Sickles with as many
replied, and with much more spirit. The artillery fire became
quite animated, soon; but the enemy was forced to withdraw
his guns farther and farther away, and ours advanced upon
him. It was not long before the cannonade ceased altogether,
the enemy having retired out of range, and Sickles, having
temporarily halted his command pending this, moved forward
again to the position he desired, or nearly that. It was now
about five o'clock, and we shall soon see what Sickles gained
by his move. First we hear more artillery firing upon Sickles's
left—the enemy seems to be opening again, and as we watch
the Rebel batteries seem to be advancing there. The cannon-

ade is soon opened again, and with great spirit upon both sides. The enemy's batteries press those of Sickles and pound the shot upon them, and this time they in turn begin to retire to position nearer the infantry. The enemy seems to be fearfully in earnest this time. And what is more ominous than the thunder or the shot of his advancing guns, this time, in the intervals between his batteries far to Sickles's left appear the long lines and the columns of the Rebel infantry, now unmistakably moving out to the attack. The position of the Third Corps becomes at once one of great peril, and it is probable that its commander by this time began to realize his true situation.

All was astir now on our crest. Generals and their staffs were galloping hither and thither—the men were all in their places, and you might have heard the rattle of ten thousand ramrods as they drove home and "thugged" upon the little globes and cones of lead. As the enemy was advancing upon Sickles's flank, he commenced a change, or at least a partial one, of front by swinging back his left and throwing forward his right in order that his lines might be parallel to those of his adversary, his batteries meantime doing what they could to check the enemy's advance; but this movement was not completely executed before new Rebel batteries opened upon Sickles's right flank—his former front—and in the same quarter appeared the Rebel infantry also. Now came the dreadful battle picture of which we for a time could be but spectators. Upon the front and right flank of Sickles came sweeping the infantry of Longstreet and Hill. Hitherto there had been skirmishing and artillery practice—now the battle began; for amid the heavier smoke and larger tongues of flame of the batteries, now began to appear the countless flashes, and the long fiery sheets of the muskets, and the rattle of the volleys mingled with the thunder of the guns. We see the long gray lines come sweeping down upon Sickles's front and mix with the battle smoke; now the same colors emerge from the bushes and orchards upon his right, and envelop his flank in the confusion of the conflict.

O, the din and the roar, and these thirty thousand Rebel wolf cries! What a hell is there down that valley!

Chapter 6

"We Ran Like a Herd of Wild Cattle"

JAMES LONGSTREET had the fight he didn't want, the fight he feared because Pickett's division had not yet come up, because the position of the Federals was too strong, because he suspected that Lee's emotions had obscured his military logic. But now as the cannon thundered, as the columns of blue and gray swept forward, as the shells burst and the horses galloped and the artillerymen wiped their sweaty faces and cursed the enemy with screaming fires of canister, the old bulldog in Longstreet sank its teeth into the ragged seat of battle. And in battle Longstreet wasn't any brass-hat general; he could take a sabre and lead a charge. Years later, as an old and querulous man who fussed for long hours over what might have been, Longstreet could still recall with eyes crackling that action on the second day at Gettysburg. It was "the best three hours of fighting by any troops on any battlefield!"

Lee's general strategy that afternoon became quickly obvious: Longstreet was to attack on the right flank and Ewell on the left while Hill held the center and kept the Union forces from the quick deployment of reinforcements on any sector of the line that might weaken. But already Lee had lost one element of the battle—time. This attack had been planned for morning! And even now, as the afternoon shadows began to lengthen, did this sudden surge of the Third Corps under Sickles force Longstreet to attack before the situation on the right flank became completely clear to him?

The outcome of a battle can depend on many elements— not alone on men and arms, not alone on ground lost or held or the timely arrival of reinforcements, but also on a frightened horse running away with a general, on the capture of the canteens of an entire regiment, on the darkness of a battlefield where men strain to catch a glimpse of their comrades between the flashes of the guns. With such factors as these Longstreet was also forced to reckon as history gave him his greatest day.

1

At the outbreak of the war Henry Edwin Tremain left Columbia Law School to enlist as a private in the Seventh Regiment of the New York National Guard. He was taken prisoner at Second Manassas and held as a hostage at Libby Prison; upon his release he was assigned to Sickles's staff, and at Gettysburg served Sickles as senior aide-de-camp. Tremain witnessed the two meetings between Meade and Sickles as the second day's battle began.

An aide of General Meade rode up and told General Sickles—and this was the second message of the same purport —that General Meade wished to see him at his headquarters. The corps commanders had been summoned there. Nothing was to be done but to comply at once. As the best trail thither—I had assayed several ways—was by that time especially familiar to me, the general directed me to lead the way and ride fast. . . .

By the time we reached headquarters the sound of musketry from Birney's front was quite marked although it had not yet attained the volume signifying battalion collisions. It was, however, to the experienced ear sufficiently significant of their approach. The interview, therefore, between General Sickles and Meade was very brief. . . . General Meade met General Sickles in front of his quarters and informed him he need not dismount, that his presence was needed at his own front. General Meade said he would meet him there in a few minutes. We were off again in short order because of the significance of the firing; and by the time we reached our starting point it was clear that the battle was thoroughly opened.

I was wondering why a battery, that I had seen at an earlier hour go into position immediately south of us and where our infantry lines were very slender and the intervening fields untimbered, had not opened on us. It enfiladed the plain where before that we had been maneuvering. But I know now that the scheme was first to force our extreme left. Besides, there was nothing special just then on that plain affording a useful mark, or specially attractive. I do not know what General Sickles thought about it, for he had made no remark when I pointed it out to him. . . .

Suddenly, to the north of where we were standing, a small body of horsemen appeared to my surprise on our open field just described, and at the place of all others most tempting to the enemy's guns thus posted. Rapidly approaching us the group proved to be General Meade and a portion of his staff.

General Sickles rode toward them, and I followed closely, necessarily hearing the brief, because interrupted, colloquy that ensued.

General Meade said, "General, I am afraid you are too far out."

General Sickles responded, "I will withdraw, if you wish, sir."

General Meade replied, "I think it is too late. The enemy will not allow you. If you need more artillery call on the reserve artillery." (Bang! a single gun sounded.) "The Fifth Corps—and a division of Hancock's—will support you."

His last sentence was caught with difficulty. It was interrupted. It came out in jerks—in sections; between the acts, to speak literally.

The conversation could not be continued. Neither the noise nor any destruction had arrested it. Attracted by the group, it was a shot at them from the battery I have mentioned. The great ball went high and harmlessly struck the ground beyond. But the whizzing missile had frightened the charger of General Meade into an uncontrollable frenzy. He reared, he plunged. He could not be quieted. Nothing was possible to be done with such a beast except to let him run; and run he would, and run he did. The staff straggled after him, and so General Meade against his own will . . . was apparently ingloriously and temporarily carried from the front at the formal opening of the furious engagement of July 2, 1863. There can be no question that for a time that frenzied horse was running away. But he bore his rider safely, and a sad misfortune under all the circumstances was happily averted.

2

While Meade, clinging to a runaway horse, was swept from the scene of action, General Gouverneur K. Warren, chief engineer of the Army of the Potomac, saw the full danger created by the unexpected movement of Sickles's Third Corps. The story now is told by Ziba B. Graham, an officer in the Sixteenth Michigan.

I went out to the front to see the line and take a view of the surrounding country. I had not returned to the regiment but a few moments before the Sixth Army Corps came up, and we moved away toward the left of the Third Corps, while the Sixth Corps took our place. While moving to our new position the ball opened and the firing became terrific. We double-quicked over the old stony ground in very short order, while shell after shell came bursting among us. We had been massed between the Emmitsburg Road and the Baltimore Pike; the First Division on the right, the Third Brigade on the right of the division, and our Sixteenth Michigan on the right of the brigade, placing our regiment on the lead of the corps.

Going into the fight we progressed near to the Trostle House (Sickles's Headquarters) in our double-quick movement to support General Birney, when General G. K. Warren came dashing to the head of the column from the direction of Little Round Top, and pointing out Little Round Top to Colonel Strong Vincent, who had command of our brigade, said, "I take the responsibility of detaching your brigade. Give the command to double-quick and ride forward with me to Little Round Top. To lose Round Top would be fatal."

The command was given. The regiments of the brigade did double-quick and moved right forward into line, formed on top, the ranks closed up. General Warren, taking position on a large boulder, pointed out to Colonel Vincent and Colonel Welch the movements of Hood's division of Longstreet's corps.

Turning to Vincent he gave him imperative orders to hold this point at all hazards, if he sacrificed every man of the Third Brigade, promising to go immediately for reinforcements.

The disposition of the regiments and battery was made as follows: Battery D., Hazlett's Fifth U. S. Artillery, on top of the mountain and on right of the brigade. The Sixteenth Michigan moved forward and down about sixty feet below the summit, its right resting under left section of battery, while Company A and the company of sharpshooters were detached and deployed as skirmishers over and on Big Round Top; Forty-fourth New York, Eighty-third Pennsylvania and Twentieth Maine in somewhat of a semicircle formation, facing in the woods and low rocky ground between the Round Tops. We remained in this position but a short time when we were attacked by Hood's column. No other troops were there when the Third Brigade made its grand charge up the rocky side of Little Round Top.

3

The situation at Little Round Top as the Union forces saw it is summarized in a single sentence by Theodore Gerrish of the Twentieth Maine: "Imagine, if you can, three hundred men on the extreme flank of an army, there to hold the key of the entire position!" To the Rebel forces advancing to the attack the scene was equally grim: the rock-strewn slopes of Little Round Top; a thousand feet away and rising 120 feet higher the steep sides of Great Round Top; and not far distant between the bases of the two the rocky caverns of Devil's Den—a sharpshooter's paradise. To Colonel William Colvin Oates, leading the Fifteenth Alabama Regiment into this labyrinth of rock and hill where death lurked in every shadow, the natural point of vantage seemed Great Round Top.

Just after we crossed Plum Run we received the first fire from the enemy's infantry. It was Stoughton's Second Regiment United States sharpshooters, posted behind a fence at or near the southern foot of Great Round Top. They reached that position as we advanced through the old field. No other troops were there nor on that mountain at that time. I did not halt at the first fire, but looked to the rear for the Forty-eighth Alabama, and saw it going under General Law's order across the rear of our line to the left, it was said, to reinforce the Texas brigade, which was hotly engaged. That left no one in my rear or on my right to meet this foe. They were in the woods and I did not know the number of them. I received the second fire. Lieutenant Colonel Feagin and one or two of the men fell.

I knew it would not do to go on and leave that force, I knew not how strong, in our rear with no troops of ours to take care of them; so I gave the command to change direction to the right. The seven companies of the Forty-seventh swung around with the Fifteenth and kept in line with it. The other three companies of that regiment were sent forward as skirmishers before the advance began. The sharpshooters retreated up the south front of the mountain, pursued by my command. In places the men had to climb up, catching to the rocks and bushes and crawling over the boulders in the face of the fire of the enemy, who kept retreating, taking shelter and firing down on us from behind the rocks and crags which covered the side of the mountain thicker than gravestones in a city cemetery. Fortunately they usually overshot us. We could see our foe only as they dodged back from one boulder to another, hence our fire was scattering. As we advanced up the mountain they ceased firing about half way up, divided, and a battalion went around the mountain on each side. Those who went up to the right fired a few shots at my flank. To meet this I deployed Company A, and moved it by the left flank to protect my right, and continued my rugged ascent until we reached the top. Some of my men fainted from heat, exhaustion, and thirst. I halted and let them lie down and rest a few minutes. My right lay exactly where the observatory now stands, and the line extended down the slope westward. I saw Gettysburg through the foliage of the trees. Saw the smoke and heard the roar of battle which was then raging at the Devil's Den, in the peach orchard, up the Emmitsburg

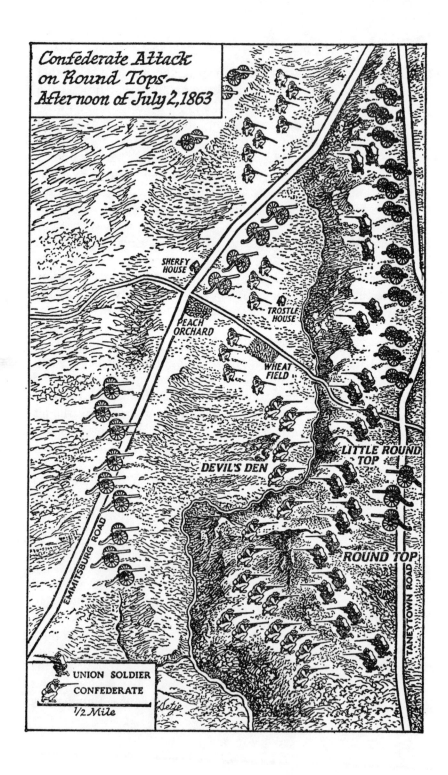

Confederate Attack on Round Tops— Afternoon of July 2, 1863

SHERFY HOUSE

TROSTLE HOUSE

PEACH ORCHARD

WHEAT FIELD

DEVIL'S DEN

LITTLE ROUND TOP

ROUND TOP

EMMITSBURG ROAD

TANEYTOWN ROAD

UNION SOLDIER
CONFEDERATE

1/2 Mile

Road, and on the west and south of the Little Round Top. I saw from the highest point of rocks that we were then on the most commanding elevation in that neighborhood. I knew that my men were too much exhausted to make a good fight without a few minutes' rest.

4

Devil's Den! One way to visualize this mass of rock piled upon rock is as Mathew Brady photographed it: the deep caverns made by the great slabs of Pennsylvania stone, a single soldier dead upon the damp floor, his arms by his side, his cap gone, his sniper's rifle resting against the wall. But Devil's Den now is the abode of a living enemy as Colonel W. F. Perry of the Forty-eighth Alabama leads a fearful charge against it.

Large rocks, from six to fifteen feet high, are thrown together in confusion over a considerable area, and yet so disposed as to leave everywhere among them winding passages carpeted with moss. Many of its recesses are never visited by the sunshine, and a cavernous coolness pervades the air within it.

A short distance to the east the frowning bastions of Little Round Top rise two hundred feet above the level of the plain. An abrupt elevation, thirty or forty feet high, itself buttressed with rocks, constitutes the western boundary of this strange formation.

The view was imposing. Little Round Top, crowned with artillery, resembled a volcano in eruption; while the hillock near the Devil's Den resembled a small one. The distance between them, diminished by the view in perspective, appeared as a secondary crater near its base. . . .

The enemy were as invisible to us as we were to them. The presence of a battery of artillery of course implied the presence of a strong supporting force of infantry. Of its strength, its position, and the nature of its defenses we were in total ignorance. . . . As the line emerged from the woods into the open space, a sheet of flame burst from the rocks less than fifty yards away. A few scattering shots in the beginning gave

warning in time for my men to fall down, and thus largely
to escape the effect of the main volley. They doubtless seemed
to the enemy to be all dead, but the volley of the fire which
they immediately returned proved that they were very much
alive.

No language can express the intensity of the solicitude with
which I surveyed the strange, wild situation which had suddenly burst upon my view. Upon the decision of a moment
depended the honor of my command, and perhaps the lives of
many brave men. I knew that, if called upon, they would follow me, and felt confident that the place could be carried by
an impetuous charge. But then what? There were no supporting troops in sight. A heavy force of the enemy might envelop
and overpower us. It was certain that we should be exposed to
a plunging, enfilading fire from Little Round Top. And yet,
the demoralization and shame of a retreat, and an exposure to
be shot in the back were not to be thought of.

Before the enemy had time to load their guns a decision
was made. Leaping over the prostrate line before me, I
shouted the order, "Forward!" and started for the rocks. The
response was a bound, a yell, and a rush, and in ten seconds
my men were pouring into the Den, and the enemy were
escaping from the opposite side. A few prisoners were taken.
Two soldiers of the Fourth Maine Regiment surrendered to
me in person at the edge of the rocks as my line overtook
and passed me.

In the charge the left wing of the regiment struck the hill
on which the artillery were stationed, and the center and the
right swept into the rocks east of it. Major George W. Carey
led the left wing up the hill, and bounding over the rocks on
its crest, landed among the artillerymen ahead of the line,
and received their surrender. . . . The Major a few moments
later found me near the foot of the hill, completely prostrated
by heat and excessive exertion. He exhibited several swords
as an evidence that the artillery had surrendered, and com-
plained that guns from both sides were playing upon the position. . . . At the very entrance of the labyrinth a spherical
case-shot from Round Top had exploded very near my head

and thrown its deadly contents against a rock almost within my reach.

5

But to Colonel Oates, resting his men on Great Round Top, any action at Devil's Den was remote, impersonal. His own problems revolved around the thirst of his men and the taking of a risk that he considered needless.

When we formed line of battle before the advance began, a detail was made of two men from each of the eleven companies of my regiment to take all the canteens to a well about one hundred yards in our rear and fill them with cool water before we went into the fight. Before this detail could fill the canteens the advance was ordered. It would have been infinitely better to have waited five minutes for those twenty-two men and the canteens of water, but generals never ask a colonel if his regiment is ready to move. The order was given and away we went. The water detail followed with the canteens of water, but when they got into the woods they missed us, walked right into the Yankee lines, and were captured, canteens and all. My men in the ranks, in the intense heat, suffered greatly for water. The loss of those twenty-two men and lack of the water contributed largely to our failure to take Little Round Top a few minutes later.

About five minutes after I halted, Captain Terrell, assistant adjutant general to General Law, rode up by the only pathway on the southeast side of the mountain and inquired why I had halted. I told him. He then informed me that General Hood was wounded, Law was in command of the division, and said for me to press on, turn the Union left, and capture Little Round Top, if possible, and to lose no time.

I then called his attention to my position. A precipice on the east and north, right at my feet; a very steep, stony, and wooded mountainside on the west. The only approach to it by our enemy was a long wooded slope on the northwest, where the pathway to the observatory now is. Within half an hour I could convert it into a Gibraltar that I could hold against ten times the number of men that I had, hence in my judgment it should be held and occupied by artillery as soon as possible, as it was higher than the other mountain and would command the entire field. Terrell replied that probably I was right, but that he had no authority to change or originate orders, which I very well knew; but with his sanction I would have remained at that point until I could have heard from Law or some superior in rank. I inquired for Law. Terrell said that as senior brigadier he was commanding the division, and along the line to the left. He then repeated that General Law had sent him to tell me to lose no time, but to press forward and drive everything before me as far as possible. . . . I felt confident that Law did not know my position, or he would not order me from it. I had not seen him or any other general officer after I received Stoughton's fire, and did not see any general or staff officer, other than Terrell, until the morning of July 3; and I am confident that no general and but the one staff officer ascended Great Round Top.

Notwithstanding my conviction of the importance of holding and occupying Big Round Top with artillery, which I endeavored to communicate to Law through Terrell (he never reached General Law until near the close of the battle), I considered it my duty to obey the order communicated to me by Terrell, whom I knew to be a trustworthy and gallant officer; but it was against my judgment to leave that strong position. It looked to me to be the key point of the field, as artillery on it would have commanded the other Round Top and the Federal line toward Gettysburg as far as it extended along Cemetery Ridge; but the order was to find and turn the left of the Union line, and that was on Little Round Top; the battle was raging below. I therefore caused both regiments to face to the left and moved to the left so as to avoid the precipice in our front, and then ordered the line by the right flank forward and passed to the left-oblique entirely down the northern side of the mountain without encountering any opposition whatever.

While descending in rear of Vincent's Spur, in plain view were the Federal wagon trains, and less than three hundred yards distant was an extensive park of Federal ordnance wagons, which satisfied me that we were then in their rear. I ordered Captain Shaaf to deploy his company, A, surround and capture the ordnance wagons, have them driven in under a spur of the mountain, and detached his company for the purpose. Advancing rapidly without any skirmishers in front, the woods being open without undergrowth, I saw no enemy until within forty or fifty steps of an irregular ledge of rocks—a splendid line of natural breastworks running about parallel with the front of the Forty-seventh regiment and my four left companies, and then sloping back in front of my center and right at an angle of about thirty-five or forty degrees. Vincent's brigade, consisting of the Sixteenth Michigan on the right, Forty-fourth New York, Eighty-third Pennsylvania, and Twentieth Maine regiments, reached this position ten minutes before my arrival, and they piled a few rocks from boulder to boulder, making the zigzag line more complete, and were concealed behind it ready to receive us. From behind this ledge, unexpectedly to us, because concealed, they poured into us the most destructive fire I ever saw. Our line halted, but did not break. The enemy were formed in line as named from their right to left. We received the fire of the three left regiments. As men fell their comrades closed the gap, returning the fire most spiritedly. I could see through the smoke men of the Twentieth Maine in front of my right wing running from tree to tree back westward toward the main body, and I advanced my right.

6

For Captain Howard L. Prince of the Twentieth Maine the action down those slopes is unforgettable.

Again and again was this mad rush repeated, each time to be beaten off by the ever-thinning line that desperately clung to its ledge of rock, refusing to yield except as it involuntarily shrunk for a pace or two at a time from the storm of lead which swept its front. Colonel Oates himself advanced close to our lines at the head of his men, and at times the hostile forces were actually at hand-to-hand distance. Twice the rebels were followed down the slope so sharply that they were obliged to use the bayonet, and in places small squads of their men in their charges reached our actual front. . . .

The front surged backward and forward like a wave. At times our dead and wounded were in front of our line, and then by a superhuman effort our gallant lads would carry the combat forward beyond their prostrate forms. Continually the gray lines crept up by squads under protecting trees and boulders, and the firing became at closer and closer range. And even the enemy's line essayed to reach around the then front of blue that stretched out in places in single rank and could not go much farther without breaking. So far had they extended, that the bullets passed beyond and into the ranks of the other regiments farther up the hill, and Captain Woodward, commanding the Eighty-third, sent his adjutant to ask if the Twentieth had been turned. Colonel Chamberlain assured him that he was holding his ground, but would like a company, if possible, to extend his line. Captain Woodward was unable to do this, but by shortening his line somewhat, he was able to cover the right of the Twentieth and enable it to take a little more ground to the left. Meanwhile the brigade in front of the hill was hard pushed to hold its own, and the heavy roar of musketry in the fitful lulls of our guns came to the anxious ears of our commander and told too plainly what would be the result if our line gave way. Not a man in that devoted band but knew that the safety of the brigade, and perhaps of the army, depended on the steadfastness with which that point was held, and so fought on and on, with no hope of assistance, but not a thought of giving up. Already nearly half of the little force is prostrate. The dead and the wounded clog the footsteps of the living.

7

The fury of the Twentieth Maine's countercharges were not sufficient to break the Rebel attack. Oates, however, realized that the final moment of decision was not far off.

I knew that the left of the Forty-seventh was disconnected, I knew not how far from the right of the Fourth Alabama, and consequently was out-flanked on its left and without sup-

port. The seven companies of that regiment present confronted the Eighty-third Pennsylvania and was enfiladed by
the left-oblique fire of the left wing of the Forty-fourth New
York, which was very destructive, and drove the men from the
obstructions behind which they were sheltering. Lieutenant
Colonel Bulger, in command of the Forty-seventh Alabama
companies, a most gallant old gentleman over sixty years of
age, fell severely wounded, and soon afterwards his seven
companies, after behaving most gallantly, broke, and in confusion retreated southward toward the position of the other
regiments of the brigade and reached their right. I aided their
gallant Major Campbell in his efforts to hold them, but having
no support on the left, they could not be rallied and held to
the position. When the Fifteenth was driven back, Colonel
Bulger was left sitting by a tree, sword in hand, shot through
one lung and bleeding profusely. A captain in the Forty-fourth
New York approached and demanded his sword. The old
Colonel said, "What is your rank?" The reply was, "I am a
captain." Bulger said, "Well, I am a lieutenant colonel, and I
will not surrender my sword except to an officer of equal
rank." The captain then said, "Surrender your sword, or I will
kill you." Coloniel Bulger promptly replied, "You may kill
and be d——d! I shall never surrender my sword to an officer
of lower rank." . . .[1]

Just as the Forty-seventh companies were being driven
back, I ordered my regiment to change direction to the left,
swing around, and drive the Federals from the ledge of rocks,
for the purpose of enfilading their line, relieving the Forty-
seventh—gaining the enemy's rear, and driving him from the
hill. My men obeyed and advanced about halfway to the
enemy's position, but the fire was so destructive that my line
wavered like a man trying to walk against a strong wind, and
then slowly, doggedly, gave back a little; then with no one
upon the left or right of me, my regiment exposed, while the
enemy was still under cover, to stand there and die was sheer
folly; either to retreat or advance became a necessity. . . . I
again ordered the advance, and knowing the officers and men

[1] A senior officer was sent to receive the colonel's sword.

of that gallant old regiment, I felt sure that they would follow their commander anywhere in the line of duty. I passed through the line waving my sword, shouting, "Forward, men, to the ledge!" and was promptly followed by the command in splendid style. We drove the Federals from their strong defensive position; five times they rallied and charged us, twice coming so near that some of my men had to use the bayonet, but in vain was their effort.

It was our time now to deal death and destruction to a gallant foe, and the account was speedily settled. I led this charge and sprang upon the ledge of rock, using my pistol within musket length, when the rush of my men drove the Maine men from the ledge along the line now indicated by stone markers on the east end of Vincent's Spur. . . . The Twentieth Maine was driven back . . . but not farther than to the next ledge on the mountainside. . . . I, with my regiment, made a rush forward from the ledge.

8

For Theodore Gerrish of the Twentieth Maine the moment had become desperate.

Our line is pressed back so far that our dead were within the lines of the enemy. Our ammunition is nearly all gone, and we are using the cartridges from the boxes of our wounded comrades. We can remain as we are no longer; we must advance or retreat. Colonel Chamberlain understands how it can be done.

"Fix bayonets!"

The steel shanks of the bayonets rattle upon the rifle barrels.

"Charge bayonets, charge!"

For a brief moment the order was not obeyed, and the little line seemed to quail under the fearful fire that was being pounded upon it.

Lieutenant H. S. Melcher, in command of Company F, sprang full ten paces to the front.

"Come on! Come on! Come on, boys!" he shouted.

With one wild yell of anguish wrung from its tortured heart, the regiment charged.

9

Gerrish continues: "We struck the Rebel lines with a fearful shock." Oates understood what was happening. This was the end, bitter and bloody.

My position rapidly became untenable. The Federal infantry were reported to be coming down on my right and certainly were closing in on my rear, while some dismounted cavalry were closing the only avenue of escape on my left rear. I sent my sergeant major with a request to Colonel Bowles, of the Fourth Alabama, the next in line to the left, to come to my relief. He returned within a minute and reported that none of our troops were in sight, the enemy was between us and the Fourth Alabama, and swarming the woods south of Little Round Top. Captain Park and Captain Hill came and informed me that the enemy were closing in on our rear. I sent Park to ascertain their number. He soon returned, and reported that two regiments were coming up behind us, and just then I saw them halt behind a fence, some two hundred yards distant, from which they opened fire on us. These . . . were the battalions of Stoughton's sharpshooters, each of which carried a flag, hence the impression that there were two regiments. They had been lost in the woods, but, guided by the firing, came up in our rear. . . .

At this moment the Fifteenth Alabama had infantry in front of them, to the right of them, dismounted cavalry to the left of them, and infantry in the rear of them. With a withering and deadly fire pouring in upon us from every direction, it seemed that the regiment was doomed to destruction. While one man was shot in the face, his right-hand or left-hand comrade was shot in the side or back. Some were struck simultaneously with two or three balls from different directions. Captains Hill and Park suggested that I should order a retreat; but this seemed impracticable. My dead and wounded were then nearly as great in number as those still on duty. They literally covered the ground. The blood stood in puddles in some places on the rocks; the ground was soaked with the blood of as brave men as ever fell on the red field of battle.

I still hoped for reinforcements or for the tide of success to turn my way. It seemed impossible to retreat and I therefore replied to my captains, "Return to your companies; we will sell out at dearly as possible." Hill made no reply, but Park smiled pleasantly, gave me the military salute, and said, "All right, sir." On reflection a few moments later I saw no hope of success and did order a retreat, but did not undertake to retire in order. I sent Sergeant Major Norris . . . . and had the officers and men advised the best I could, that when the signal was given we would not try to retreat in order, but everyone should run in the direction whence we came, and halt on the top of the Big Round Top Mountain. . . . I waited until the next charge of the Twentieth Maine was repulsed, as it would give my men a better chance to get out unhurt, and then ordered the retreat. . . .

When the signal was given we ran like a herd of wild cattle, right through the line of dismounted cavalrymen. Some of the men as they ran through seized three of the cavalrymen by the collar and carried them out prisoners. As we ran, a man named Keils, of Company H, from Henry County, who was to my right and rear had his throat cut by a bullet, and he ran past me breathing at his throat and the blood spattering. His windpipe was entirely severed, but notwithstanding he crossed the mountain and died in the field hospital that night or the next morning.

10

For Ziba B. Graham the victory on Little Round Top had cost the Sixteenth Michigan a terrible price.

When darkness covered us we held the same ground we planted ourselves upon at four-thirty P.M., holding the ground that Warren had entrusted us with, and with what sacrifice! The losses sustained by the brigade in this desperate en- counter, as reported July 3 were 491 officers and men, or 62 per cent of those of the command actually engaged; our beloved Brigade Commander Vincent mortally wounded; General Weed killed, falling over the dead body of brave Artillery Hazlett; O'Rourke, the dashing and brave commander of the One Hundred and Fortieth, just fresh from West Point, also lay dead among the rocks. Our own regimental losses were fearful—349 men for duty on June 30, a twenty-two hours' almost continuous march on July 1, the natural falling out on such a forced march. Two of our strongest companies on detached duty left us no more than 150 fighting men. Of that number, 60 had fallen, 30 never to rise again. Of my own Company B, of which I had command, just one-half were killed.

During the lulls in our own vicinity, we could, from our vantage ground witness the fierce struggle of the balance of our corps and the Third Corps in the peach orchard and the wheatfield. We could see line after line of Longstreet's men forming and advancing; also the close contact, the repulses, the fierce havoc of artillery, the close range of musketry, the break of the lines, the gallant unbroken second line still pushing forward, the gradual pressure upon Sickles, his stubborn falling back, the hand-to-hand conflict in the wheatfield where the gallant Fourth Michigan fought so stubbornly, and where their brave and noble Colonel Jefferds lost his life by a bayonet thrust, still holding to the flag. All this and more passed before our eyes. So fierce was our own fight that we could spare no men to take off the field our own wounded. I engaged part of my time in securing from them the ammunition they had not used in loading the guns for those who could fire.

Although unable to describe the fight, the memory of what I saw, the bravery, heroism and fearful grandeur of it all, I never shall forget. The fighting was sharp and did not quiet until after dark. We who had survived the battle thanked God that we had been spared, whilst so many of our comrades had fallen, and as we groped around in the darkness for our wounded on the rock-bound mountainside, friend grasped the hand of friend and congratulated each other that they had been spared.

Chapter 7

"Hurl Forward Your Howling Lines"

THE SITUATION as it develop at Little Round Top scarcely pleased Longstreet, but that failure alone, coming in the late afternoon while the furious impact of Longstreet's attack through the Peach Orchard and the Wheatfield was ripping Sickles's Third Corps to shreds, did not dispel the hope that a Confederate wedge could be driven through the Union lines and the Army of the Potomac split in two. The old bulldog in Longstreet growled and snapped. If the accusation had been made that a distinct edge had crept into his voice, he could have answered with asperity that it was small wonder. Time and again that day he had been irked—by Lee, by Hood, by McLaws and Barksdale.

But Lafayette McLaws, whose division joined the Confederate line at Devil's Den and the Round Tops, could not feel that he had been wrong in his altercation with Longstreet. Their dispute had developed when Longstreet had met Mc-Laws at a place on the Emmitsburg Road where there was open front. "Why is not a battery placed here?" Longstreet demanded, and when McLaws argued that a battery at that point would draw the enemy's artillery among his men forming for the charge and thus tend to demoralize them, Longstreet replied with a peremptory order to place the battery there, anyhow. The result had been precisely as McLaws had predicted; he rode among his men "directing them to lie down so as to escape as much as possible the shot and shell which were being rained around us from a very short range."

Longstreet's complaint—McLaws's, too—against William Barksdale, commanding the Mississippians, was simply that Barksdale was overanxious. Three times he came forward, pleading "General, let me go; General, let me charge!" and

134

each time he had been sent back to wait with his men at the
base of Peach Orchard Hill where the Emmitsburg Road
dipped between two high rail fences. Underneath, perhaps,
Longstreet was immensely satisfied with Barksdale, understanding his fiery, impetuous nature, knowing he was loved
by his men even if he had been born in Tennessee and was
only a Mississippian by adoption. The longer Barksdale waited
the tighter he would coil for the eventual spring into action;
Longstreet could relish the impact that charge would make
when it was finally released.

And so the brittle moments ran on—with tempers short,
nerves frayed, faces strained. First from McLaws's division
Joe Kershaw's brigade of South Carolinians strikes—strikes
with Longstreet himself going forward on foot with them
as far as the Emmitsburg Road. Now Barksdale—but somewhere the timing has gone awry. Kershaw is left alone, forced
to split his brigade into two columns to cover the left flank
that Barksdale has left exposed.

1

At last the order to charge reaches Barksdale. Captain G. B.
Lamar, Jr., aide-de-camp to McLaws, standing upon a summit, watches the furious impact of the attack.

I had witnessed many charges marked in every way by unflinching gallantry—in some I had the honor of participating
when in line with the First Georgia Regulars—but I never
saw anything equal the dash and heroism of the Mississippians.
You remember how anxious General Barksdale was to attack
the enemy, and his eagerness was participated in by all his
officers and men and when I carried him the order to advance
his face was radiant with joy. He was in front of his brigade,
hat off, and his long white hair reminded me of the "white
plume of Navarre." I saw him as far as the eye could follow,
still ahead of his men, and leading them on. Do you remember
the picket fence in front of his brigade? I was anxious to see
how they would get over it. When they reached it the fence

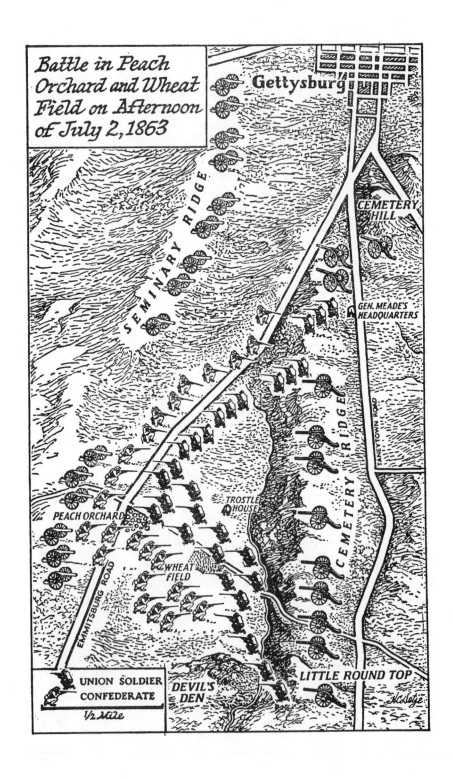

Battle in Peach Orchard and Wheat Field on Afternoon of July 2, 1863

Gettysburg

SEMINARY RIDGE

CEMETERY HILL

GEN. MEADE'S HEADQUARTERS

CEMETERY RIDGE

TANEYTOWN ROAD

PEACH ORCHARD

TROSTLE HOUSE

EMMITSBURG ROAD

WHEAT FIELD

DEVIL'S DEN

LITTLE ROUND TOP

UNION SOLDIER
CONFEDERATE
½ Mile

disappeared as if by magic, and the slaughter of the "red-breeched zouaves" on the other side was terrible!

2

As Barksdale's Mississippians slashed into the enemy three men saw a barn, but for each of them it held a different meaning.

[*J. S. McNeily retained only a fleeting memory of the barn*]: At top speed, yelling at the top of their voices, without firing a shot, the brigade sped swiftly across the field and literally rushed the goal. Our men began to drop as soon as they came to attention, and were well peppered in covering the distance to the enemy. The Twenty-first struck and flanked the Peach Orchard angle. Our left regiment, the Eighteenth, breasted a hot fire from a large brick oven—converted into a fortress by a Zouave regiment of Graham's brigade—which they captured and burned. The Thirteenth and Seventeenth swept the line between these two salients. . . . When the bluecoats saw us swarming over the fences and across the Emmitsburg Road without pausing, they began to "back out." Though they fought back bravely, retiring slowly until the firing was at close quarters, the retreat became a rout in which our men took heavy toll for the losses inflicted on them. So hot was our fire that many of the enemy hid behind boulders, which were numerous, and as our charging line passed over them surrendered and were sent to the rear. General Graham . . . rode out of the orchard behind his men. His horse was wounded and pitched the general over his head, leaving him in a dazed state of mind. Thus he was passed over and captured by the Twenty-first Mississippi and sent to the rear.

*

[*But to Major G. B. Gerald the barn had unforgettable meaning.*] Before us lay open fields dotted with houses and right in our front were some farmhouses with a grove of trees to the left, and the enemy drawn up in a double line of battle and supported by artillery. We steadily advanced, driving the enemy before us until we reached the houses with the trees on the left. . . . On one end of the orchard was a barn in which a part of the enemy had taken refuge. I was on the left of the regiment and the colonel and lieutenant colonel were somewhat to my right and partially protected by other buildings and I with most of the regiment was directly in front of the barn . . . I called to the men that the barn must be captured and to follow me and that I would open the door. They followed me with a rush and I forced the door open and within less than two minutes we had killed, wounded or captured every man in the barn. The barn was filled with smoke so dense that it was very nearly impossible to distinguish a man's body in it, such a continuous fire had the enemy within kept up. We left the barn and the brigade moved through the orchard toward the heights, still driving the enemy before them. General Barksdale encouraged the men by shouting "Forward, men, forward," which was the only command I ever heard him give after a battle commenced.

*

[*And to J. C. Lloyd of the Thirteenth Mississippi the barn was both the beginning and the end.*] Scarcely a minute and we were at the barn and scaling the fences at the lane and right across and in among the enemy, literally running over him. A divergence to the left and we run over and capture a battery. Then a divergence to the right to face a foe not yet driven back. Then on and on until no enemy was seen in our front. Then still on to Plum River. And did our gallant Barksdale ride into our midst and still say, "Forward, through the bushes." Did I hear him make a sound and see men rush to him; see him taken off his horse and started off the field? I turn again to the front and see the enemy bursting through the bushes and firing on us. They had come out from the top of the hill and were fresh.

A shock, as if I had a rail in my left hand and one end had struck the ground. I sat down with the other hand up to show surrender. That line marches over me and I go down into the bushes to find a rest for my arm and for protection from further damages.

Did that line soon retreat over me and one of them fix a sling for my arm, leaving with a "Wish you well?" Then I reasoned that no enemy was between me and our troops and I pulled out. Not a single Confederate was to be seen anywhere. I hear a weak hail to my right, and, turning to it, find General Barksdale, and what a disappointment when I hold my canteen to his mouth for a drink of water and found a ball had gone through and let it all out. I took his last message to his brigade and left him, with a promise to send the litter bearers. . . . I was safe now, but the first thing I knew I was in the lines of a regiment of Yankees. It was so smoky they did not notice me and I tacked back and made a wide circuit around and came in again at the barn and then made my way on to the field hospital.

3

Such savage fighting as this can only go on when the stakes are high. Henry Tremain, senior aide-de-camp to General Sickles, describes one price the Union's Third Corps must pay for it.

Approaching the spot, I observed [General Sickles] . . . reclining with apparent suffering against the wall of the barn, while a soldier was engaged under the general's directions in buckling a saddle strap, which had been tightly wound around his leg above the knee—thus forming an improvised tourniquet to prevent the flow of blood.

Throwing myself from the saddle with the exclamation, "General, are you hurt?" I found myself at his side, instantly realizing, as perhaps he might have realized, the possibly fatal nature of the injury. His voice was clear, and he responded, "Tell General Birney he must take command. . . ."

Saying I would send for an ambulance, I started to find Birney. As I was mounting, General Birney rode up. I exclaimed, "Here is General Birney now, sir." Stepping to the latter's side I said that "General Sickles was seriously wounded and directs me to notify you, sir, to assume command of the corps." General Sickles, if he did not hear, inferred what I was saying, and himself sung out in his ringing tones: "General Birney, you will take command, sir."

With an affirmative response, and an inquiry softly of myself if I had sent for an ambulance, General Birney at once rode off to his work, for it needed him, and he knew it. . . .

The man I sent for an ambulance surely could not so quickly have found one, except by accident; but an ambulance immediately appeared, doubtless sent by someone else. I thought it would be shattered to pieces by shot and shell before the patient could be placed in it. But strange to relate, not man or beast concerned with it was injured during the process.

Obviously the general was growing weaker, and I dared not ride away from the jolting ambulance to find a surgeon lest the sufferer expire in utter loneliness. So at a signal from the attendant I dismounted and sprung to the side of the general. Brandy was given as often as possible. I thought the end had come. Solemn words, not to be written in my story, were softly spoken amid the din of cannon. Father O'Fagan, chaplain of the Fifth Excelsior (Seventy-fourth New York) Regiment, rode up, and dismounting, came into the wagon to the patient's side. The memory of those prayerful moments cannot be effaced.

It seemed to me a long while before a halt was made, and Surgeon Thomas Sim, the corps medical director, took charge of the case. The other aides by this time had come up. It was fast growing dark, and the scene and actors need not be recalled. An improvised operating table, candles in bayonets, lanterns, sponges, the odor of medicines, of chloroform, a few idlers who belonged elsewhere—all are vaguely assembled in uncertain memory certain only of the distant sound of the continuing battle.

4

And yet a general in an ambulance can be but an interruption as the battle rages. Men at the guns, they must tell the story. War is wrought in incidents such as the one now seen by Whitelaw Reid, war correspondent for the *Cincinnati Gazette*.

Let me give one phase of the fight, fit type of many more. Some Massachusetts batteries—Captain Bigelow's, Captain

Philips's, two or three more under Captain McGilvray of Maine—were planted on the extreme left, advanced now well down to the Emmitsburg Road, with infantry in their front —the first division of Sickles's Corps. A little after five a fierce Rebel charge drove back the infantry and menaced the batteries. Orders are sent to Bigelow, on the extreme left, to hold his position at every hazard short of sheer annihiliation till a couple more batteries could be brought to his support. Reserving his fire a little, then with depressed guns opening with double charges of grape and canister, he smites and shatters but cannot break the advancing. His grape and canister are exhausted and still, closing grandly up over the slain, on they come. He falls back on spherical case, and pours this in at the shortest range. On, still onward comes the artillery— defying line, and still he holds his position. They are within six paces of the guns—he fires again. Once more, and he blows devoted soldiers from his very muzzles. And still mindful of that solemn order, he holds his place. They spring upon his carriages and shoot down his forces! And then, his Yankee artillerists still around him, he seizes the guns by hand and from the very front of that line drags two of them off. The caissons are further back—five out of six are saved.

That single company in that half-hour's fight lost thirty-three of its men, including every sergeant it had. The captain himself was wounded. Yet it was the first time it was ever under fire! I gave it simply as a type. So they fought along that fiery line!

5

But war is not won by bravery alone. Up on Cemetery Ridge Meade watches the battle unfolding, and his hollow, weary eyes are red and worried. How critical the moment has become can no longer be doubted. The lines have begun to break, guns and caissons are abandoned and in the hands of the enemy, organization is all but lost, and the Third Corps literally is being swept from the field. To young George Meade, who serves his father as an aide-de-camp, there is only one person to watch.

General Meade has been nearly continuously on the field, making the most strenuous exertions for establishing the line, in person bringing up and placing reinforcements, exposing himself in the reckless manner dictated by the emergency, during which he has his faithful old horse Baldy shot under him. He is now returning from headquarters, to which he has been for a brief period, and while there he had ordered Newton to bring up Robinson and Doubleday quickly to the gap in the line to the left of the Second Corps. For a few minutes affairs seem critical in the extreme. The Confederates appear determined to carry everything before them. A vigorous attack is made by them at various points along the whole front. Gibbon's line becomes heavily engaged along the whole front, while on his left, as we know, there is a space unoccupied.

At this gap, waiting for the coming of Newton, surrounded by a few aides and orderlies, stands Meade. The crash of musketry and the shouts of contending troops resound on all sides, and the air seems filled with shot and shell. At this moment Meade sees a short distance of a line of the enemy heading for the gap. Will nothing stop these people? He glances anxiously in the direction of the cemetery, whence succor should come. It will be a disaster if nothing can stop these troops, if only for a brief space of time. The general realizes the situation but too well. He straightens himself in his stirrups, as do also his aides, who ride closer to him, bracing themselves up to meet the crisis. It is in the minds of those who follow him that he is going to throw himself into the breach—anything to gain a few moments' time. Suddenly someone cries out, "There they come, General," and looking to the right, Newton is seen in advance of Doubleday's division, followed by Robinson. In close column by division, at a sharp double-quick, with muskets at a right shoulder, the two divisions sweep down the Taneytown Road, swing around to the right, and as, amidst the wildest excitement and shouting, they press forward to the line of battle, Meade rides ahead with the skirmish line, waving his hat, saying to those about him, "Come on, gentlemen," and someone remarking that it seemed at one time pretty desperate, it is pleasant to hear him reply in his hearty way, "Yes, but it is all right now, it is all right now."

6

To Haskell the moment is equally joyous.

Up to this hour General Gibbon had been in command of the Second Corps since yesterday, but General Hancock, relieved of his duties elsewhere, now assumed command. Five or six hundred yards away the Third Corps was making its last opposition; and the enemy was hotly pressing his advantages there, and throwing in fresh troops whose line extended still more along our front, when Generals Hancock and Gibbon rode along the lines of their troops; and at once cheer after cheer—not Rebel, mongrel cries, but genuine cheers—rang out all along the line, above the roar of battle, for "Hancock" and "Gibbon" and "our generals." These were good. Had you heard their voices, you would have known these men would fight. Just at this time we saw another thing that made us glad: we looked to our rear, and there, and all up the hillside which was the rear of the Third Corps before it went forward, were rapidly advancing large bodies of men from the extreme right of our line of battle, coming to the support of the part now so hotly pressed. There was the whole Twelfth Corps, with the exception of about one brigade, that is, the larger portion of the divisions of Generals Williams and Geary; the Third Division of the First Corps, General Doubleday; and some other brigades from the same corps—and some of them were moving at the double-quick. They formed lines of battle at the foot of the Taneytown Road, and when the broken fragments of the Third Corps were swarming by them toward the rear, without halting or wavering they came sweeping up, and with glorious old cheers, under fire, took their places on the crest in line of battle to the left of the Second Corps. Now Sickles's blunder is repaired. Now, Rebel chief, hurl forward your howling lines and columns! Yell out your loudest and your last, for many of your best will never yell, or wave the spurious flag again!

The battle still rages all along the left, where the Fifth Corps is, and the west slope of Round Top is the scene of the conflict; and nearer us there was but short abatement, as the last of the Third Corps retired from the field, for the enemy is flushed with his success. He has been throwing forward brigade after brigade, and division after division, since the battle began, and his advancing line now extends almost as far to our right as the right of the Second Division of the Second Corps. The whole slope in our front is full of them; and in various formations, in line, in column, and in masses which are neither, with yells and thick volleys, they are rushing toward our crest. The Third Corps is out of the way.

Now we are in for it. The battery men are ready by their loaded guns. All along the crest is ready. Now Arnold and Brown—now Cushing, and Woodruff, and Rorty!—you three shall survive today! They drew the cords that moved the friction primers, and gun after gun, along the batteries, in rapid succession, leaped where it stood and bellowed its canister upon the enemy. The enemy still advance. The infantry open fire—first the two advance regiments, the Fifteenth Massachusetts and the Eighty-second New York—then here and there throughout the length of the long line, at the points where the enemy comes nearest, and soon the whole crest, artillery and infantry, is one continued sheet of fire. From Round Top to near the Cemetery stretches an uninterrupted field of conflict. There is a great army upon each side, now hotly engaged.

To see the fight, while it went on in the valley below us, was terrible—what must it be now, when we are in it and it is all around us, in all its fury?

All senses for the time are dead but the one of sight. The roar of the discharges and the yells of the enemy all pass unheeded; but the impassioned soul is all eyes, and sees all things that the smoke does not hide. How madly the battery men are driving home the double charges of canister in those broad-mouthed Napoleons, whose fire seems almost to reach the enemy. How rapidly these long, bluecoated lines of infantry deliver their file fire down the slope.

But there is no faltering—the men stand nobly to their

work. Men are dropping dead or wounded on all sides, by scores and by hundreds, and the poor mutilated creatures, some with an arm dangling, some with a leg broken by a bullet, are limping and crawling toward the rear. They make no sound of complaint or pain, but are as silent as if dumb and mute. A sublime heroism seems to pervade all, and the intuition that to lose that crest, all is lost. How our officers, in the work of cheering on and directing the men, are falling.

We have heard that General Zook and Colonel Cross, in the First Division of our corps, are mortally wounded—they both commanded brigades—now near us Colonel Ward of the Fifteenth Massachusetts—he lost a leg at Balls Bluff—and Lieutenant Colonel Horton of the Eighty-second New York, are mortally struck while trying to hold their commands, which are being forced back; Colonel Revere, Twentieth Massachusetts, grandson of old Paul Revere, of the Revolution, is killed, Lieutenant Colonel Max Thomann, commanding the Fifty-ninth New York, is mortally wounded, and a host of others that I cannot name. These were of Gibbon's division. Lieutenant Brown is wounded among his guns—his position is a hundred yards in advance of the main line—the enemy is upon his battery, and he escapes, but leaves three of his six guns in the hands of the enemy.

The fire all along our crest is terrific, and it is a wonder how anything human could have stood before it, and yet the madness of the enemy drove them on, clear up to the muzzle of the guns, clear up to the lines of our infantry—but the lines stood right in their places. General Hancock and his aides rode up to Gibbon's division under the smoke. General Gibbon, with myself, was near, and there was a flag dimly visible, coming toward us from the direction of the enemy.

"Here, what are these men falling back for?" said Hancock.

The flag was no more than fifty yards away, but it was the head of a Rebel column, which at once opened fire with a volley. Lieutenant Miller, General Hancock's aide, fell, twice struck, but the general was unharmed, and he told the First Minnesota, which was near, to drive these people away. That splendid regiment, the less than three hundred that are left out of fifteen hundred that it has had, swings around upon the enemy, gives them a volley in their faces, and advances upon them with the bayonet. The Rebels fled in confusion, but Colonel Colville, Lieutenant Colonel Adams, and Major Downie are all badly, dangerously wounded, and many of the other officers and men will never fight again. More than two-thirds fell.

Such fighting as this cannot last long. It is now near sundown, and the battle has gone on wonderfully long already. But if you will stop to notice it, a change has occurred. The Rebel cry has ceased, and the men of the Union begin to shout there, under the smoke, and their lines to advance. See, the Rebels are breaking! They are in confusion in all our front! The wave has rolled upon the rock, and the rock has smashed it. Let us shout, too!

First upon their extreme left the Rebels broke, where they had almost pierced our lines; thence the repulse extended rapidly to their right. They hung longest about Round Top, where the Fifth Corps punished them, but in a space of time incredibly short, after they first gave signs of weakness, the whole force of the Rebel assault along the whole line, in spite of waving red flags, and yells, and the entreaties of officers, and the pride of the chivalry, fled like chaff before the whirlwind, back down the slope, over the valley, across the Emmittsburg Road, shattered, without organization in utter confusion, fugitive into the woods, and victory was with the arms of the Republic. The great Rebel assault, the greatest ever made upon this continent, has been made and signally repulsed, and upon this part of the field the fight of today is now soon over. Pursuit was made as rapidly and as far as practicable, but owing to the proximity of night, and the long distance which would have to be gone over before any of the enemy, where they would be likely to halt, could be overtaken, further success was not attainable today. Where the Rebel rout first commenced, a large number of prisoners, some thousands at least, were captured; almost all their dead, and such of their wounded as could not themselves get to the rear, were within our lines; several of their flags were gathered up, and a good many thousand muskets, some nine or ten guns and some caissons lost by the Third Corps, and the three of Brown's

battery—these last were in Rebel hands but a few minutes—
were all safe now with us, the enemy having had no time to
take them off.

7

Now as Haskell looks down onto those fields of slaughter
there is only a strange, tense stillness.

The whole air roared with the conflict but a moment since
—now all is silent; not a gunshot sound is heard, and the
silence comes distinctly, almost painfuly to the senses. And
the sun purples the clouds in the west, and the sultry evening
steals on as if there had been no battle, and the furious shout
and the cannon's roar had never shaken the earth. And how
look these fields? We may see them before dark—the ripening grain, the luxuriant corn, the orchards, the grassy meadows,
and in their midst the rural cottage of brick or wood. They
were beautiful this morning. They are desolate now—trampled
by the countless feet of the combatants, plowed and scored
by the shot and shell, the orchards splintered, the fences
prostrate, the harvest trodden in the mud.

And more dreadful than the sight of all this, thickly strewn
over all their length and breadth, are the habiliments of the
soldiers, the knapsacks cast aside in the stress of the fight,
or after the fatal lead had struck; haversacks, yawning with
the rations the owner will never call for; canteens of cedar of
the Rebel men of Jackson, and of cloth-covered tin of the
men of the Union; blankets and trousers, and coats and caps,
and some are blue and some are gray; muskets and ramrods,
and bayonets, and swords, and scabbards and belts, some
bent and cut by the shot or shell; broken wheels, exploded
caissons, and limber-boxes, and dismantled guns, and all these
are sprinkled with blood; horses, some dead, a mangled heap
of carnage, some alive, with a leg shot clear off, or other frightful wounds, appealing to you with almost more than brute
gaze as you pass; and last, but not least numerous, many
thousands of men—and there was no rebellion here now—
the men of South Carolina were quiet by the side of those
of Massachusetts, some composed, with upturned faces, sleep-

ing the last sleep, some mutilated and frightful, some wretched, fallen, bathed in blood, survivors still and unwilling witnesses of the rage of Gettysburg.

And yet with all this before them, as darkness came on, and the dispositions were made and the outposts thrown out for the night, the Army of the Potomac was quite mad with joy. No more light-hearted guests ever graced a banquet than were these men as they boiled their coffe and munched their soldiers' supper tonight. Is it strange?

Otherwise they would not have been soldiers. And such sights as all these will be certain to be seen as long as war lasts in the world, and when war is done, then is the end and the days of the millenium are at hand.

The ambulances commenced their work as soon as the battle opened—the twinkling lanterns through the night, and the sun of tomorrow saw them still with the same work unfinished.

Chapter 8

"Such Then is the Decision"

THE LONG, BITTER DAY that had ended for Longstreet was not yet over for Ewell. Old Bald Head, entrusted with guarding the Confederate's left flank and with striking the enemy when he could, had waited throughout the morning and afternoon for the sound of Longstreet's guns as a signal to action. As Ewell surveyed the Federal entrenchments that now opposed him from the crests of Cemetery, Culp's, and Wolf hills he hardly needed to be told by Lee: "We did not or could not pursue our advantage of yesterday, and now the enemy are in good position." Not only did these hills bristle with the cannons and rifles of the Union's Eleventh Corps, but the bluecoats also had spent a night and day building breastworks, felling trees, blocking them up into a close log fence, battening with cordwood from piles near at hand, and surmounting the whole with "head-logs" so that these works when finally in place appeared so formidable to the Confederates that they reported them to be log forts requiring scaling ladders for successful assault. But the holding of these ridges had become a necessity for Meade's men since not more than one hundred and twenty rods behind them lay the Baltimore Pike —the line of retreat for more than two-thirds of the Army of the Potomac!

For Ewell, gazing up at these well-protected heights, the thought of what might have been must have proved a sore aggravation. Sometime between four and five o'clock in the afternoon, with Longstreet attacking through the Peach Orchard and at the Round Tops, Ewell ordered the Confederate batteries to open on Cemetery Hill. The Union guns at once answered—answered so effectively, reported Captain Edward N. Whittier from his vantage point on Culp's Hill, that "in less than half an hour four of the Confederate limbers or caissons were exploded, the men driven from the guns, and the batteries silenced."[1] The Union artillerymen were using a French "ordnance glass," the nearest approach to a range finder for light artillery at that time known, with the result—again to quote Whittier—that "nowhere on the field of Gettysburg was such havoc wrought by artillery on artillery, and the wreck of Andrew's (Confederate) Battalion, in dead horses, shattered guns, and ammunition carriages left on the field, was for months a noteworthy feature."

What Ewell found in this bombardment to encourage an assault never has been explained, but to go forward he was determined. He had conceived the notion that if Johnson's and Early's Divisions would attack simultaneously, with the divisions of Rodes and Pender cooperating as best they could, Culp's Hill might be taken. The entire plan misfired: darkness had fallen (and Longstreet's attack had been virtually repulsed) before any of Johnson's troops could be brought across Rock Creek. Rodes, advancing from Gettysburg, was unable to reach the scene of action before the fighting ended while Pender, wounded in midafternoon, had not left explicit orders to co-operate in the assault. To Douglas Southall Freeman the situation could best be described as "a part of a perversity of Fate that strengthened the fine Federal defense." In the end, although this nighttime duel was vicious, its results were small: a brigade under Steuart clung to the base of East Cemetery Hill throughout the night, and although Hays' Louisiana Tigers and Hoke's North Carolinians succeeded in finding a gap in the Union lines only eighty-seven of them found their way to the top of the crest. A few guns were taken. At one point the flashes of the rifles revealed to Whittier the sight of a Union battery defending its position "with trail-handspikes, spongers and rammers, rock, and whatever else they could find on the ground." Both Hays and Hoke were forced to call back their brigades for want of the help that never came. It was now past ten o'clock; the

---

[1] Quotations here and later attributed to Whittier are from an article appearing in *Civil War Papers*, Volume I. Boston: Privately Printed, 1900, pp. 75-108.

gunfire perhaps went on sporadically until eleven; and then there was silence and again Old Bald Head had failed, principally because he was twenty-four hours too late in making up his mind.

Freeman gives a good summary of the Confederate position when the fighting ceased on July 2: "On the extreme right, along the western slope of Little Round Top, some of Hood's men were building with boulders a fortification to protect the barren ground they had won. Peach Orchard remained in Confederate hands. Far to the left, in the darkness, 'Maryland' Steuart's men still were holding a section of the front trenches of the enemy. These three strips of Pennsylvania soil might be, as Lee hoped, the points of departure for a decisive attack the next day but if anyone in the exhausted Confederate Army remembered a corresponding night two months before, when Jackson was wounded near Chancellorsville, their contrast must have been worse than a humiliation."[2]

And yet the omens for the Army of the Potomac, as Whittier evaluates them, were far from encouraging: "The First Corps had left 60 per cent, the Eleventh Corps, 33 per cent, and the Third Corps, 38 per cent, dead and wounded on the field, or prisoners in the enemy's hands; throngs of stragglers had not yet fallen into line, while along our right flank, and a mile in rear of our right center, Rebel yells and the rattle of musketry awoke the slumbering echoes of Culp's and Wolf and Powers's Hills; the night fell on a loss inflicted by the enemy, of more than twenty thousand men, without counting the men dispersed by the contest and not yet able to rejoin their colors. The conviction was strong that the enemy had not yet spoken his last word; while General Meade was made to fear that another day's fighting, equally murderous, might cause his whole army literally to melt away."

In the gloom of the night, General Birney, who had taken over the command of the shattered Third Corps when Sickles had been wounded, watched his men gathering among the wounded and the dying. Birney's throat tightened. To one

[2] Freeman, Douglas Southall. *Lee's Lieutenants*, Volume III. Pp. 135-6.

of his lieutenants he whispered sadly: "I wish I were already dead!"

1

Although the darkened hours are filled with such fearful echoes, around the silent countryside only the affairs of the living—in the town, down a dark country road, and on the battlefield—give meaning to the night or to the day to come. For Sallie Robbins Broadhead it had seemed throughout the long afternoon and evening as though the cannonading would never cease.

About four o'clock P.M. the storm burst again with terrific violence.

It seemed as though heaven and earth were being rolled together.

For better security we went to the house of a neighbor and occupied the cellar, by far the most comfortable part of the house. Whilst there a shell struck the house, but mercifully did not burst, but remained one half embedded in the wall. About six o'clock the cannonading lessened, and we, thinking the fighting for the day was over, came out.

Then the noise of the musketry was loud and constant, and made us feel quite as bad as the cannonading, though it seemed to me less terrible. Very soon the artillery joined in the din, and soon became as awful as ever and we again retreated to our friend's underground apartment, and remained until the battle ceased, about ten o'clock at night. I have just finished washing a few pieces for my child, for we expect to be compelled to leave town tomorrow, as the Rebels say it will most likely be shelled. I cannot sleep, and as I sit down to write, to while away the time, my husband sleeps as soundly as though nothing was wrong. I wish I could rest so easily, but it is out of the question for me to either sleep or eat under such terrible excitement and painful suspense.

We gain no information from the Rebels, and are shut off from all communication with our soldiers. I think little has been gained by either side so far.

"Has our army been sufficiently reinforced?" is our anxious question. A few minutes since we had a talk with an officer of the staff of General Early, and he admits that our army has the best position, but says we cannot hold it much longer. The Rebels do so much bragging that we do not know how much to believe. At all events, the manner in which this officer spoke indicates that our troops have the advantage so far. Can they keep it? The fear that they may not be able to causes our anxiety and keeps us in suspense.

2

For Billy Bayly the coming of the night brought high adventure.

Evening came and with it, to me, the most impressive incidents of the battle. A ceaseless thunder of artillery and the scream peculiar to shot and shell when hurtling though the air, the flashes of fire from bursting shells as darkness came on—all of this make upon my mind a picture, the strongest and most vivid of the battle. I had stood during the day looking from a point of vantage over the battlefield, but the movements of the forces fighting there could not be distinguished, partly because of distance, but more particularly, perhaps, because of the clouds of smoke that hung over the whole field. A flash of flame and the angry crack of guns a few seconds afterwards indicated where the opposing forces were engaged. But that was all that the eye could distinguish save here and there a wagon train or reinforcements of artillery moving into position.

Just before nightfall I went alone to the portico roof above the main porch in front of our house and fixed myself there undisturbed, to get the feeling of things. During the day I hardly had time to do anything but respond to countless, as it seemed to me, demands on my services. It was do this or get that, and I was not getting my money's worth of the show.

On this portico roof alone for half an hour or more I had the sensation of a lifetime, and the pity is I cannot tell in words the emotions the great drama aroused in the boy that was me. Of course, I have stated there was a thunder of guns; a shrieking, whistling, moaning, if you will, of shells before they burst, sometimes like rockets in the air. But that is not all. While I was alone and all was enwrapped in that silence that late twilight casts over field and meadow, I do not remember seeing a soldier or a body of soldiers at the time. The family was in the back part of the house (or out-houses) engaged in domestic duties. No results of the conflicts could be noted; no shifting of scenes or movement of actors in the great struggle could be observed. It was simply noise, flash and roar, the roar of a continuous thunderstorm and the sharp angry crashes of the thunderbolt, for it must be remembered that the noise of battle was in a decreasing diminuendo along a line of battle, the nearest battery of which was about two miles distant, and the more remote about five miles south. There were guns in action that evening, the reverberation from whose discharges shook the windows in the house. I did not know then nor do I know where these guns were located, but I know that the windows rattled and the house shook. Had I emotions that could be reduced to expression? No, not that I now recall. I would have to draw on subsequent experience and more matured judgment for that, and this is supposed to be only the narrative of what a boy saw and felt with the fewest possible historical details and deductions. As darkness gathered the firing ceased and all was quiet, uncanny in its silence as the noise had been satanic in its volume.

Early in the night a Confederate officer and a couple of his lieutenants asked for accommodations for the night and were shown to the spare room, containing two beds, where they spent the night leaving early in the morning before I was out of bed.

I remember when passing the door of the spare room where these officers were quartered noticing a sword in its scabbard, the belt and, I think, pistol holsters standing outside the door which was shut. I marveled that a man should be so careless when in the house of an enemy. I really was sorely tempted to grab the warlike trappings and run (and perhaps the idea did enter my head to capture the officers within but such a bold thought did not materialize into action), but I feared for the rest of the family if I should confiscate the trappings, and did not altogether relish the idea of staying out all night or of the search that might be instituted for me next morning by the despoiled officers.

3

But where Billy had found excitement sitting on his roof only uncertainty and ill-boding filled the heart of Michaels Jacobs, professor of mathematics at Gettysburg College and inventor of the process for canning fruits still widely used.

To us, however, who were at the time within the Rebel lines, the results seemed doubtful; and gloomy foreboding filled our minds as we laid ourselves down to catch, if possible, a little sleep. The unearthly yells of the exultant and defiant enemy had, during the afternoon, been frequently heard even amidst the deafening sounds of exploding cannon, of screaming and bursting shells, and of the continuous roar of musketry; and it seemed to us, judging from the character and direction of these mingled noises that the enemy had been gaining essentially on our flanks. At about six P.M. it is true, we heard cheering different from that which had so often fallen dolefully upon our ears, and some of the Rebels said to each other, "Listen, the Yankees are cheering." But whilst this—which we afterwards found to be the cheering of General Crawford's men as they charged and drove the Rebels down the face of Little Round Top—afforded us temporary encouragement, the movement of Rodes' division, which we saw hurried forward on a "doublequick" for the purpose of uniting in a combined attack up our right center and flank, the incessant and prolonged musketry fire, and the gradual cessation of the report of our artillery on Cemetery Hill, caused us to fear that our men had been badly beaten, and that our guns had either been captured or driven back from the advantageous position they had occupied. The battle ceased, and the outer world sank into its "usual repose"; but we lay down, not to sleep, but to indulge in sad and gloomy reflections. Intensely anxious to know, we had no means of finding out the relative condition of the two armies; and, like drowning men, were ready to catch at straws.

The Rebels returned to our street at ten P.M., and prepared their supper; and soon we began to hope that all was not lost. Some of them expressed their most earnest indignation at the foreigners—the Dutchmen—for having shot down so many of their men. This led us to believe that the Eleventh Corps, of whom many were foreign Germans, and whom, on the previous evening, they tauntingly told us they met at Chancellorsville—had done their duty, and had nobly redeemed their character. We afterwards found this explanation of their indignation when we learned what had taken place that evening, on the eastern flank on Cemetery Hill. Then again, soon after this, some were heard to say: "The Yankees have a *good position,* and we must drive them out of it tomorrow." This assured us that our men had been able to hold their position and that our lines were unbroken. There seemed now to be an entire absence of that elation and boastfulness which they manifested when they entered the town on the evening of the first of July. Still later at night, one said to another in tones of great earnestness, "I am very much discouraged," from which we learned that the results of the day were not in accordance with their high expectations, although they said, during the evening, they had been driving us on our right and on our left.

Sometime after supper, about midnight, nearly all of those who had returned to the town, instead of lying down to sleep, moved eastward again to our right. Soon afterwards, some of those who remained as a guard and for the purpose of plundering the houses and cellars of the citizens, said to us, "Tomorrow, Longstreet, who just arrived this evening, and has not yet been in the fight, will give the Yankees something to do." Of course this was mere boasting, for two of Longstreet's divisions had been in position during the day and

McLaws's was active in the fight. Only Pickett's division had arrived during the evening.

4

Now it is eleven o'clock and no shot is heard in all the armies. But the quiet night is filled with hidden drama and Haskell glimpses a scene to inspire an artist's brush.

After evening came on, and from reports received, all was known to be going satisfactorily upon the right, General Meade summoned his corps commanders to his headquarters for consultation. A consultation is held upon matters of vast moment to the country, and that poor little farmhouse is honored with more distinguished guests than it ever had before, or than it will ever have again, probably.

Do you expect to see a degree of ceremony and severe military aspect characterize this meeting, in accordance with strict military rules and commensurate with the moment of the matters of their deliberation? Name it "Major General Meade, Commander of the Army of the Potomac, with his Corps Generals, holding a Council of War, upon the field of Gettysburg," and it would sound pretty well—and that was what it was; and you might make a picture of it and hang it up by the side of "Napoleon and his Marshals" and "Washington and his Generals" maybe, at some future time. But for the artist to draw his picture from, I will tell how this council appeared. Meade, Sedgwick, Slocum, Howard, Hancock, Sykes, Newton, Pleasonton—commander of the cavalry—and Gibbon, were the generals present. Hancock, now that Sickles is wounded, has charge of the Third Corps, and Gibbon again has the Second.

Meade is a tall, spare man, with full beard which with his hair, originally brown, is quite thickly sprinkled with gray—has a Romanish face, very large nose, and a white, large forehead, prominent and wide over the eyes, which are full and large and quick in their movements, and he wears spectacles. His *fibres* are all of the long and sinewy kind. His habitual personal appearance is quite careless, and it would be rather difficult to make him look well dressed. Sedgwick is quite a heavy man, short, thickset and muscular, with florid complexion, dark, calm, straight-looking eyes, with full, heavyish features, which, with his eyes, have plenty of animation when he is aroused. He has a magnificent profile, well cut, with the nose and forehead forming almost a straight line, curly, short, chestnut hair and full beard, cut short, with a little gray in it. He dresses carelessly, but can look magnificent when he is well dressed. Like Meade, he looks and is honest and modest. You might see at once why his men, because they love him, call him "Uncle John," not to his face, of course, but among themselves. Slocum is small, rather spare, with black, straight hair and beard, which latter is unshaven and thin; large, full, quick, black eyes, white skin, sharp nose, wide cheek bones, and hollow cheeks and small chin. His movements are quick and angular, and he dresses with a sufficient degree of elegance.

Howard is medium in size, has nothing marked about him, is the youngest of them all, I think—has lost an arm in the war, has straight brown hair and beard, shaves his short upper lip over which his nose slants down, dim blue eyes, and on the whole appears a very pleasant, affable, well-dressed little gentleman. Hancock is the tallest and most shapely, and in many respects is the best-looking officer of them all. His hair is very light brown, straight and moist, and always looks well; his beard is of the same color, of which he wears the moustache and a tuft upon the chin; complexion ruddy, features neither large nor small, but well cut with full jaw and chin, compressed mouth, straight nose, full, deep blue eyes, and a very mobile, emotional countenance. He always dresses remarkably well, and his manner is dignified, gentlemanly and commanding. I think if he were in citizens' clothes and should give commands in the army to those who did not know him, he would be likely to be obeyed at once, and without any question as to his right to command.

Sykes is a small, rather thin man, well dressed and gentlemanly, brown hair and beard which he wears full, with a red, pinched, rough-looking skin, feeble blue eyes, long nose, and the general air of one who is weary and a little ill-natured. Newton is a well-sized, shapely, muscular, well-dressed man, with brown hair, a very ruddy, clean-shaved, full face, blue eyes, blunt, round features; walks very erect, curbs in his chin, and has somewhat of that smart sort of swagger that people are apt to suppose characterizes soldiers. Pleasonton is quite a nice little dandy, with brown hair and beard, a straw hat with a little jockey rim which he cocks upon one side of his head, with an unsteady eye that looks slyly at you and then dodges.

Gibbon, the youngest of them all save Howard, is about the same size as Slocum, Howard, Sykes and Pleasonton, and there are none of these who will weigh one hundred and fifty pounds. He is compactly made, neither spare nor corpulent, with ruddy complexion, chestnut brown hair, with a clean-shaved face, except his moustache which is decidedly reddish in color, medium-sized, well-shaped head, sharp, moderately jutting brow; deep blue, calm eyes, sharp, slightly equiline nose, compressed mouth, full jaws and chin, with an air of calm firmness in his manner. He always looks well dressed. I suppose Howard is about thirty-five and Meade about forty-five years of age; the rest are between these ages, but not many under forty.

As they come to the council now, there is the appearance of fatigue about them which is not customary, but is only due to the hard labors of the past few days. They all wear clothes of dark blue, some have top boots and some not, and except the two-starred straps upon the shoulders of all save Gibbon, who has but one star, there was scarcely a piece of regulation uniform about them all. They wore their swords, of various patterns, but no sashes, the Army hat, but with the crown pinched into all sorts of shapes and the rim slouched down and shorn of all its ornaments but the gilt band—except Sykes who wore a blue cap, and Pleasonton with his straw hat with broad black band. Then the mean little room where they met—its only furniture consisted of a large, wide bed in one corner, a small pine table in the center, upon which was a wooden pail of water with a tin cup for drinking, and a candle, stuck to the table by putting the end in tallow melted down from the wick, and five or six straight-backed rush-buttomed chairs. The generals came in—sat, some kept walking or standing, two lounged upon the bed, some were constantly smoking cigars. And thus disposed, they deliberated whether the army should fall back from its present position to one in the rear which it was said was stronger, should attack the enemy on the morrow, wherever he could be found, or should stand there upon the horseshoe crest, still on the defensive, and await the further movements of the enemy.

5

Self-consciously, John Gibbon sat through that council. Despite his long years of army service—fighting the Seminoles in Florida, suppressing the Mormon uprising in Utah, commanding a division at Fredericksburg—he felt himself as untested as when he had first entered West Point as an appointee from North Carolina. But his record of those moments of decision is clearly told.

A staff officer from army headquarters met General Hancock and myself and summoned us both to General Meade's headquarters where a council of war was to be held. We at once proceeded there and soon after our arrival all the corps commanders were assembled in the little front room of the Liester House—Newton who had been assigned to the command of Doubleday, his senior; Hancock, Second; Birney, Third; Sykes, Fifth; Sedgwick, who had arrived during the day with the Sixth, after a long march from Manchester; Howard, Eleventh, and Slocum, Twelfth beside General Meade, General Butterfield, chief of staff; Warren, chief of engineers; A. S. Williams, Twelfth Corps; and myself, Second. It will be seen that two corps were doubly represented, the Second by Hancock and myself and the Twelfth by Slocum and Williams. These twelve were all assembled in a little room not more than ten or twelve feet square, with a bed in one corner, a small table on one side, and a chair or two.

Of course, all could not sit down; some did, some lounged on the bed and some stood up, while Warren, tired out and suffering from a wound in the neck, where a piece of shell had struck him, lay down in a corner of the room and went fast asleep and I don't think heard any of the proceedings.

The discussion was at first very informal and . . . each one made comments on the fight and told what he knew of the condition of affairs. In the course of this discussion Newton expressed the opinion that "this was no place to fight a battle in." General Newton was an officer of engineers (since chief engineer of the army) and was rated by me, and I suppose most others, most highly as a soldier. The assertion, coming from such a source, rather startled me and I eagerly asked what his objections to the position were. The objections he stated, as I recollect them, related to some minor details of the line of which I knew nothing except so far as my own front was concerned, and with those I was satisfied; but the prevailing impression seemed to be that the place for the battle had been selected for us. Here we are; now what is the best thing to do? It soon became evident that everybody was in favor of staying where we were and giving battle there. General Meade himself said very little excepting now and then to make some comment, but I cannot recall that he had any decided opinion on any point, preferring apparently to listen to the conversation. After the discussion had lasted some time, Butterfield suggested it would perhaps be well to formulate the question to be asked, and, General Meade assenting, he took a piece of paper on which he had made some memoranda and wrote down a question; when he had done this he read it off and formally proposed it to the council.

I had never been a member of a council of war before (nor have I been since) and did not feel very confident I was properly a member of this one; but I was engaged in the discussion and found myself (Warren being asleep) the junior member in it. By the customs of war the junior member votes first, as on courts-martial; and when Butterfield read off his question, the substance of which was: "Should the army remain in its present position or take up some other?"

he addressed himself first to me for an answer. To say "Stay and fight" would be to ignore the objections made by General Newton, and I therefore answered somewhat in this way: "Remain here, and make such correction in our position as may be deemed necessary, but take no step which even looks like retreat." The question was put to each member and his answer taken down, and when it came to Newton who was first in rank, he voted pretty much the same way I did, and we had some playful sparring as to whether he agreed with me or I with him; the rest voted to remain.

The next question put by Butterfield was: "Should the army attack or await the attack of the enemy?" I voted not to attack, and all the others voted substantially the same way; and on the third question, "How long shall we wait?" I voted "Until Lee moves." The answer to this last question showed the only material variation in the opinion of the members.

When the meeting was over, General Meade said, quietly but decidedly, "Such then is the decision" and certainly he said nothing which produced a doubt in my mind as to his being in accord with the members of the council.

6

The day that closed with John Gibbon walking from his first council of war, with Billy Bayly resisting the chance to pilfer a Confederate officer's scabbard and pistol holsters, and with Michaels Jacobs rolling on his bed, sleepless and worried, found Frank Haskell still on the battlefield.

Night, sultry and starless, droned on, and it was almost midnight that I found myself peering my way from the line of the Second Corps, back down to the general's headquarters, which was an ambulance in the rear in a little peach orchard. All was silent now but the sound of the ambulances as they were bringing off the wounded, and you could hear them rattle here and there about the field and see their lanterns.

I am weary and sleepy, almost to such an extent as not to be able to sit on my horse. And my horse can hardly move

—the spur will not start him—what can be the reason? I know that he has been touched by two or three bullets today, but not to wound or lame him to speak of. Then, in riding by a horse that is hitched, in the dark I got kicked; had I not a very thick boot, the blow would have been likely to have broken my ankle—it did break my temper as it was—and, as if it would cure matters, I foolishly spurred my horse again. No use, he would but walk.

I dismounted; I could not lead him along at all, so out of temper I rode at the slowest possible walk to the headquarters, which I reached at last. Generals Hancock and Gibbon were asleep in the ambulance. With a light I found what was the matter with "Billy." A bullet had entered his chest just in front of my left leg, as I was mounted, and the blood was running down all his side and leg, and the air from his lungs came out of the bullet hole. I begged his pardon mentally for my cruelty in spurring him, and should have done so in words if he could have understood me. Kind treatment as is due to the wounded he could understand and he had it. Poor Billy! He and I were first under fire together, and I rode him at the second Bull Run and the first and second Fredericksburg, and at Antietam after brave "Joe" was killed; but I shall never mount him again—Billy's battles are over.

"George, make my bed here upon the ground by the side of this ambulance. Pull off my sabre and my boots—that will do!" Was ever princely couch or softest down so soft as those rough blankets there upon the unroofed sod? At midnight they received me for four hours delicious, dreamless oblivion of weariness and of battle. So to me ended the Second of July.

Chapter 9

"We Dozed in the Heat"

FOR EWELL the third of July completed a tragic cycle: hesitation and the loss of the heights on the first day, an assault too feeble and too late on the second, and now as the dawn began to break over the crests of the hills rising out of the bed of Rock Creek another attack too early in its timing to support Lee's revised plan for the day. Again a "perversity of Fate" seemed to be working against the Confederates; thirty minutes after Ewell's assault started a courier from Lee's headquarters brought Old Bald Head a message asking him to wait—Longstreet's attack would be delayed until later in the morning and Lee wished the two actions co-ordinated. But Old Bald Head's troops already were engaged and the assault could not be stopped; Freeman comments sadly, "The message came too late to assure any co-ordination of attack, but the fault was neither Lee's nor Ewell's."

This time Old Bald Head gave the Federals a stiff fight for Culp's Hill. Johnson's division had been strengthened by a brigade from Early's division and two from Rodes', so that Johnson had six brigades to throw behind Steuart and his men clinging to the side of East Cemetery Hill.

For Maryland Steuart that precious perch only three hundred and thirty yards from the Baltimore Pike proved precarious in the extreme. At times during the night Steuart had enheartened himself and his men with the conviction that the bluecoats were evacuating Culp's Hill, but dawn brought quick and bitter disillusionment. At five-thirty o'clock Federal guns opened a furious bombardment, raking Steuart's trenches all along the line; and after a brief pause while Steuart waited helplessly, hoping this was the end since, in Freeman's words, the Confederates could not oppose the bombardment with "anything heavier than a rifle," the Federals resumed fire with six fieldpieces added to the twenty they had previously employed.

The moment was desperate. Johnson's other brigades charged the hill, supporting Steuart to the right and north, but the slaughter from the Union artillery went on. Then Junius Daniel, who had gotten astride the railroad cut on the first day and saved Rodes at Seminary Ridge, brought his brigade up beside Steuart. The slim hope of another miracle persisted; Steuart and Daniel agreed on a supreme effort—their two brigades would make a charge in unison. Steuart leaped the breastworks first, sabre drawn, a single command thrown back to his men: "Charge bayonets!"

1

Captain Edward N. Whittier braced himself on the crest of Culp's Hill to meet the assault. It was now past seven o'clock. To engage the enemy the Federals must traverse an open meadow—action that fell upon the troops of the Second Massachusetts and Twenty-seventh Indiana. As Lieutenant Colonel Mudge of the Second Massachusetts looked across the meadow he said grimly, "It's murder, but it's the order!" Mudge, turning, snapped, "Up, men, over the works!"—and through Whittier's eyes the charge begins.

Up and out from behind well-built life-saving entrenchments the men of the Second Massachusetts dashed across the swale, where even a skirmish line could not live, into death-dealing woods. Driven out, fighting their way back through a line of the enemy thrown behind them to compel their surrender, forming anew under the protection of a low detached piece of stonewall about halfway across the meadow, they cleared the ground of the enemy in their new front, then fell back to their new position. . . . Five times the colors changed hands, and the next day when the regiment took its place in column to march away, as it passed General Slocum's headquarters, he and a large group of general and staff officers uncovered their heads. . . .

Until ten o'clock, charge followed charge in swift succession—assault and counter assault served only to multiply the windrows of the dead and wounded in the Confederate ranks; the cross-fire of artillery and musketry barely held in check the savage onslaught of Johnson's men.

Never before in the history of the Army of the Potomac, and never again until this same Edward Johnson's division had been gathered in, artillery, battle flags, and all—prisoners of war at Spottsylvania—did men so nearly thrust the smoking muzzles of their rifles into each other's faces; nowhere before and not again, until the Brock Road had been reached, and the tangled thickets of the Wilderness concealed lines of battle almost in contact, was volleying so heavy and so continuous from so small a front as Greene's on the crest of Culp's Hill during the hard fighting, urged with varying fortune to gain and to maintain possession of the Baltimore Pike.

Directly in my rear, their left resting close to the foot of the knoll I occupied, I counted twelve lines of infantry crouching in the grass and behind the rocks and stonewalls in the narrow fields separating Greene's right from the pike, so great was the danger of the enemy's breaking through at this point.

Nothing that I have ever read describes the situation so well as the poet Stedman's versification of the words of the gallant Kearney at the Seven Pines—

"Up came the reserves to the mêlée infernal,
Shouting, 'Where to go in, through opening or pine,'
'Anywheres, forward, 'tis all the same, Colonel,
You'll find lovely fighting along the whole line.' "

Just at this time the enemy showed signs of yielding—then came the rush, the grand rush to recapture our breastworks; then cheers, for the entrenchments were once more in our possession, and the enemy had been driven out and down the slopes. The right flank was safe. . . .

No place on the field of Gettysburg presented such terrible effect of battle as the portion of Culp's Hill in front of Greene's line, and along the works vacated on the evening of the second by McDougall's Brigade of the First Division. From under our works down the hill to the creek, the open places were covered with Confederate dead, every exposed place holding groups, and behind the rocks many wounded had been dragged only to die a lingering death.

About eleven A.M. a considerable number of the enemy in front of Greene's entrenchments and close up to our lines displayed a white flag. Major Leigh, Johnson's chief of staff, galloped into the throng, and endeavored to prevent the surrender, but fell shot to pieces almost by a volley from our works. I remember well on the morning of the fourth, crossing from my position the short distance to the front of Greene's line, and there seeing Major Leigh pinned to the ground by his horse, shot at the same time with his rider and falling on him.

Of all those lying there, whose leader he seemed to be, who would watch no more for the coming of Longstreet's mighty hosts; who would listen no longer for Hill's bugles sounding the charge, or the volleying rifles of Stonewall Jackson's old corps hurrying to their support; of all the uncounted dead covering the ground; of the dying, tenderly cared for by hands which but the day before had given mortal wounds; of all the signs of battle, in trees stripped by bullets and torn by shot and shell; of all these, no memory is so vivid as that of this dead soldier, still astride his horse, borne, as it were, on the crest of the highest wave of the Rebellion up into the flame of our guns, almost seizing our flags swaying in the smoke of that fierce, uncertain struggle.

2

Ewell's failure was complete, the effect of his assault on the entrenchments and the morale of the Army of the Potomac so slight that Haskell could dismiss the entire action with the wry comment, "He had Stonewall Jackson's Corps, and possibly imagined himself another Stonewall . . . . but all the Rebel's efforts were fruitless, save in one thing, slaughter to his own men." For Haskell the third of July began when General Gibbon awakened him by pulling his foot and saying, "Come, don't you hear that?" Brisk skirmish-firing sounded to the front and right of the Second Corps, but Haskell was inclined now to dismiss such annoyances of battle with a shrug.

At the commencement of the war such firing would have awaked the whole army and roused it to its feet and to arms;

not so now. The men upon the crest lay snoring in their blankets, even though some of the enemy's bullets dropped among them, as if bullets were as harmless as the drops of dew around them. As the sun arose today, the clouds became broken, and we had once more glimpses of sky, and fits of sunshine—a rarity, to cheer us. From the crest, save to the right of the Second Corps, no enemy, not even his outposts could be discovered along all the position where he so thronged upon the Third Corps yesterday. All was silent there —the wounded horses were limping about the field; the ravages of the conflict were still fearfully visible—the scattered arms and the ground thickly dotted with the dead—but no hostile foe.

The men were roused early, in order that the morning meal might be out of the way in time for whatever should occur. Then ensued the hum of an army, not in ranks, chatting in low tones, and running about and jostling among each other, rolling and packing their blankets and tents. They looked like an army of rag-gatherers while shaking these very useful articles of the soldier's outfit, for you must know that rain and mud in conjunction have not had the effect to make them clean, and the wear and tear of service have not left them entirely whole. But one could not have told by the appearance of the men that they were in battle yesterday, and were likely to be again today. They packed their knapsacks, boiled their coffee and munched their hard bread, just as usual—just like old soldiers who know what campaigning is; and their talk is far more concerning their present employment—some joke or drollery—than concerning what they saw or did yesterday. . . .

It is the opinion of many of our generals that the Rebel will not give us battle today—that he had enough yesterday —that he will be heading toward the Potomac at the earliest practicable moment, if he has not already done so; but the better and controlling judgment is that he will make another grand effort to pierce or turn our lines—that he will either mass and attack the left again, as yesterday, or direct his operations against the left of our center, the position of the Second Corps, and try to sever our line. I infer that General

Meade was of the opinion that the attack today would be upon the left—this from the disposition he ordered. I know that General Hancock anticipated the attack upon the center.

The dispositions today upon the left are as follows:

The Second and Third Divisions of the Second Corps are in the position of yesterday; then on the left come Doubleday's—the Third Division and Colonel Stannard's brigade of the First Corps; then Caldwell's—the First Division of the Second Corps; then the Third Corps, temporarily under the command of Hancock since Sickles's wound. The Third Corps is upon the same ground in part, and on the identical line where it first formed yesterday morning, and where, had it stayed instead of moving out to the front, we should have many more men today and should not have been upon the brink of disaster yesterday. On the left of the Third Corps is the Fifth Corps, with a short front and deep line; then comes the Sixth Corps, all but one brigade, which is sent over to the Twelfth.

The Sixth, a splendid corps, almost intact in the fight of yesterday, is the extreme left of our line, which terminates to the south of Round Top and runs along its western base in the woods, and thence to the Cemetery. This corps is burning to pay off the old scores made on the fourth of May, there back of Fredericksburg. Note well the position of the Second and Third Divisions of the Second Corps—it will become important. There are nearly six thousand men and officers in these two divisions here upon the field—the losses were quite heavy yesterday, some regiments are detached to other parts of the field—so all told there are less than six thousand men now in the two divisions, who occupy a line of about a thousand yards. The most of the way along this line upon the crest was a stone fence, constructed of small rough stones, a good deal of the way badly pulled down, but the men had improved it and patched it with rails from the neighboring fences and with earth, so as to render it in many places a very passable breastwork against musketry and flying fragments of shells.

These works are so low as to compel the men to kneel or lie down generally to obtain cover. Near the right of the

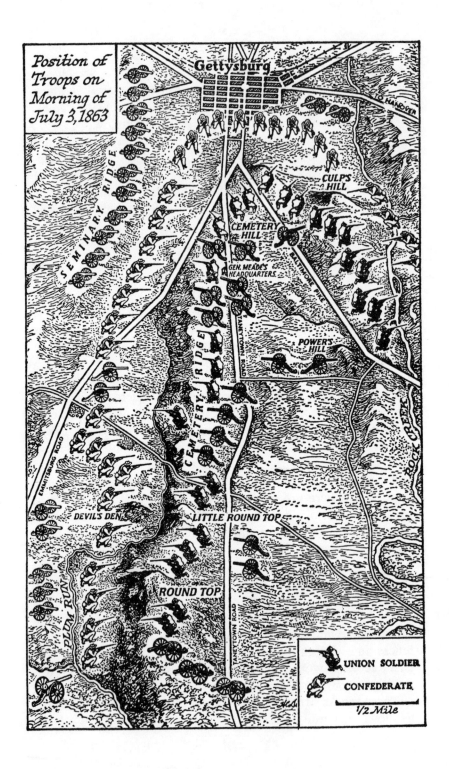

Position of Troops on Morning of July 3, 1863

Gettysburg

SEMINARY RIDGE

CULP'S HILL

CEMETERY HILL

GEN. MEADE'S HEADQUARTERS

POWER'S HILL

CEMETERY RIDGE

TANEYTOWN ROAD

EMMITSBURG ROAD

DEVIL'S DEN

LITTLE ROUND TOP

PLUM RUN

ROUND TOP

TANEYTOWN ROAD

ROCK CREEK

O HANOVER

UNION SOLDIER

CONFEDERATE

1/2 Mile

Second Division, and just by the little group of trees that I have mentioned there, this stone fence made a right angle, and extended thence to the front about twenty or thirty yards, where with another less than a right angle it followed along the crest again.

The lines were conformed to these breastworks and to the nature of the ground upon the crest so as to occupy the most favorable places to be covered and still be able to deliver effective fire upon the enemy should he come there. In some places a second line was so posted as to be able to deliver its fire over the heads of the first line behind the works; but such formation was not practicable all of the way. But all the force of these two divisions was in line, in position, without reserves, and in such a manner that every man of them could have fired his piece at the same instant.

The division flags, that of the Second Division being a white trefoil upon a square blue field and of the Third Division a blue trefoil upon a white rectangular field, waved behind the divisions at the points where the generals of division were supposed to be; the brigade flags, similar to these but with a triangular field, were behind the brigades; and the national flags of the regiments were in the lines of their regiments. To the left of the Second Division, and advanced something over a hundred yards, were posted a part of Stannard's brigade, two regiments or more, behind a small bush-crowned crest that ran in a direction oblique to the general line. These were well covered by the crest, and wholly concealed by the bushes, so that an advancing enemy would be close upon them before they could be seen. Other troops of Doubleday's division were strongly posted in rear of these in the general line.

I could not help wishing all the morning that this line of the two divisions of the Second Corps was stronger; it was, so far as numbers constitute strength, the weakest part of our whole line of battle. What if, I thought, the enemy should make an assault here today with two or three heavy lines—a great overwhelming mass; would he not sweep through that thin six thousand?

But I was not General Meade, who alone had power to

send other troops there; and he was satisfied with that part of the line as it was. He was early on horseback this morning, and rode along the whole line, looking to it himself, and with glass in hand sweeping the woods and fields in the direction of the enemy to see if aught of him could be discovered. His . manner was calm and serious, but earnest. There was no arrogance of hope or timidity of fear discernible in his face; but you would have supposed he would do his duty conscientiously and well, and would be willing to abide the result. You would have seen this in his face. He was well pleased with the left of the line today, it was so strong with good troops. He had no apprehension for the right where the fight now was going on, on account of the admirable position of our forces there. He was not of the opinion that the enemy would attack the center, our artillery had such sweep there, and this was not the favorite point of attack with the Rebel. Besides, should he attack the center, the general thought he could reinforce it in good season. I heard General Meade speak of these matters to Hancock and some others at about nine o'clock in the morning while they were up by the line near the Second Corps. . . .

Save the operations upon the right, the enemy so far as we could see was very quiet all the morning. Occasionally the outposts would fire a little, and then cease. Movements would be discovered which would indicate the attempt on the part of the enemy to post a battery. Our Parrotts would send a few shells to the spot, then silence would follow.

3

Behind the Confederate lines where a battery could be quickly silenced by a few shells from the Union Parrotts, a bitter dispute continued—again between Longstreet and Lee. To Longstreet there was only one sane course now: "To move around the right of Meade's army, and maneuver him into attacking us." But Lee stood firm for another attack on Cemetery Ridge; the Army of Northern Virginia was not yet ready to confess repulse, and the whole of the First Corps must be thrown into the new assault. Longstreet remonstrated violently; he knew what soldiers could and could not achieve: "It is my opinion that no 15,000 men ever arrayed for battle can take that position!" Lee could not be moved from his plan; to Longstreet's argument that 1,400 yards was too great a distance for a successful assault Lee replied that a bombardment would clear the way; and although Longstreet was never reconciled to the plan he had no choice but to accept it. Years afterwards he recalled that he never had been "so depressed as upon that day"; and to the very last moment, as the following exchange of communications between Longstreet and Colonels Alexander and Walton of the Confederate artillery indicates, he hoped for some other way out of his melancholy dilemma.

Colonel: If the artillery fire does not have the effect to drive off the enemy or greatly demoralize him so as to make our efforts pretty certain, I would prefer that you should not advise General Pickett to make the charge. I shall rely a great deal on your good judgment to determine the matter, and shall expect you to let General Pickett know when the moment offers.

Respectfully,
J. Longstreet,
Lieut.-General

To Colonel E. P. Alexander, Artillery.

General: I will only be able to judge of the effect of the fire on the enemy by his return fire, for his infantry is but little exposed to view and the smoke will obscure the whole field. If, as I infer from your note, there is any alternative to this attack, it should be carefully considered before opening our fire, for it will take all the ammunition we have left to test this one thoroughly, and if the result is unfavorable, we will have none left for another effort. And even if this is entirely successful it can only be so at bloody cost.

Very respectfully, &c.,
E. P. Alexander, Colonel Artillery
Hd. Qrs., July 3rd, 1863.

Colonel: The intention is to advance the infantry if the

artillery has the desired effect of driving the enemy's off, or having other effect such as to warrant us in making the attack. When that moment arrives advise General P., and of course advance such artillery as you use in aiding the attack.

Respectfully,

J. Longstreet, Lieut.-General, Commanding
To Colonel Alexander.

General: When our artillery fire is doing its best I shall advise General Pickett to advance.

Hdqrs., July 3rd, 1863.

Colonel: Let the batteries open; order great care and precision in firing. If the batteries in the peach-orchard cannot be used against the point we intend attacking, let them open on the rocky hill.

Most respectfully,

J. Longstreet, Lieut.-General, Commanding
To Col. Walton, Chief of Artillery.

4

Longstreet's depression clung with him; gone was the growling bulldog of yesterday who had barked at McLaws and Barksdale and in person had led Kershaw's brigade as far as the Emmitsburg Road. Fremantle's diary records an astonishing act for a general on the point of so great an assault: "At noon all Longstreet's dispositions were made; his troops for attack were deployed into line and lying down in the woods; his batteries were ready to open. The general then dismounted and *went to sleep* for a short time." But Colonel E. Porter Alexander reflects something of the same depressed glumness as he checks over the batteries for the impending bombardment.

I was directed by Longstreet to post all of his artillery for a preliminary cannonade, and then to take a position whence I could best observe the effect of our fire, and determine the proper moment to give the signal to Pickett to advance. The signal for the opening of the cannonade would be given by Longstreet himself after the infantry brigades were all in position.

A clump of trees in the enemy's line was pointed out to me as the proposed point of attack . . . and about 9 A.M. I began to revise our line and post it for the cannonade. The enemy very strangely interfered with only an occasional cannon-shot, to none of which did we reply, for it was easily in their power to drive us to cover or to exhaust our ammunition before our infantry column could be formed. I can only account for their allowing our visible preparations to be completed by supposing that they realized into what a trap we would find ourselves. Of Longstreet's eighty-three guns eight were left on our extreme right to cover our flank, and the remaining seventy-five were posted on an irregular line about 1,300 yards long beginning in the Peach Orchard and ending near the northeast corner of Spangler wood.

While so engaged, General Pendelton offered me the use of nine 12-Pr. howitzers of Hill's corps, saying that that corps could not use guns of such short range. I gladly accepted and went to receive the guns under command of Major Richardson. I placed them under cover in rear of the forming column with orders to remain until sent for, intending to take them with the column when it advanced.

A few hundred yards to the right and rear of my line began the artillery of the Third Corps under Colonel Walker. It comprised sixty guns, extending on Seminary Ridge as far as the Hagerstown Road, and two Whitworth rifles located nearly a mile farther north of the same ridge. In this interval was located twenty rifle guns of the Second Corps under Colonel Carter. Four more rifles of the corps under Captain Graham were located about one and a half miles northeast of Cemetery Hill. These twenty-four guns of the Second Corps were ordered to fire only solid shot as their fuses were unreliable.

There remained unemployed of the Second Corps twenty-five rifles and sixteen Napoleons, and of the Third Corps, fifteen 12-Pr. howitzers. It is notable that of the eighty-four guns of the Second and Third Corps to be engaged, eighty

were in the same line *parallel to the position of the enemy
and fifty-six guns stood idle.* It was a phenomenal oversight
not to place these guns, and many beside, in and near the
town to enfilade the "shank of the fish-hook" [i.e., the shape of
the Federal lines] and cross-fire with the guns from the west.

The Federal guns in position on their lines at the commencement of the cannonade were 166, and during it ten
batteries were brought up from the reserves, raising the number engaged to 220 against 172 used upon our side for the
same time.

The formation of our infantry line consumed a long time,
and the formation used was not one suited for such a heavy
task. Six brigades, say 10,000 men, were in the first line.
Three brigades only were in the second line—very much
shorter on the left. It followed about 200 yards in rear of
the first. The remaining brigade, Wilcox's, posted in rear of
the right of the column, and being ordered forward twenty
minutes or more later, was much too late to be of any assistance whatever. Both flanks of the assaulting column left
without any support in the rear. It was sure to crumble away
rapidly under fire. The arrangement may be represented
thus:—

Brockenbrough, Davis, McGown, Archer, Garnett,
Kemper, Lane, Scales, Armistead
Wilcox

No formation, however, could have been successful and the
light one doubtless suffered fewer casualties than one com-
pact and deeper would have had.

5

Unconscious of the dispute between Lee and Longstreet
or of the lethargy that had seized Longstreet so that he could
go to sleep—perhaps to sleep in disgust, as the saying goes—
John Dooley was up early that morning and in good spirits
marched with his comrades in Pickett's division to the line
of battle.

Before the day has fully dawned we are on our way to
occupy the position assigned to us for the conflict of the

third day. As we turn from the main road to the right, General Lee, or better known as Uncle Robert, silent and motionless, awaits our passing by, and anxiously does he gaze upon the only division of his army whose numbers have not been thinned by the terrible fires of Gettysburg. I must confess that the General's face does not look as bright as though he were certain of success. But yet it is impossible for us to be any otherwise than victorious and we press forward with beating hearts. . . .

How long we take to gain our position, what delays, what suspense! We are soon passing over the battlefield of yesterday, and the details of burying parties are digging graves to receive the freshly fallen comrades, and, in many instances, they have only the ghastly and mangled remnants of their gallant friends to deposit in these hastily dug pits. I pass very close to a headless body; the boy's head being torn off by a shell is lying around in bloody fragments on the ground.

A little further we take temporary position in the hollow of a field. Before us is a rising slope which hides the Yankee position from view. To the right of our front some quarter of a mile is a brick house near which one of our batteries now and then opens on the enemy who are generally ready to respond to the harsh greeting. Around us are some trees with very small green apples; and while we are resting here we amuse ourselves by pelting each other with green apples. So frivolous men can be even in the hour of death.

Now Generals Lee, Longstreet, and Pickett are advising together and the work of the day is arranged. Soon we are ordered to ascend the rising slope and pull down a fence in our front, and this begins to look like work.

Again, orders come for us to lie down in line of battle; *that all the cannon* on our side will open at a given signal, will continue for an hour and upon their ceasing we are to charge straight ahead over the open field and *sweep from our path* anything in the shape of a Yankee that attempts to oppose our progress. This order is transmitted from regiment to regiment, from brigade to brigade, and we rest a long time awaiting the signal.

6

Upon the crest of Cemetery Ridge—across those 1,400 yards that Longstreet fears with all his heart—Haskell does not suspect the terrible storm soon to break.

Eleven o'clock came. The noise of battle has ceased upon the right; not a sound of a gun or musket can be heard on all the field; the sky is bright, with only the white fleecy clouds floating over from the west. The July sun streams down its fire upon the bright iron of the muskets in stacks upon the crest and the dazzling brass of the Napoleons. The Army lolls and longs for the shade, of which some get a hand's breadth from a shelter tent stuck upon a ramrod. The silence and sultriness of a July noon are supreme. Now it so happened that just about this time of day a very original and interesting thought occurred to General Gibbon and several of his staff; that it would be a very good thing, and a very good time, to have something to eat.

When I announce to you that I had not tasted a mouthful of food since yesterday noon, and that all I had to drink since that time but the most miserable muddy warm water was a little drink of whisky that Major Biddle, General Meade's aide-de-camp, gave me last evening, and a cup of strong coffee that I gulped down as I was first mounting this morning, and further, save the four or five hours in the night there was scarcely a moment since that time but that I was in the saddle, you may have some notion of the reason of my assent to this extraordinary proposition. Nor will I mention the doubts I had as to the feasibility of the execution of this very novel proposal, except to say that I knew this morning that our larder was low; not to put too fine a point upon it, that we had nothing but some potatoes and sugar and coffee in the world.

And I may as well say here that of such in scant proportion would have been our repast had it not been for the riding of miles by two persons, one an officer, to procure supplies; and they only succeeded in getting some few chickens, some butter, and one huge loaf of bread, which last was bought of a soldier because he had grown faint in carrying it and was afterwards rescued with much difficulty and after a long race from a four-footed hog which had got hold of and had actually eaten a part of it. "There is a divinity," etc. . . .

Of the absolute quality of what we had to eat I could not pretend to judge, but I think an unprejudiced person would have said of the bread that it was good; so of the potatoes before they were boiled. Of the chickens he would have questioned their age, but they were large and in good *running* order. The toast was good and the butter. There were those who, when coffee was given them, called for tea, and vice versa, and were so ungracious as to suggest that the water that was used in both might have come from near a barn. Of course it did not.

We all came down to the little peach orchard where we had stayed last night, and, wonderful to see and tell, ever mindful of our needs, of faithful John [had the meal all ready]. There was an enormous pan of stewed chickens and the potatoes and toast, all hot, and the bread and the butter, and tea and coffee. There was satisfaction derived from just naming them all over. We called John an angel, and he snickered and said he "knowed" we'd come. General Hancock is of course invited to partake, and without delay we commence operations. Stools are not very numerous, two in all, and these the two generals have by common consent. Our table was the top of a mess chest. By this the generals sat. The rest of us sat upon the ground, cross-legged, like the picture of a smoking Turk, and held our plates upon our laps. How delicious was the stewed chicken. I had a cucumber pickle in my saddle bags, the last of a lunch left there two or three days ago, which George brought, and I had half of it.

We were just well at it when General Meade rode down to us from the line, accompanied by one of his staff, and by General Gibbon's invitation they dismounted and joined us. For the general commanding the Army of the Potomac, George, by an effort worthy of the person and the occasion, finds an empty cracker box for a seat. The staff officer must sit upon the ground with the rest of us. Soon Generals Newton and Pleasonton, each with an aide, arrive. By an almost super-human effort a roll of blankets is found, which, upon a pinch, is long enough to seat these generals both, and room is made for them. The aides sit with us. And, fortunate to relate, there was enough cooked for us all, and from General Meade to the youngest second lieutenant we all had a most hearty and well-relished dinner. . . .

The generals ate, and after, lighted cigars and under the flickering shade of a very small tree discoursed of the incidents of yesterday's battle and of the probabilities of today. General Newton humorously spoke of General Gibbon as "this young North Carolinian," and how he was becoming arrogant and above his position because he commanded a corps. General Gibbon retorted by saying that General Newton had not been long enough in such a command, only since yesterday, to enable him to judge of such things. General Meade still thought that the enemy would attack his left again today toward evening; but he was ready for them. General Hancock thought that the attack would be upon the position of the Second Corps. It was mentioned that General Hancock would again assume command of the Second Corps from that time so that General Gibbon would again return to the Second Division.

General Meade spoke of the provost guards, that they were good men, and that it would be better today to have them in the works [ranks] than to stop stragglers and skulkers, as these latter would be good for but little even in the works; and so he gave the order that all the provost guards should at once temporarily rejoin their regiments. Then General Gibbon called up Captain Farrell, First Minnesota, who commanded the provost guards of his division, and directed him for that day to join the regiment. "Very well, sir," said the captain, as he touched his hat and turned away. He was a quiet, excellent gentleman and thorough soldier. I knew him well and esteemed him. I never saw him again. He was killed in two or three hours from that time, and over half of his splendid company were either killed or wounded.

And so the time passed on, each general now and then dispatching some order or message by an officer or orderly until about half-past twelve, when all the generals, one by one, first General Meade, rode off their several ways, and General Gibbon and his staff alone remained.

We dozed in the heat and lolled upon the ground with half-open eyes. Our horses were hitched to the trees munching some oats. A great lull rests upon all the field. Time was heavy, and for want of something better to do, I yawned and looked at my watch. It was five minutes before one o'clock. I returned my watch to my pocket and thought possibly that I might go to sleep, and stretched myself upon the ground accordingly. *Ex uno disce omnes.* My attitude and purpose were those of the general and the rest of the staff.

What sound was that? There was no mistaking it. The distinct sharp sound of one of the enemy's guns, square over to the front, caused us to open our eyes and turn them in that direction, when we saw directly above the crest the smoke of the bursting shell, and heard its noise. In an instant, before a word was spoken, as if that was the signal gun for general work, loud, startling, booming, the report of gun after gun in rapid succession smote our ears and their shells plunged down and exploded all around us. We sprang to our feet. In briefest time the whole Rebel line to the west was pouring out its thunder and its iron upon our devoted crest.

Chapter 10

"The Great Hoarse Roar of Battle"

AMONG THE UNION forces only the wildest confusion holds sway. Shells now are bursting everywhere. Horses, hitched to the trees or held by the slack hands of orderlies, plunge riderless through the fields. Haskell sees Gibbon snatch his sword and start for the front on foot. Haskell calls for his own horse; there is no response. But the horse is by the tree where Haskell tied him—"eating oats with an air of the greatest composure." Alone of all beasts or men this horse is cool, and Haskell is not sure but that he has learned a lesson from the animal. While he is being bridled, the animal keeps his head down, anxious still for only his oats, and as Haskell adjusts the halter he sees one of the horses of the mess wagon struck and torn by a shell. The pair plunge —the driver has lost the reins—the horses, driver, and wagon end in a heap by a tree. Close at hand two mules, packed with ammunition boxes, are knocked all to pieces by a shell.

1

Haskell continues.

General Gibbon's groom has just mounted his horse and is starting to take the general's horse to him, when the flying iron meets him and tears open his breast. He drops dead and the horses gallop away. No more than a minute since the first shot was fired, and I am mounted and riding after the general. The mighty din that now rises to heaven and shakes the earth is not all of it the voice of the rebellion; for our guns, the guardian lions of the crest, quick to awake when danger comes, have opened their fiery jaws and begun to roar—the great hoarse roar of battle. I overtake the general half way up to the line. Before we reach the crest his horse is brought by an orderly. Leaving our horses just behind a sharp declivity of the ridge, on foot we go up among the batteries. How the long streams of fire spout from the guns, how the rifled shells hiss, how the smoke deepens and rolls.

But where is the infantry? Has it vanished in smoke? Is this a nightmare or a juggler's devilish trick? All too real. The men of the infantry have seized their arms, and behind their works, behind every rock, in every ditch, wherever there is any shelter, they hug the ground, silent, quiet, unterrified, little harmed. The enemy's guns now in action are in position at their front of the woods along the second ridge that I have before mentioned and toward their right behind a small crest in the open field, where we saw the flags this morning. Their line is some two miles long, concave on the side toward us, and their range is from one thousand to eighteen hundred yards.

A hundred and twenty-five Rebel guns, we estimate, are now active, firing twenty-four pound, twenty-, twelve-, and ten-pound projectiles, solid shot and shells, spherical, conical, spiral. The enemy's fire is chiefly concentrated upon the position of the Second Corps. From the Cemetery to Round Top, with over a hundred guns, and to all parts of the enemy's line, our batteries reply, of twenty- and ten-pound Parotts, ten-pound rifled ordnance, and twelve-pound Napoleons, using projectiles as various in shape and name as those of the enemy. Captain Hazard commanding the artillery brigade of the Second Corps was vigilant among the batteries of his command, and they were all doing well. . . . We had nothing to do, therefore, but to be observers of the grand spectacle of battle. Captain Wessels, Judge Advocate of the Division, now joined us, and we sat down behind the crest, close to the left of Cushing's Battery, to bide our time, to see, to be ready to act when the time should come, which might be at any moment.

Who can describe such a conflict as is raging around us? To say that it was like a summer storm, with the crash of thunder, the glare of lightning, the shrieking of the wind, and the clatter of hailstones, would be weak. The thunder and lightning of these two hundred and fifty guns and their shells, whose smoke darkens the sky, are incessant, all pervading, in the air above our heads, on the ground at our feet, remote, near, deafening, ear-piercing, astounding; and these hail-stones are massy iron, charged with exploding fire. And there is little of human interest in a storm; it is an absorbing element of this. You may see flame and smoke, and hurrying men, and human passion at a great conflagration; but they are all earthly and nothing more. These guns are great infuriate demons, not of the earth, whose mouths blaze with smoky tongues of living fire, and whose murky breath, sulphur-laden, rolls around them and along the ground, the smoke of Hades. These grimy men, rushing, shouting, their souls in frenzy, plying the dusky globes and the igniting spark, are in their league, and but their willing ministers.

We thought that at the second Bull Run, at the Antietam, and at Fredericksburg on the eleventh of December we had heard heavy cannonading; they were but holiday salutes compared with this. Besides the great ceaseless roar of the guns, which was but the background of the others, a million various minor sounds engaged the ear. The projectiles shriek long and sharp. They hiss, they scream, they growl, they sputter; all sounds of life and rage; and each has its different note, and all are discordant. Was ever such a chorus of sound before? We note the effect of the enemies' fire among the batteries and along the crest. We see the solid shot strike axle, or pole, or wheel, and the tough iron and heart of oak snap and fly like straws. The great oaks there by Woodruff's guns heave down their massy branches with a crash, as if the lightning smote them. The shells swoop down among the battery horses standing there apart. A half a dozen horses start, they stumble, their legs stiffen, their vitals and blood smear the ground. And these shot and shells have no respect for men either. We see the poor fellows hobbling back from the crest, or unable to do so, pale and weak, lying on the ground with the mangled stump of an arm or leg, dripping their life-blood away; or with a cheek torn open, or a shoulder mashed. And many, alas! hear not the roar as they stretch upon the ground with upturned faces and open eyes, though a shell should burst at their very ears. Their ears and their bodies this instant are only mud. We saw them but a moment since there among the flame, with brawny arms and muscles or iron, wielding the rammer and pushing home the cannon's plethoric load.

2

Strange freaks these round shots play, and Haskell finds it difficult to believe that what he sees is true.

We saw a man coming up from the rear with his full knapsack on, and some canteens of water held by the straps in his hands. He was walking slowly and with apparent unconcern, though the iron hailed around him. A shot struck the knapsack, and it and its contents flew thirty yards in every direction, the knapsack disappearing like an egg thrown spitefully against a rock. The soldier stopped and turned about in puzzled surprise, put up one hand to his back to assure himself that the knapsack was not there, and then walked slowly on again unharmed, with not even his coat torn.

Near us was a man crouching behind a small disintegrated stone, which was about the size of a common water bucket. He was bent up, with his face to the ground in the attitude of a Pagan worshipper before his idol. It looked so absurd to see him thus, that I went and said to him, "Do not lie there like a toad. Why not go to your regiment and be a man?"

He turned up his face with a stupid, terrified look upon me, and then without a word turned his nose again to the ground.

An orderly that was with me at the time told me a few moments later that a shot struck the stone, smashing it in a thousand fragments, but did not touch the man, though his head was not six inches from the stone.

All the projectiles that came near us were not so harmless. Not ten yards away from us a shell burst among some small bushes, where sat three or four orderlies holding horses. Two of the men and one horse were killed. Only a few yards off a shell exploded over an open limber box in Cushing's battery, and at the same instant another shell over a neighboring box. In both the boxes the ammunition blew up with an explosion that shook the ground, throwing fire and splinters and shells far into the air and all around, and destroying several men.

We watched the shells bursting in the air as they came hissing in all directions. Their flash was a bright gleam of lightning radiating from a point, giving place in the thousandth part of a second to a small, white, puffy cloud, like a fleece of the lightest, whitest wool. These clouds were very numerous. We could not often see the shell before it burst; but sometimes, as we faced toward the enemy and looked above our heads, the approach would be heralded by a prolonged hiss which always seemed to me to be a line of something tangible, terminating in a black globe, distinct to the eye as the sound had been to the ear. The shell would seem to stop and hang suspended in the air an instant, and then vanish in fire and smoke and noise.

We saw the missiles tear and plow the ground. All in the rear of the crest for a thousand yards, as well as among the batteries, was the field of their blind fury. Ambulances, passing down the Taneytown Road with wounded men, were struck. The hospitals near this road were riddled. The house which was General Meade's headquarters was shot through several times, and a great many horses of officers and orderlies were lying dead around it. Riderless horses, galloping madly through the fields, were brought up, or down rather, by these invisible horse-tamers, and they would not run any more. Mules with ammunition, pigs wallowing about, cows in the pastures, whatever was animate or inanimate in all this broad range, were no exception to their blind havoc. The percussion shells would strike and thunder, and scatter the earth with their whistling fragments; the Whitworth bolts would pound and ricochet, and bowl far away, sputtering, with the sound of a mass of hot iron plunged in water; and the great solid shot would smite the unresisting ground with a sounding "thud," as the strong boxer crashes his iron fist into the jaws of his unguarded adversary. . . .

Our artillerymen upon the crest budged not an inch, nor

intermitted, but, though caisson and limber were smashed, and guns dismantled, and men and horses killed there amidst smoke and sweat, they gave back, without grudge or loss of time in the sending, in kind whatever the enemy sent, globe, and cone, and bolt, hollow or solid, an iron greeting to the rebellion, the compliments of the wrathful Republic.

An hour has droned its flight since the war began. There is no sign of weariness or abatement on either side. So long it seemed, that the din and crashing around began to appear the normal condition of nature there, and fighting man's element. The general proposed to go among the men and over to the front of the batteries, so at about two o'clock he and I started. We went along the lines of the infantry as they lay there flat upon the earth, a little to the front of the batteries. They were suffering little, and were quiet and cool. How glad we were that the enemy were no better gunners, and that they cut the shell fuses too long. To the question asked the men, "What do you think of this?" the replies would be, "O, this is bully," "We are getting to like it," "O, we don't mind this." And so they lay under the heaviest cannonade that ever shook the continent, and among them a thousand times more jokes than heads were cracked.

3

Haskell and Gibbon go down the line and Haskell hears the general speak of God.

We went down in front of the line some two hundred yards, and as the smoke had a tendency to settle upon a higher plain than where we were, we could see near the ground distinctly all over the fields, as well back to the crest where were our own guns as to the opposite ridge where were those of the enemy. No infantry was in sight save the skirmishers, and they stood silent and motionless—a row of gray posts through the field on one side confronted by another of blue.

Under the grateful shade of some elm trees where we could see much of the field, we made seats of the ground and sat down. Here all the more repulsive features of the fight were unseen by reason of the smoke. Man had arranged the scenes

and for a time had taken part in the great drama; but at last,
. . . conscious of his littleness and inadequacy to the mighty
part, he had stepped aside and given place to more powerful
actors. So it seemed, for we could see no men about the batteries. On either crest we could see the great flaky streams of
fire, and they seemed numberless, of the opposing guns, and
their white banks of swift, convolving smoke; but the sound
of the discharges was drowned in the universal ocean of
sound. Over all the valley the smoke, a sulphury arch,
stretched its lurid span; and through it always, shrieking on
their unseen courses, thickly flew a myriad iron deaths. With
our grim horizon on all sides round toothed thick with battery flame, under that dissonant canopy of warring shells, we
sat and heard in silence. What other expression had we that
was not mean, for such an awful universe of battle?

A shell struck our breastwork of rails up in sight of us, and
a moment afterwards we saw the men bearing some of their
wounded companions away from the same spot; and directly
two men came from there down toward where we were and
sought to get shelter in an excavation near by where many
dead horses, killed in yesterday's fight, had been thrown.
General Gibbon said to these men, more in a tone of kindly
expostulation than of command: "My men, do not leave
your ranks to try to get shelter here. All these matters are in
the hands of God, and nothing that you can do will make you
safer in one place than in another."

The men went quietly back to the line at once.

The general then said to me: "I am not a member of any
church, but I have always had a strong religious feeling; and
so in all these battles I have always believed that I was in the
hands of God, and that I should be unharmed or not, according to His will. For this reason, I think it is, I am always
ready to go where duty calls, no matter how great the danger."

Half-past two o'clock, an hour and a half since the commencement, and still the cannonade did not in the least abate;
but soon thereafter some signs of weariness and a little slack-
ing of fire began to be apparent upon both sides. First we
saw Brown's battery retire from the line, too feeble for further
battle. Its position was a little to the front of the line. Its

commander was wounded, and many of its men were so or worse; some of its guns had been disabled, many of its horses killed; its ammunition was nearly expended. Other batteries in similar case had been withdrawn before to be replaced by fresh ones, and some were withdrawn afterwards. Soon after the battery named had gone, the general and I started to return, passing toward the left of the division and crossing the ground where the guns had stood. The stricken horses were numerous, and the dead and wounded men lay about, and as we passed these latter, their low, piteous call for water would invariably come to us, if they had yet any voice left. I found canteens of water near—no difficult matter where a battle has been—and held them to livid lips, and even in the faintness of death the eagerness to drink told of their terrible torture of thirst.

4

Behind the Confederate lines the cannonade was but the respite. The gathering tension, the undaunted spirit, the quickening hope of Pickett's men as they waited for the moment of attack is described by Captain W. W. Wood.

Pickett's division and the artillery were all in position by eleven A.M. The battle, however, did not begin for some hours later. The day was clear and bright. There was not a cloud in the sky, and the sun, from whose rays there was no shelter, shone intensely hot. There was no water near us, and not knowing how soon the battle might begin, no details could be sent for any. The canteens which had been filled at the last water we passed, were soon emptied, and there was a great suffering from thrist. But there was no help for it. It had to be endured. While waiting for the expected signal we saw Generals Lee, Longstreet, and Pickett riding up and down the line and occasionally approaching the crest of the hill to take a look at the enemy's position. It was then whispered among us that Longstreet disapproved of the proposed charge and had earnestly protested against it. His protest was heard, but overruled by the council of war.

At one P.M. a single shot was fired from a Confederate gun

and in two minutes afterward another. It was the preconcerted signal, and hearing the first gun, every man threw himself flat on the ground in obedience to orders. The echoes of the sound of the second gun had not died away when all the Confederate artillery on that part of the field opened fire on Cemetery Heights with a salvo the like of which had never been heard in America till then. The Federal batteries must have been surprised, for it was several minutes before they replied to it. Yet when they did reply their fire was very effective and deadly, and seemed to be fully equal to that of the Confederates. . . .

The smoke from the Confederate batteries, although they were but a little ways from me, soon obscured them from my sight. This smoke was lit up by red, angry flares of flame as the successive discharges left the muzzles of the guns. The firing was so rapid and continuous that the report of a single gun could not be distinguished. Over the space intervening between the infantry and artillery passed some mounted officer and his staff—notably once General Lee, and several times Generals Longstreet and Pickett. The Federal batteries were returning Confederate fire with great vigor, and when General Lee passed over the ground it was being swept with a deadly hail of every missile known to the nomenclature of artillerists. His appearance at a place of such eminent danger both thrilled and horrified the line, and men shouted to him to go away to shelter. Always regardless of himself when duty called, he had but one attendant with him. When the men yelled to him to go away he took off his hat in acknowledgment of their affectionate solicitude, and then rode on quickening the pace of his noble gray.

Major James E. Dearing, chief of artillery of Pickett's division, boasted that the flag of his battalion should not that day touch the ground. Accompanied by his flag-bearer, he galloped incessantly from one end of the guns to the other, cheering the cannoneers by his presence, and giving them directions where to direct their fire. While galloping along the line at full speed, a round shot struck and killed the horse of the latter, and threw him to the ground. Major Dearing turned and saw his flag falling, but so quick was he that before it had reached the ground he seized it from the stand-ard-bearer and carried it for the remainder of the battle himself. This gallant act performed in full view of the line of battle was greeted with such a Confederate yell as not even the infernal roar of the guns could drown. General Pickett, while tarrying unnecessarily long, as some of his staff thought, at a point where the death missiles came the thickest, was urged by a captain of his staff to move to some other portion of the field where the danger was not so great and operations could equally as well be directed. . . .

The combat between the artillery of the two armies must have been of two hours' duration. Throughout it all the officers and men of that portion of the line where I was were stretched flat upon the ground with their hands toward the firing. . . . Not a breath of air was in motion and the sun shone down intensely hot. The bursting of innumerable shells added to the heat. My company, numbering fifty men present, lost four killed and some fifteen wounded while in this posi-tion. The enemy shot hurtled among us and clipped off the clover heads by our side.

The fire was so terrible that when a man cried out "Wounded" the ambulance corps would not go to his relief. To have taken anyone to the rear while that firing was in progress would have been almost certain death. At last the Federal batteries began to slacken their fire, and not long afterwards ceased entirely. Soon the Confederate guns ceased firing too, and then all knew the supreme moment had come. Each surviving commandant of a company sprang to his feet and ordered his men into line. All who could got into line, but there were many dead and wounded and sunstricken poor fellows who were left upon the ground.

The order to go forward was given and obeyed with alacrity and cheerfulness, for we believed that the battle was prac-tically over, and we had nothing to do but to march unop-posed to Cemetery Heights and occupy them. The ascent to the crest of the hill, which had hitherto concealed us from the enemy's view, was made speedily and in good order. While making the ascent it was seen that the supports to our left and right flanks were not coming forward, as we had been told they would. Mounted officers were dashing frantically up and down their line, apparently endeavoring to get them to move forward, but we could see that they could not move. Their failure to support us was discouraging, but did not dishearten us. Some of our men cursed them for being cowards but still our charge was kept up and no man fell out.

Soon we were past the crest of the hill and out of sight of them. Before us stood Cemetery Heights, of which we could get glimpses through rifts in the clouds of powder-smoke which enveloped them. We could not see whether or not there were troops there to defend them against us.

Somewhere further on, perhaps a hundred and fifty yards beyond the crest of the hill we had just passed, a post-and-rail fence some five feet high was encountered. This fence was quickly mounted, and a little distance beyond it my regiment and, I supposed, the whole line of battle, was halted for the purpose of rectifying the alignment. From the time the charge began, up to this moment, not a shot had been fired at us, nor had we been able to see, because of the density of the smoke which hung over the field like a pall, that there was an enemy in front of us. But directly afterward, just as the line started forward again, a shot, fired from somewhere to our left, struck the center company of my regiment, and, enfilading its right wing as it did, killed and wounded a large number of men and officers.

The smoke now lifted from our front and there, right before us stood Cemetery Heights in awful grandeur. At their base was a double line of Federal infantry and several pieces of artillery planted behind stone walls, and infantry supports were hurriedly coming up. We fully realized that Pickett's three little brigades, already greatly reduced by heavy casualties, were making alone and without possibility of succor, a desperate charge against the whole power of the Federal army.

5

On the crest of Cemetery Ridge the advancing Rebel infantry is seen by Haskell.

We were near our horses when we noticed Brigadier General Hunt, Chief of Artillery of the Army, near Woodruff's Battery, swiftly moving about on horseback, and apparently in a rapid manner giving some orders about the guns. Thought we, what could this mean? In a moment afterwards we met Captain Wessels and the orderlies who had our horses; they were on foot leading the horses. Captain Wessels was pale, and he said, excited: "General, they say the enemy's infantry is advancing."

We sprang into our saddles, a score of bounds brought us upon the all-seeing crest. To say that men grew pale and held their breath at what we and they there saw, would not be true. Might not six thousand men be brave and without shade of fear, and yet, before a hostile eighteen thousand, armed, and not five minutes' march away, turn ashy white? None on that crest now need be told that *the enemy is advancing.* Every eye could see his legions, an overwhelming resistless tide of an ocean of armed men sweeping upon us!

Regiment after regiment and brigade after brigade move from the woods and rapidly take their places in the lines forming the assault. Pickett's proud division, with some additional troops, hold their right; Pettigrew's (Worth's) their left. The first line at short interval is followed by a second, and that a third succeeds; and columns between support the lines. More than half a mile their front extends; more than a thousand yards the dull gray masses deploy, man touching man, rank pressing rank, and line supporting line. The red flags wave, their horsemen gallop up and down; the arms of eighteen thousand men, barrel and bayonet, gleam in the sun, a sloping forest of flashing steel. Right on they move, as with one soul, in perfect order, without impediment of ditch, or wall or stream, over ridge and slope, through orchard and meadow and cornfield, magnificent, grim, irresistible.

All was orderly and still upon our crest; no noise and no confusion. The men had little need of commands, for the survivors of a dozen battles knew well enough what this array in front portended, and already in their places, they would be prepared to act when the right time should come. The click of the locks as each man raised the hammer to feel with his fingers that the cap was on the nipple; the sharp jar as a

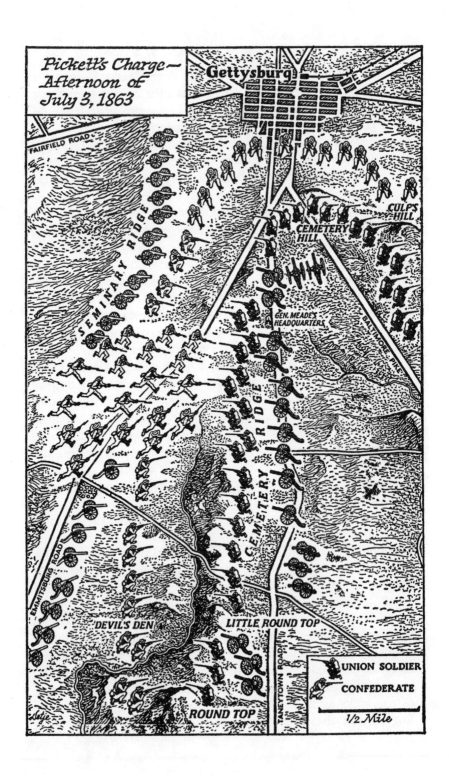

Pickett's Charge—
Afternoon of
July 3, 1863

Gettysburg

FAIRFIELD ROAD

SEMINARY RIDGE

CULP'S
HILL

CEMETERY
HILL

GEN. MEADE'S
HEADQUARTERS

BALTIMORE PIKE

CEMETERY RIDGE

EMMITSBURG ROAD

DEVIL'S DEN

LITTLE ROUND TOP

TANEYTOWN ROAD

ROUND TOP

UNION SOLDIER

CONFEDERATE

1/2 Mile

musket touched a stone upon the wall when thrust in aiming over it, and the clicking of the iron axles as the guns were rolled up by hand a little further to the front, were quite all the sounds that could be heard. Cap-boxes were slid around to the front of the body; cartridge boxes opened, officers opened their pistol-holsters. Such preparations, little more was needed. The trefoil flags, colors of the brigades and divisions moved to their places in rear; but along the lines in front the grand old ensign that first waved in battle at Saratoga in 1777, and which these people coming would rob of half its stars, stood up, and the west wind kissed it as the sergeants sloped its lance toward the enemy. I believe that not one above whom it then waved but blessed his God that he was loyal to it, and whose heart did not swell with pride toward it, as the emblem of the Republic before that treason's flaunting rag in front.

General Gibbon rode down the lines, cool and calm, and in an unimpassioned voice he said to the men, "Do not hurry, men, and fire too fast, let them come up close before you fire, and then aim low and steadily."

The coolness of their general was reflected in the faces of his men. Five minutes has elapsed since first the enemy have emerged from the woods—no great space of time surely, if measured by the usual standard by which men estimate duration—but it was long enough for us to note and weigh some of the elements of mighty moment that surrounded us; the disparity of numbers between the assailants and the assailed; that few as were our numbers we could not be supported or reinforced until support would not be needed or would be too late; that upon the ability of the two trefoil divisions to hold the crest and repel the assault depended not only their own safety or destruction, but also the honor of the Army of the Potomac and defeat or victory at Gettysburg. Should these advancing men pierce our line and become the entering wedge, driven home, that would sever our army asunder, what hope would there be afterwards, and where the blood-earned fruits of yesterday? It was long enough for the Rebel storm to drift across more than half the space that had at first separated it from us. None, or all, of these considerations either depressed or elevated us. They might have done the former had we been timid; the latter had we been confident and vain. But, we were there waiting, and ready to do our duty—that done, results could not dishonor us.

Chapter 11

"My God, It was True!"

THE FEDERAL SKIRMISHERS do their work, opening a spattering fire along the line, retiring. Then the thunder of Federal guns—Arnold's, Cushing's, Woodruff's and the rest—screaming shells that smite the advancing enemy. As the range grows shorter and shorter, the artillerymen change to shrapnel, from shrapnel to canister.

1

A correspondent for the *Richmond Enquirer* captures the frightfulness of those moments.

The cannonade still goes on with intense fury; our batteries are handled with great skill. This battery and that limber up, advance to the front, wheel into action, and again the roar of cannon becomes almost deafening. Our shells seem to burst with terrible accuracy; now a caisson of the enemy's is blown up—quickly another follows—their fire slackens—the order comes to advance. That flag which waved amid the wild tempest of battle of Gaines's Mill, Frayser's Farm, and Manassas, never rose more proudly. Kemper, with as gallant men as ever trod beneath that flag, leads the right; Garnett, with his heroes, brings up the left; and the veteran Armistead, with his brave troops, moves forward in support. The distance is more than half a mile. As they advance, the enemy fire with great rapidity; shell and solid shot give place to grape and canister; the very earth quivers beneath the heavy roar; wide gaps are made in this regiment and that brigade; yet they quickly close up and move steadily onward. That flag goes down. See how quickly it again mounts upward, borne by some gallant man who feels keenly the honor of his old Commonwealth in this hour which is to test her manhood. The line

197

moves onward, straight onward—cannons roaring, grape and canister plunging and ploughing through the ranks—bullets whizzing as thick as hailstones in winter, and men falling as leaves fall when shaken by the blasts of autumn.

2

Haskell shakes his head, almost not daring to believe. But in spite of shells or shrapnel or canister, without wavering or halting, the lines of the enemy continue to move on.

The Rebel guns make no reply to ours, and no charging shout rings out today, as is the Rebel wont; but the courage of these silent men amid our shots seems not to need the stimulus of other noise. The enemy's right flank sweeps near Stannard's bushy crest, and his concealed Vermonters rake it with a well-delivered fire of musketry. The gray lines do not halt or reply, but withdrawing a little from that extreme, they still move on. And so across all that broad open ground they have come, nearer and nearer, nearly half the way, with our guns bellowing in their faces, until now a hundred yards, no more, divide our ready left from their advancing right.

The eager men there are impatient to begin. Let them. First, Harrow's breastworks flame; then Hall's; then Webb's. As if our bullets were the fire coals that touched off their muskets, the enemy in front halts, and his countless level barrels blaze back upon us. The Second Division is struggling in battle. The rattling storm soon spreads to the right, and the blue trefoils are vying with the white. All along each hostile front, a thousand yards, with narrowest space between, the volleys blaze and roll; as thick the sound as when a summer hailstorm pelts the city roofs; as thick the fire as when the incessant lightning fringes a summer cloud.

When the Rebel infantry had opened fire our batteries soon became silent, and this without their fault, for they were foul by long previous use. They were the targets of the concentrated Rebel bullets, and some of them had expended all their canister. But they were not silent before Rorty was killed, Woodruff had fallen mortally wounded, and Cushing, firing almost his last canister, had dropped dead among his

guns shot through the head by a bullet. The conflict is left
to the infantry alone.

Unable to find my general when I had returned to the crest
after transmitting his message to General Meade, and while
riding in the search having witnessed the development of the
fight, from the first fire upon the left by the main lines until
all of the two divisions were furiously engaged, I gave up
hunting as useless—I was convinced General Gibbon could
not be on the field; I left him mounted; I could easily have
found him now had he so remained—but now, save myself,
there was not a mounted officer near the engaged lines—and
was riding toward the right of the Second Division, with purpose to stop there, as the most eligible position to watch the
further progress of the battle, there to be ready to take part
according to my own notions whenever and wherever occasion
was presented. The conflict was tremendous, but I had seen
no wavering in all our line.

Wondering how long the Rebel ranks, deep though they
were, could stand our sheltered volleys, I had come near my
destination, when—great heaven! were my senses mad? The
larger portion of Webb's brigade—my God, it was true—
there by the group of trees and the angles of the wall, was
breaking from the cover of their works, and, without orders
or reason, with no hand lifted to check them, was falling back,
a fear-stricken flock of confusion! The fate of Gettysburg
hung upon a spider's single thread!

A great magnificent passion came on me at the instant, not
one that overpowers and confounds, but one that blanches
the face and sublimes every sense and faculty. My sword,
that had always hung idle by my side, the sign of rank only
in every battle, I drew, bright and gleaming, the symbol of
command. Was not that a fit occasion, and these fugitives
the men on whom to try the temper of the Solinzen steel?
All rules and proprieties were forgotten; all considerations of
person, and danger and safety despised; for, as I met the tide
of these rabbits, the damned red flags of the Rebellion began
to thicken and flaunt along the wall they had just deserted,
and one was already waving over one of the guns of the
dead Cushing.

I ordered these men to "halt," and "face about" and "fire," and they heard my voice and gathered my meaning, and obeyed my commands. On some unpatriotic backs of those not quick of comprehension, the flat of my sabre fell not lightly, and at its touch their love of country returned, and, with a look at me as if I were the destroying angel, as I might have become theirs, they again faced the enemy.[1]

General Webb soon came to my assistance. He was on foot, but he was active, and did all that one could do to repair the breach, or to avert its calamity. The men that had fallen back, facing the enemy, soon regained confidence in themselves, and became steady. This portion of the wall was lost to us, and the enemy had gained the cover of the reverse side, where he now stormed with fire.

But Webb's men, with their bodies in part protected by the abruptness of the crest, now sent back in the enemies' faces as fierce a storm. Some scores of venturesome Rebels, that in their first push at the wall had dared to cross at the further angle, and those that had desecrated Cushing's guns, were promptly shot down, and speedy death met him who should raise his body to cross it again. At this point little could be seen of the enemy by reason of his cover and the smoke, except the flash of his muskets and his waving flags.

These red flags were accumulating at the wall every moment, and they maddened us as the same color does the bull. Webb's men are falling fast, and he is among them to direct and to encourage; but, however well they may now do, with that walled enemy in front, with more than a dozen flags to Webb's three, it soon becomes apparent that in not many minutes they will be overpowered, or that there will be none alive for the enemy to overpower.

[1] Bruce Catton, editing a modern edition of Haskell's classic memoirs, recalls a pamphlet, published in 1910 by survivors of Webb's brigade, that denied they either broke and ran or Haskell was forced to rally them; and Catton concludes it is "probable" Haskell "slightly overstated the extent of the rout." The contemporary account in the *Richmond Enquirer,* however, recalled how, as the Union line began "yielding," a Federal officer "with flashing sword" dashed forward and urged the men to stand. *Rebellion Record,* VII, 114.

Webb has but three regiments, all small, the Sixty-ninth, Seventy-first and Seventy-second Pennsylvania . . . and he must have speedy assistance, or this crest will be lost. Oh, where is Gibbon? where is Hancock?—some general—anybody with the power and the will to support that wasting, melting line? No general came, and no succor! I thought of Hays upon the right, but from the smoke and war along his front, it was evident that he had enough upon his hands, if he stayed the in-rolling tide of the Rebels there. Doubleday upon the left was too far off and too slow, and on another occasion I had begged him to send his idle regiments to support another line battling with thrice its numbers, and this "Old Sumpter Hero" had declined. As a last resort I resolved to see if Hall and Harrow could not send some of their commands to reinforce Webb.

3

Haskell gallops to the left, and as he attains the rear of Hall's lines it was easy to discover the reason and the manner of this gathering of Rebel flags in front of Webb.

The enemy, emboldened by his success in gaining our line by the group of trees and the angle of the wall, was concentrating all his right against and was further pressing that point. There was the stress of his assault; there would he drive his fiery wedge to split our line. In front of Harrow's and Hall's Brigades he had been able to advance no nearer than when he first halted to deliver fire, and these commands had not yielded an inch. To effect the concentration before Webb, the enemy would march the regiment on his extreme right of each of his lines by the left flank to the rear of the troops, still halted and facing to the front, and so continuing to draw in his right, when they were all massed in the position desired, he would again face them to the front, and advance to the storming. This was the way he made the wall before Webb's line blaze red with his battle flags, and such was the purpose there of his thick-crowding battalions. Not a moment must be lost.

Colonel Hall I found just in rear of his line, sword in hand, cool, vigilant, noting all that passed and directing the battle of his brigade. The fire was constantly diminshing now in his front, in the manner and by the movement of the enemy that I have mentioned, drifting to the right.

"How is it going?" Colonel Hall asked me, as I rode up.

"Well, but Webb is hotly pressed and must have support, or he will be overpowered. Can you assist him?"

"Yes."

"You cannot be too quick."

"I will move my brigade at once."

"Good."

He gave the order, and in briefest time I saw five friendly colors hurrying to the aid of the imperilled three; and each color represented true, battle-tried men, that had not turned back from Rebel fire that day nor yesterday, though their ranks were sadly thinned. To Webb's brigade, pressed back as it had been from the wall, the distance was not great from Hall's right. The regiments marched by the right flank. Colonel Hall superintended the movement in person. Colonel Devereux coolly commanded the Nineteenth Massachusetts. His major, Rice, had already been wounded and carried off. Lieutenant Colonel Macy, of the Twentieth Massachusetts, had just had his left hand shot off, and so Captain Abbott gallantly led over this fine regiment. The Forty-second New York followed their excellent Colonel Mallon. Lieutenant Colonel Steele, Seventh Michigan, had just been killed, and his regiment, and the handful of the Fifty-ninth New York followed their colors.

The movement, . . . attracting the enemy's fire and executed in haste as it must be, was difficult; but in reasonable time, and in order that is serviceable if not regular, Hall's men are fighting gallantly side by side with Webb's before the all important point. I did not stop to see all this movement of Hall's, but from him I went at once further to the left to the First brigade. General Harrow I did not see, but his fighting men would answer my purpose as well. The Nineteenth Maine, the Fifteenth Massachusetts, the Thirty-second New York and the shattered old thunderbolt, the First Minnesota—poor

Farrell was dying then upon the ground where he had fallen —all men that I could find I took over to the right at the *double quick.*

As we were moving to and near the other brigade of the division, from my position on horseback I could see that the enemy's right, under Hall's fire, was beginning to stagger and to break.

"See," I said to the men. "See the *chivalry!* See the gray-backs run!"

The men saw, and as they swept to their places by the side of Hall and opened fire, they roared, and this in a manner that said more plainly than words—for the deaf could have seen it in their faces, and the blind could have heard it in their voices—*the crest is safe!*

The whole division concentrated, and changes of position and new phases as well on our part as on that of the enemy having as indicated occurred, for the purpose of showing the exact present posture of affairs some further description is necessary. Before the Second Division the enemy is massed, the main bulk of his force covered by the ground that slopes to his rear, with his front at the stonewall. Between his front and us extends the very apex of the crest. All there are left of the White Trefoil Division . . . are below or behind the crest, in such a position that by the exposure of the head and upper part of the body above the crest they can deliver their fire in the enemy's faces along the top of the wall.

By reason of the disorganization incidental in Webb's brigade . . . formation of companies and regiment in regular ranks is lost; but commands, companies, regiments and brigades are blended and intermixed—an irregular extended mass—men enough, if in order, to form a line of four or five ranks along the whole front of the division. The twelve flags of the regiments wave defiantly at intervals along the front; at the stonewall, at unequal distances from ours of forty, fifty or sixty yards, stream nearly double this number of the battle flags of the enemy. . . . Although no cessation or abatement in the general din of conflict since the commencement had at any time been appreciable, now it was as if a new battle,

deadlier, stormier than before, had sprung from the body of
the old—a young Phoenix of combat, whose eyes stream
lightning, shaking his arrowy wings over the yet glowing
ashes of his progenitor.

4

Doggedly, John Dooley, the Confederate soldier who makes
this charge for Uncle Robert, walks into the face of the
murderous Federal fire.

On, men, on! Thirty more yards and the guns are ours;
but who can stand such a storm of hissing lead and iron?
What a relief if earth, which almost seems to hurl these
implements of death in our faces, would open now and afford
a secure retreat from threatening death. Every officer is in
front . . . . colonels, lieutenant colonels, majors, captains, all
press on and cheer the shattered lines.

Just here—from right to left the remnants of our braves
pour in their long reserved fire; until now no shot had been
fired, no shout of triumph had been raised; but as the cloud
of smoke rises over the heads of the advancing divisions the
well-known southern battle cry which marks the victory
gained or nearly gained bursts wildly over the blood-stained
field and *all that line of guns is ours.*

Shot through both thighs, I fall about thirty yards from the
guns. By my side lies Lieutenant Kehoe, shot through the
knee. Here we lie, he in excessive pain, I fearing to bleed
to death, the dead and dying all around, while the division
sweeps over the Yankee guns. Oh, how I long to know the
result, the end of this fearful charge! We seem to have victory
in our hands; but what can our poor remnant of a shattered
division do if they meet beyond the guns an obstinate
resistance?

There—listen—we hear a new shout, and cheer after cheer
rends the air. Are those fresh troops advancing to our support? No! no! That huzza never broke from Southern lips.
Oh God! Virginia's bravest, noblest sons have perished here
today and perished all in vain!

5

The terrible sacrifice tore the heart of the reporter for the *Richmond Enquirer.*

General Pickett, seeing the splendid valor of his troops, moves among them as if courting death by his own daring intrepidity. The noble Garnett is dead, Armistead wounded, and the brave Kemper, with hat in hand, still cheering on his men, falls from his horse into the ranks of the enemy. His men rush forward, rescue their General, and he is borne mortally wounded from the field. Where is the gallant Williams? The First is there, but his clear voice is no longer heard —he has fallen lifeless, and there goes his horse now riderless. There stand the decimated ranks of the Third; and Mayo, though struck, stands firm with his faithful men, animating them to yet more daring deeds; but Callcott, the Christian soldier, who stood unmoved amid this carnival of death, has fought his last battle; no sound shall awake him to glory again, 'till the summons of the great Judge, announcing to him the reward of the faithful soldier, who has fought the good fight. Patton, Otey, and Terry, who, but a moment since, stood at their respective regiments, are wounded. The brave Hunton, hero of Leesburgh, most worthy succcessor of the noble Garnett, Stewart, and Gant, lies wounded. Carrington, his gallant regiment shattered, stands firmly, flaunting defiantly his colors in the very face of the enemy. Allen and Ellis are killed. Hodges, too, has fallen, and the modest, chivalrous Edmunds lies numbered with the noble dead; Aylett wounded, and Magruder has gone down in the shock of battle. The fight goes on—but few are left; and the shrinking columns of the enemy gain confidence from the heavy reenforcements advanced to their support. They, too, are moving in large force on the right flank. This division, small at first, with ranks now torn and shattered, most of its officers killed or wounded, no valor able to rescue victory from such a grasp, annihilation or capture inevitable, slowly, reluctantly fell back.

6

Exultantly, Haskell senses that the moment of victory is near.

The jostling, swaying lines on either side boil and roar and dash their flaming spray, two hostile billows of a fiery ocean. Thick flashes stream from the wall, thick volleys answer from the crest. No threats or expostulations now, only example and encouragement. All depths of passion are stirred, and all combatives fire, down to their deep foundations. Individuality is drowned in a sea of clamor, and timid men, breathing the breath of the multitude, are brave. The frequent dead and wounded lie where they stagger and fall—there is no humanity for them now, and none can be spared to care for them. The men do not cheer or shout; they growl, and over that uneasy sea, heard with the roar of musketry, sweeps the muttered thunder of a storm of growls.

Webb, Hall, Devereux, Mallon, Abbott among the men where all are heroes, are doing deeds of note. Now the loyal wave rolls up as if it would overleap its barrier, the crest. Pistols flash with the muskets. My "Forward to the wall" is answered by the Rebel counter-command, "Steady, men!" and the wave swings back. Again it surges, and again it sinks.

These men of Pennsylvania, on the soil of their own homesteads, the first and only to flee the wall, must be the first to storm it.

"Major ——, *lead* your men over the crest, they will follow."

"By the tactics I understand my place is in rear of the men."

"Your pardon, sir; I see *your* place is in rear of the men. I thought you were fit to lead."

"Captain Sapler, come on with your men."

"Let me first stop this fire in the rear, or we shall be hit by our own men."

"Never mind the fire in the rear; let us take care of this in front first."

"Sergeant, forward with your color. Let the Rebels see it close to their eyes once before they die."

The color sergeant of the Seventy-second Pennsylvania, grasping the stump of the severed lance in both his hands, waved the flag above his head and rushed toward the wall.

"Will you see your color storm the wall alone?"

One man only starts to follow. Almost half way to the wall, down go color bearer and color to the ground—the gallant sergeant is dead.

The line springs—the crest of the solid ground with a great roar, heaves forward its maddened load, men, arms, smoke, fire, a fighting mass. It rolls to the wall—flash meets flash, the wall is crossed—a moment ensues of thrusts, yells, blows, shots, and undistinguishable conflict, followed by a shout universal that makes the welkin ring again, and the last and bloodiest fight of the great battle of Gettysburg is ended and won.

7

Now as the shattered Rebel infantry falls back, Colonel E. Porter Alexander, who commanded the great cannonade, stands beside the saddest man in the Army of Northern Virginia—General Robert E. Lee.

While Wilcox's brigade was making its charge, General Lee rode up and joined me. He was entirely alone, which could scarcely have happened, except by design on his part. We were not firing, but holding position to prevent pursuit by the enemy. I have no doubt but that Lee was apprehensive of this, and had come to the front to help rally the fugitives if that happened. He remained with us perhaps an hour and spoke to nearly every man who passed, using expressions such as: "Don't be discouraged." "It was my fault this time." "Form your ranks again when you get under cover." "All good men must hold together now."

I had with me an aide, Lieutenant Colston, ordnance officer of my battalion. At one time loud cheering was heard in the Federal line and Lee asked Colston to ride to the front and find out the cause. Colston's horse was unused to the spur and balking, Colston had a stick handed him and used it. Lee said: "Oh, don't do that. I once had a foolish horse and I found gentle measures so much the best." Colston presently reported the Federals were cheering an officer riding along their line. Lee remarked that he had thought it possible that Johnson's division in the Federal rear might have gained some success. Evidently he was not yet informed that Johnson, about noon, had withdrawn to a defensive position.

Kemper was brought by on a litter. Lee rode up and said, "General, I hope you are not badly hurt." Kemper replied, "Yes, General, I'm afraid they have got me this time." Lee pressed his hand, saying, "I trust not! I trust not." Colonel Fremantle of Her Majesty's Coldstream Guards had also joined the party. We sat on horseback, on the slope behind the guns where we could see over the crest, but the group of horses were not visible to the enemy.

8

In defeat Longstreet seemed to have regained his ability to bark and growl. Fremantle describes his meeting with him.

When I got close up to General Longstreet, I saw one of his regiments advancing through the woods in good order; so, thinking I was just in time to see the attack, I remarked to the general that *"I wouldn't have missed this for anything!"* Longstreet was seated on top of a snake fence at the edge of the wood, and looking perfectly calm and imperturbed. He replied, laughing, *"The devil you wouldn't! I would like to have missed it very much; we've attacked and been repulsed; look there!"*

For the first time I viewed the open space between the two positions and saw it covered with Confederates, slowly and sulkily returning toward us in small, broken parties, under a heavy fire of artillery. But the fire where we were was not so bad as further to the rear; for although the air seemed alive with shell, the greater number burst behind us.

The General told me that Pickett's division had succeeded in carrying the enemy's position and capturing his guns, but after remaining there twenty minutes, it had been forced to retire on the retreat of Heth and Pettigrew on its left. No person could have been more calm or self-possessed than General Longstreet under these trying circumstances, aggravated as they now were by the movements of the enemy, who began to show a strong disposition to advance. I could now fully appreciate the term bulldog, which I heard applied to him by the soldiers. Difficulties seem to make no other impression upon him than to make him a little more savage.

Major Walton was the only one with him when I came up —all the rest had been put into the charge. In a few minutes Major Latrobe arrived on foot, carrying his saddle, having just had his horse killed. Colonel Sorrell was also in the same predicament, and Captain Gorel's horse was wounded in the mouth.

The General was making the best arrangements in his power to resist the threatened advance, by advancing some artillery, rallying the stragglers, etc. I remember seeing a General (Pettigrew, I think it was) come up to him and report that "he was unable to bring his troops up again." Longstreet turned upon him, and replied with some sarcasm, *"Very well, never mind then, General; just let them remain where they are: the enemy's going to advance and will spare you the trouble."*

9

Haskell stands beside another general.

General Meade rode up accompanied alone by his son, who is his aide-de-camp, an escort, if select, not large for a commander of such an army. The principal horseman was no bedizened hero of some holiday review, but he was a plain man, dressed in a serviceable summer suit of dark blue cloth, without badge or ornament, save the shoulder-straps of his grade, and a light, straight sword of a general or general staff officer. He wore heavy, high-top boots and buff gauntlets, and his soft black felt hat was slouched down over his eyes. His face was very white, not pale, and the lines were marked and earnest and full of care.

As he arrived near me, coming up the hill, he asked in a sharp, eager voice: "How is it going here?"

"I believe, general, the enemy's attack is repulsed," I answered.

Still approaching, and a new light began to come in his face, of gratified surprise with a touch of incredulity, of which his voice was also the medium, he further asked: *"What! Is the assault already repulsed?"* his voice quicker and more eager than before.

"It is, sir," I replied.

By this time he was on the crest, and when his eye had for a instant swept over the field, taking in just a glance of the whole—the masses of prisoners, the numerous captured flags which the men were derisively flaunting about, the fugitives of the routed enemy disappearing with the speed of terror in the woods—partly at what I had told him, partly at what he saw, he said impressively, and his face lighted: "Thank God." And then his right hand moved as if it would have caught off his hat and waved it; but this gesture he suppressed, and instead he waved his hand and said "Hurrah!"

The son, with more youth in his blood and less rank upon his shoulders, snatched off his cap and roared out his three "hurrahs" right heartily. The general then surveyed the field, some minutes, in silence. He at length asked who was in command—he had heard that Hancock and Gibbon were wounded —and I told him that General Caldwell was the senior officer of the corps and General Harrow of the division. He asked where they were, but before I had time to answer that I did not know, he resumed: "No matter; I will give my orders to you and you will see them executed." He then gave direction that the troops should be reformed as soon as practicable and kept in their places, as the enemy might be mad enough to attack again. He also gave directions concerning the posting of some reinforcements which he said would soon be there, adding: "If the enemy does attack, charge him in the flank and sweep him from the field."

The general then, a gratified man, galloped in the direction of his headquarters.

Chapter 12

"Your Sorrowing Soldier"

DISASTROUS THOUGH July 3 became to everyone in the Army of Northern Virginia the results of the day were to prove no more disheartening to anyone than to Jeb Stuart. Finally reaching Gettysburg on the night before the last day of fighting, Stuart still was filled with bravado. Perhaps he already suspected what Lee would write in his official report concerning his part in the invasion of Pennsylvania: "The movements of the army preceding the battle of Gettysburg had been much embarrassed by the absence of the cavalry"; but it is inconceivable that either Stuart's conscience or his pride was greatly affected by the threat of such action. To the end Stuart saw himself as blameless in any criticism that could be leveled at his foray into Maryland, and now that he was actually on the field at Gettysburg he was confident that his performance would more than compensate for any "embarrassment" he may have caused Lee and the army.

No eagerness was ever more genuine than that with which Stuart looked forward to settling scores with the Federal cavalry for the surprise attack at Brandy Station. His big chance had come at last and now on the home soil of the Army of the Potomac he would strike his blow of vengeance. If Ewell couldn't give Lee possession of the Baltimore Pike, Stuart would; the scene of his attack would be behind Benner's Hill where Anderson's artillery had been emplaced, and he would charge at the precise moment when Pickett's Division was engaging the Federal infantry along Cemetery Ridge. In good heart he rode out to battle; to his men he never had seemed in finer spirit.

1

But the Federal cavalry was equally eager to carry on where it had left off at Brandy Station. Under Alfred Pleasonton, the

Union horsemen set themelves for an engagement that later was described as "the finest cavalry fight of the war." From a point of concealment in a woods the Federals watched Stuart's men advancing to the attack, and this account of the battle, as seen from that place of vantage, is by Colonel William Brooke-Rawle.

In close columns of squadrons, advancing as if in review, with sabres drawn and glistening like silver in the bright sunlight, the spectacle called forth a murmur of admiration. It was, indeed, a memorable one. Chester, being nearest, opened at once with his section at the distance of three-fourths of a mile. Pennington and Kinney soon did the same. Canister and percussion shell were put into the steadily approaching columns as fast as the guns could fire. The dismounted men fell back to the right and left, and such as could got to their horses. The mounted skirmishers rallied and fell into line. Then Gregg rode over to the First Michigan, which, as it had come upon the field some time before, had formed close column of squadrons between and supporting the batteries, and ordered it to charge. As Town ordered sabres to be drawn and the column to advance, Custer dashed up with similar orders, and placed himself at its head. The two columns drew nearer and nearer, the Confederates outnumbering their opponents as three or four to one.

The gait increased—first the trot, then the gallop. Hampton's battle flag floated in the van of the brigade. The orders of the Confederate officers could be heard by those in the woods on their left: "Keep to your sabres, men, keep to your sabres!" for the lessons they had learned at Brandy Station and at Aldie had been severe. There the cry had been: "Put up your sabres! Draw your pistols and fight like gentlemen!" But the sabre was never a favorite weapon with the Confederate cavalry, and now, in spite of the lessons of the past, the warnings of the present were not heeded by all.

As the charge was ordered the speed increased, every horse on the jump, every man yelling like a demon. The columns of the Confederates blended, but the perfect alignment was maintained. Chester put charge after charge of canister into their midst, his men bringing it up to the guns by the armful. The execution was fearful, but the long rents closed up at once. As the opposing columns drew nearer and nearer, each with perfect alignment, every man gathered his horse well under him, and gripped his weapon the tighter. Though ordered to retire his guns, toward which the head of the assaulting column was directed, Chester kept on until the enemy was within fifty yards and the head of the First Michigan had come into the line of his fire. Staggered by the fearful execution from the two batteries, the men in the front line of the Confederate column drew in their horses and wavered. Some turned, and the column fanned out to the right and left, but those behind came pressing on. Custer, seeing the front men hesitate, waved his sabre and shouted, "Come on, you Wolverines!" and with a fearful yell the First Michigan rushed on, Custer four lengths ahead.

McIntosh, as he saw the Confederate column advancing, sent his Adjutant General, Captain Walter S. Newhall, to the left with orders to rally men for a charge on the flank as it passed. But sixteen men could get their horses, and with five officers they made for the battle flag. Newhall, back once more with the men of his own regiment, who, as he knew well, would go anywhere, and sharing the excitement of the moment, rushed at the head of the little band. Miller, whose squadron of the Third Pennsylvania was already mounted and had rallied, fired a volley from the woods on the right as the Confederate column passed parallel with his line but one hundred yards off, and then, with sabres drawn, charged down into the overwhelming masses of the enemy.

The small detachment of the Third Pennsylvania struck the enemy first, all making for the color guard. Newhall was about seizing the flag when a sabre blow, directed at his head, compelled him to parry it. At the same moment the color-bearer lowered his spear and struck Newhall full in the face, tearing open his mouth and knocking him senseless to the ground. Every officer and nearly every man in the little band was killed or wounded, although some succeeded in cutting their way clear through. Almost at the same moment Miller, with his squadron of the Third Pennsylvania, struck the left flank about two-thirds of the way down the column. Going through and through, he cut off the rear portion and drove it almost up to the Confederate battery, and nothing but the heavy losses which he had suffered and the scattering of his men prevented his going further, wounded though he was.

In the meantime, the two columns had come together with a crash—the one led by Hampton and Fitz Lee (for he, too, was there), and the other by Custer—and were fighting hand-to-hand. McIntosh, with his staff and orderlies, and such scattered men from the Michigan and other regiments as he could get together, charged in with their sabres. For minutes which seemed like hours, amid the clashing of the sabres, the rattle of the small arms, the frenzied imprecations, the demands to surrender, the undaunted replies, and the appeals for mercy, the Confederate column stood its ground. Captain Thomas of the staff, seeing that a little more was needed to turn the tide, cut his way over to the woods on the right, where he knew he could find Hart with his fresh squadron of the First New Jersey. In the mêlée near the colors was an officer of high rank, and the two headed the squadron for that part of the fight. They came within reach of him with their sabres, and then it was that Wade Hampton was wounded.

By this time the edges of the Confederate column had begun to fray away, and the outside men to draw back. As Hart's squadron and the other small parties who had rallied and mounted charged down from all sides, the enemy turned. Then followed a pell-mell rush, our men in close pursuit. Many prisoners were captured, and many of our men, through their impetuosity, were carried away by the overpowering current of the retreat.

2

Thus Stuart failed and the fighting on July 3 ended. To Sallie Robbins Broadhead, however, the outcome of the battle was still unknown as she set down in her diary the experiences of the day.

Today the battle opened with fierce cannonading before

four o'clock A.M. Shortly after the battle began we were told to leave this end of town, for likely it would be shelled.

My husband declared he would not go while one brick remained upon another, and as usual we betook ourselves to the cellar, where we remained until 10 o'clock when the firing ceased. We could not get breakfast on account of our fears and the great danger. During the cessation we managed to get a cold bite. Again the battle began with unearthly fury.

Nearly all afternoon it seemed as if the heavens and earth were crashing together.

The time we sat in the cellar seemed long, listening to the terrific sound of the strife; more terrible never greeted human ears. We knew that with every explosion, and the scream of each shell, human beings were hurried through excruciating pain into another world, and that many more were torn, and mangled, and lying in torment worse than death, and no one able to extend relief. The thought made me very sad, and feel that, if it was God's will, I would rather be taken away than remain to see the misery that would follow. Some thought this afternoon would never come to a close.

We knew that the Rebels were putting forth all their might, and it was a dreadful thought that they might succeed.

Who is victorious, or with whom the advantage rests, no one here can tell. It would ease the horror if we knew our arms were successful. Some think the Rebels were defeated, as there has been no boasting as on yesterday, and they look uneasy and by no means exultant. I hope they are correct, but I fear we are too hopeful. We shall see tomorrow. It will be the fourth of July, and the Rebels have promised us a glorious day. If it only ends the battle and drives them off it will be glorious, and I will rejoice.

3

For Billy Bayly, seeing the gray columns turning in retreat, there was no uncertainty.

The temper of our guests changed materially; while they insisted that the Yanks were being whipped and driven from their defensive position we knew to the contrary and so told

them. Then the drift of the wagon trains, stragglers and camp
followers in general was back in the direction whence they
came, and inquiries as to the most direct route to Chambersburg and Hagerstown highways were of promising portent.

Standing that afternoon on the high part of the farm with
father, Uncle William Hamilton and his son John, and the
deserter, we saw long wagon trains moving westward in the
valley below and although the battle was raging at the time,
my uncle remarked, "That is a good sign; the enemy are retreating, I am sure!" And such was really the fact. Uncle
William Hamilton was at the time looking over the smoke-
embowered field where two of his sons were with their commands in the Army of the Potomac, one lying seriously
wounded in a field hospital back of Round Top at the time.

Presently my uncle and cousin left for home and while the
others of us were standing there two Confederate cavalrymen
rode up and asked the nearest route to Hagerstown, which
information father willingly gave them only to be rewarded
with a tirade of abuse, punctuated with oaths. Then is the
only time I was fighting mad during the strenuous days that
had passed and I forgot self-restraint and everything else
except the wild desire to pull the "Reb" from his horse. What
I said I do not know, but I was jerked back by my deserter
friend and told to shut up. The "Rebs" spurred off, not in
fear of the youth sputtering below but in fear of capture and
imprisonment by a mightier force than the impotent little
Yank, who would have cursed them in turn if he could have
found voice and proper curse words to suit the occasion.

I recall nothing of special note during the evening and
night and when morning came we found that our host of
visitors had, like the Arab, folded their tents and quietly
stolen away. At least so far as the Southern Army was concerned, the evening before was the last we saw of them and
then, as I have stated, they were showing their heels.

4

George Edward Pickett relived the agony of the day in a
letter to his sweetheart.

My letter of yesterday, my darling, written before the battle, was full of hope and cheer; even though it told you of the long hours of waiting from four in the morning, when Gary's pistol rang out from the Federal lines signaling the attack upon Culp's Hill, to the solemn eight o'clock review of my men, who rose and stood silently lifting their hats in loving reverence as Marse Robert, Old Peter [1] and your own Soldier reviewed them—on then to the deadly stillness of the five hours following, when the men lay in the tall grass in the rear of the artillery line, the July sun pouring its scorching rays almost vertically down upon them, till one o'clock when the awful silence of the vast battlefield was broken by a cannon shot which opened the greatest artillery duel in the world. The firing lasted two hours. When it ceased we took advantage of the blackened field and in the glowering darkness formed our attacking column just before the brow of Seminary Ridge.

I closed my letter to you a little before three o'clock and rode up to Old Peter for orders. I found him like a great lion at bay. I have never seen him so grave and troubled. For several minutes after I had saluted him he looked at me without speaking. Then in an agonized voice, the reserve all gone, he said:

"Pickett, I am being crucified at the thought of the sacrifice of life which this attack will make. I have instructed Alexander to watch the effect of our fire upon the enemy, and when it begins to tell he must take the responsibility and give you your orders, for I can't."

While he was yet speaking a note was brought to me from Alexander. After reading it I handed it to him, asking if I should obey and go forward. He looked at me for a moment, then held out his hand. Presently, clasping his other hand over mine without speaking he bowed his head upon his breast. I shall never forget the look in his face nor the clasp of his hand when I said: "Then, General, I shall lead my division on." I had ridden only a few paces when I remembered your letter and (forgive me) thoughtlessly scribbled in a corner

[1] Longstreet.

of the envelope, "If Old Peter's nod means death, then goodby and God bless you, little one," turned back, and asked the dear old chief if he would be good enough to mail it for me. As he took your letter from me, my darling, I saw tears glisten on his cheeks and beard. The stern old warhorse, God bless him, was weeping for his men, and, I know, praying too that this cup might pass from them. I obeyed the silent assent of his bowed head, an assent given against his own convictions—given in anguish and with reluctance.

My brave boys were full of hope and confident of victory as I led them forth, forming them in column of attack, and though officers and men alike knew what was before them—knew the odds against them—they eagerly offered up their lives on the altar of duty, having absolute faith in their ultimate success. Over on Cemetery Ridge the Federals beheld a scene never before witnessed on this continent—a scene which has never previously been enacted and can never take place again—an army forming in line of battle in full view, under their very eyes—charging across a space nearly a mile in length over fields of waving grain and anon of stubble and then a smooth expanse—moving with the steadiness of a dress parade, the pride and glory soon to be crushed by an overwhelming heartbreak. . . .

Well, it is all over now. The battle is lost, and many of us are prisoners, many are dead, many wounded, bleeding and dying. Your Soldier lives and mourns and, but for you, my darling, he would rather, a million times rather, be back there with his dead, to sleep for all time in an unknown grave.

Your sorrowing
Soldier.

5

Haskell describes how he brought the news of the great Union victory to wounded men behind the lines.

At about six o'clock on the afternoon of the third of July, my duties done upon the field, I quitted it to go to the general. My brave horse *Dick*—poor creature, his good conduct in the battle that afternoon had been complimented by a brigadier—was a sight to see. He was literally covered with blood. Struck repeatedly, his right thigh had been ripped open in a ghastly manner by a piece of shell, and three bullets were lodged deep in his body, and from his wounds the blood oozed and ran down his sides and legs and with the sweat formed a bloody foam. Dick's was no mean part in that battle. Good conduct in men under such circumstances as he was placed in might result from a sense of duty—his was the result of his bravery. Most horses would have been unmanageable with the flash and roar of arms about and the shouting. Dick was utterly cool, and would have obeyed the rein had it been a straw. To Dick belongs the honor of first mounting that stormy crest before the enemy, not forty yards away, whose bullets smote him, and of being the only horse there during the heat of the battle.

Even the enemy noticed Dick, and one of their reports of the battle mentions the *"solitary horseman"* who rallied our wavering line. He enabled me to do twelve times as much as I could have done on foot. It would not be dignified for an officer on foot to run; it is entirely so, mounted, to gallop. I do not approve of officers dismounting in battle, which is the time of all when they most need to be mounted, for thereby they have so much greater facilities for being everywhere present. Most officers, however, in close action, dismount. Dick deserves well of his country, and one day should have a horse monument. If there be *"ut sapientibus placit,"* an equine elysium, I will send to Charon the brass coin, the fee for Dick's passage over, and on the other side of the Styx in those shadowy clover fields he may nibble the blossoms forever.

I had been struck upon the thigh by a bullet which I think must have glanced and partially spent its force upon my saddle. It had pierced the thick cloth of my trousers and two thicknesses of underclothing, but had not broken the skin, leaving me with an enormous bruise that for a time benumbed the entire leg. At the time of receiving it I heard the thump and noticed it and the hole in the cloth into which I thrust my finger, and I experienced a feeling of relief, I am sure, when I found that my leg was not pierced. I think when I dismounted my horse after that fight that I was no very comely specimen of humanity. Drenched with sweat, the white of battle, by the reaction, now turned to burning red. I felt like a boiled man; and had it not been for the exhilaration at results I should have been miserable. This kept me up, however, and having found a man to transfer the saddle from poor Dick, who was not disposed to lie down by loss of blood and exhaustion, to another horse, I hobbled on among the hospitals in search of General Gibbon. . . .

At last I found the generals. General Gibbon was sitting on a chair that had been borrowed somewhere, with his wounded shoulder bare, and an attendant was bathing it with cold water. General Hancock was near by in an ambulance. They were at the tents of the Second Corps hospitals, which were on Rock Run. As I approached General Gibbon, when he saw me, he began to hurrah and wave his right hand. He had heard the result. I said: "O, General, long and well may you wave"—and he shook me warmly by the hand.

General Gibbon was struck by a bullet in the left shoulder, which had passed from the front through the flesh and out behind, fracturing the shoulder blade and inflicting a severe but not dangerous wound. He thinks he was the mark of a sharpshooter of the enemy hid in the bushes near where he and I had sat so long during the cannonade; and he was wounded and taken off the field before the fire of the main lines of infantry had commenced, he being at the time he was hit near the left of his division. General Hancock was struck a little later near the same part of the field by a bullet, piercing and almost going through his thigh, without touching the bone, however. His wound was severe also. He was carried back out of range, but before he would be carried off the field, he lay upon the ground in sight of the crest, where he could see something of the fight until he knew what would be the result.

And then, at General Gibbon's request, I had to tell him and a large voluntary crowd of the wounded who pressed around now . . . the story of the fight. I was nothing loath;

and I must say though I used sometimes before the war to make speeches, that I never had so enthusiastic an audience before. Cries of "good," "glorious," frequently interrupted me, and the storming of the wall was applauded by enthusiastic tears and the waving of battered, bloody hands.

6

Schoolgirl Tillie Alleman, who had taken refuge on a farm and now returned home, found nothing "glorious" in the aftermath of battle.

I fairly shrank back aghast at the awful sight presented. The approaches were crowded with wounded, dying and dead. The air was filled with moanings and groanings. As we passed on toward the house, we were compelled to pick our steps in order that we might not tread on the prostrate bodies. . . .

Amputating benches had been placed about the house. I must have become inured to seeing the terrors of battle, else I could hardly have gazed upon the scenes now presented. I was looking out one of the windows facing the front yard. Near the basement door, and directly under the window I was at, stood one of these benches. I saw them lifting the poor men upon it, then the surgeons cutting and sawing off legs, then again probing and picking bullets from the flesh.

Some of the soldiers fairly begged to be taken next, so great was their suffering, so anxious were they to obtain relief.

I saw the surgeons hastily put a cattle horn over the mouths of the wounded ones, after they were placed upon the bench. At first I did not understand the meaning of this, but upon inquiry, soon learned that that was their mode of administering chloroform in order to produce unconsciousness. But the effect in some instances was not produced; for I saw the wounded throwing themselves wildly about, and shrieking with pain while the operation was going on.

To the south of the house and just outside of the yard, I noticed a pile of limbs higher than the fence. It was a ghastly sight! Gazing upon these, too often the trophies of the amputating bench, I could have no other feeling than that the whole scene was one of cruel butchery.

7

On the Fourth of July the President of the United States issued a message.

WASHINGTON CITY, *July 4, 10 a.m.—1863*

The President announces to the country that news from the Army of the Potomac, up to 10 P.M. of the 3d is such as to cover that Army with the highest honor, to promise a great success to the cause of the Union, and to claim the condolences of all for the many gallant fallen. And that for this, he especially desires that on this day, He whose will, not ours, should ever be done, be everywhere remembered and reverenced with profoundest gratitude.

ABRAHAM LINCOLN.

8

Now for Sallie Robbins Broadhead the victory was to become certain, but joy is not nourished on human suffering.

July 4. This morning about six o'clock I heard a great noise in the street, and going to the door I saw a Rebel officer on horseback hallooing to some soldiers on foot, to "Hurry up, the Yankees have possession of the town and all would be captured." I looked up street and saw our men in the public square, and it was a joyful sight, for I knew we were now safe. Soon after, the Rebels sent in a flag of truce, but what was communicated we did not know, and, in consequence, the people were more scared than ever, the report spreading that it was to give notice to remove the women and children before shelling the town. As soon as the flag of truce had gone, our sharpshooters were pushed out to this side of town, and were all around us. We were between two fires and were kept close prisoners all day, not daring either to go out, or even look out of the windows on account of the bullets being fired at every moving object.

The people of other parts of town could go where they pleased. It has been a dreadfully long day. We know, however, that the Rebels are retreating, and that our army has been victorious. I was anxious to help care for the wounded, but the day is ended and all is quiet, and for the first time for a week I shall go to bed feeling safe.

July 5. What a beautiful morning! It seems as though nature was smiling on thousands suffering. One might think, if he saw only the sky, and earth, and trees, that everyone must be happy; but just look around and behold the misery made in so short time by man. Early this morning I went out to the Seminary, just outside of town, and which, until the retreat, was in the hands of the enemy.

What horrible sights present themselves on every side, the roads being strewn with dead horses and the bodies of some men, though the dead have nearly all been buried, and every step of the way giving evidence of the dreadful contest.

Shall we—for I was not alone—enter the building or return home? Can we endure the spectacle of hundreds of men wounded in every conceivable manner, some in the head, and limbs, here an arm off and there a leg, and just inside a poor fellow with both legs shot away? It is dreadful to behold, and, to add to the misery, no food has been served for several days. The little we have will not go far with so many.

What can we do? is the only question, and the little we brought was distributed.

It is heart-sickening to think of these noble fellows sacrificing everything for us, and saving us, and it out of our power to render any assistance of consequence.

I turned away and cried. We returned to town to gather up more food if possible, and to get soft material to place under their wounded limbs to help make them more comfortable. As we returned, our Cavalry was moving out to follow the Rebels, and the street was all in an uproar. When I reached home, I found my husband's brother, who had passed through the battle unhurt and had come to see us. I rejoiced at seeing him, for we feared he had fallen, and at once set to work to prepare a meal to appease his hunger. As I was baking cakes for him a poor prisoner came to the door and asked me to give him some, for he had had nothing to eat for the last two or three days. Afterward more joined him and made the same statement and request. I was kept baking cakes until nearly noon, and, in consequence, did not return to the Seminary. The poor fellows in my house were so hungry they could hardly wait until the cakes were baked.

Chapter 13

"We Have Our House to Ourselves"

ON THE FOURTH OF JULY, while rain fell steadily and the muddy roads slowed down the movements of the wagons and the ambulances, the Army of Northern Virginia began its retreat down the Fairfield Road. Ragged, graycoated soldiers who not a week before had marched along this same road with high hopes of reaching Philadelphia and Baltimore now trudged wearily through the dismal night toward the Potomac and home. Exhausted, downhearted, haunted by the dread that Meade's army might strike at any moment, the Confederates pushed their thin, wavering lines over the mountains and on the afternoon of the sixth and on the morning of the seventh assembled on Maryland soil at Hagerstown. Lee's men at once prepared to cross the Potomac between Williamsport and Falling Waters, but with flood tides the river was past fording. The Army of Northern Virginia settled down to wait for the high waters to recede, expecting attack, digging rifle pits to meet it. And so the shadow of war passed beyond Gettysburg and Pennsylvania; for a brief time it was to hover over these flooded shores of Maryland, and then the shadow moved on into Virginia, there to linger and to merge with other shadows until over all the Confederacy there spread the bitter darkness of final defeat.

With the armies gone, Gettysburg turned to the task of returning to its normal habits of living. Families that had fled with the first sound of the guns came home, red embers glowed again in the forge of the blacksmith's shop, and the streets were cleared of the litter of knapsacks and canteens, torn clothing and empty cartridge belts left behind by the fleeing soldiers. But the dead remained to be buried, the wounded to be healed, and the suffering of three long days of war to be softened in memory.

1

No one turned to the rebuilding of an interrupted life with greater fortitude of mind and heart than Sallie Robbins Broadhead.

July 7. This morning we started out to see the wounded, with as much food as we could scrape together and some old quilts and pillows. It was very little, but yet better than nothing. We found on reaching the hospital that a wagon-load of bread and fifty pounds of butter had arrived, having been sent in from the country, and a supply of what the soldiers call "hard tack" had been distributed. All got some to eat, but not as much as they desired. Government meat is promised for tomorrow, and a full supply of provisions. I assisted in feeding some of the severely wounded when I perceived that they were suffering on account of not having their wounds dressed. I did not know whether I could render any assistance in that way, but I thought I would try. I procured a basin and water, and went to a room where there were seven or eight, some shot in the arms, others in the legs, and one in his back, and another in the shoulder. I asked if anyone would like to have his wounds dressed? Someone replied, "There is a man on the floor who cannot help himself, you would better see to him." Stooping over him, I asked him for his wound, and he pointed to his leg. Such a horrible sight I had never seen and hope never to see again. His leg was all covered with worms. I inquired, Was there no doctor in the building? If there was, I must see him. One was brought, and I asked how the men ever came to be in such a condition.

He said enough men had not been detailed to care for the wounded, and that that man had been wounded in the first day's fight and held by the Rebels until the day previous, and that the surgeons had not yet had time to attend to all, and, at any rate, there were not enough surgeons, and what few there were could do little as the Rebels had stolen their instruments. He declared further that many would die from sheer lack of timely attendance.

We fixed the man as comfortably as we could, and when the doctor told me he could not live, I asked him for his home and if he had a family. He said I should send for his wife, and when I came home I wrote to her, as he told me, but I fear she may never see him alive, as he is very weak and sinking rapidly. I did not return to the hospital today, being very much fatigued and worn out, and having done what I never expected to do or thought I could. I am becoming more used to sights of misery.

July 8. Again at the hospital early this morning. Several physicians and lady nurses had come on from Washington the previous evening, and under their care things already began to look better. The work of extracting balls and of amputating shattered limbs had begun, and an effort at regular cooking. I aided a lady to dress wounds until soup was made, and then I went to distribute it. I found that I had only seen the lighter cases, and worse horrors met my eyes on descending to the basement of the building. Men, wounded in three and four places, not able to help themselves the least bit, lay almost swimming in water. I hunted up the lady whom I had been helping, and told her to come and see how they were situated. When she came down she reverently exclaimed, "My God! they must be gotten out of this or they will drown." I gladly, in answer to her request, consented to assist her.

She called some nurses to help and getting some stretchers the work was begun. There were somewhere near one hundred to be removed to the fourth story of the building. The way they happened to be in such a place was this. On the first day during the battle they had been taken into the building for shelter. On Thursday and Friday the Rebels planted a battery just behind this hospital, which annoyed our troops not a little, who, in endeavoring to silence it, could not avoid throwing some shells into the building. Some entered several of the rooms and injured one of the end walls, and the basement became the only safe place to which our wounded could betake themselves, and the heavy rains, following the engagement, flooded the floor. I did not think all could be removed today, but the lady said it must be done, and by hard work she had it accomplished. We had the satisfaction of seeing them more comfortably fixed, though they lay on the bare floor with only their gum blankets under them, but dry and thankful for so little. I fed one poor fellow who had both legs and one arm taken off and though he is very weak and surely cannot live, he seems in right good spirits.

Some weeks since I would have fainted had I seen as much blood as I have today, but I am proof now, only caring to relieve suffering. I now begin to feel fatigued, but I hope rest may restore me.

2

The first nurse to reach Gettysburg was Cornelia Hancock, a young Quakeress from Hancock's Bridge, New Jersey. She recalled that when she reached Philadelphia "the city was wild with excitement over news of a terrible battle which had just been fought on Pennsylvania soil"; and on arriving in Baltimore her experiences were no less exciting although more acutely personal: "Here Dorothea Dix appeared on the scene. She looked the nurses over and pronounced them all suitable except me. She immediately objected to my going further on the score of my youth and rosy cheeks. I was then just twenty-three years of age. In those days it was considered indecorous for angels of mercy to appear otherwise than gray-haired and spectacled. Such a thing as a hospital corps of comely young maiden nurses, possessing grace and good looks, was then unknown. Miss Farnham explained that she was under obligations to my friends who had helped her get proper credentials. The discussion waxed warm and I have no idea what conclusions they came to, for I settled the question myself by getting on the car and staying in the seat until the train pulled out of the city of Baltimore." The picture which Cornelia Hancock gives of her ministrations among the wounded at Gettysburg is extracted from letters written to her cousin, her sister, and her mother.

I am very tired tonight; have been on the field all day— went to the Third Division, Second Army Corps. I suppose there are about five hundred wounded belonging to it. They have one patch of woods devoted to each army corps for a hospital. I being interested in the Second, because Will [her brother] had been in it, got into one of its ambulances and went out at eight this morning and came back at six this evening. There are no words in the English language to express the sufferings I witnessed today. The men lie on the ground; their clothes have been cut off them to dress their wounds; they are half naked, have nothing but hard-tack to eat only as Sanitary Commissions, Christian Associations, and so forth give them.

I was the first woman who reached the Second Corps after the three days fight at Gettysburg. I was in that corps all day, not another woman within a half mile. Mrs. Harris was in First Division of Second Corps. I was introduced to the surgeon of the post, went anywhere through the corps, and received nothing but the greatest politeness from even the lowest private.

You can tell Aunt that there is every opportunity for "secesh" sympathizers to do a good work among the butternuts; we have lots of them here suffering fearfully. To give you some idea of the extent and numbers of the wounds, four surgeons, none of whom was idle fifteen minutes at a time, were busy all day amputating legs and arms. I gave to every man that had a leg or arm off a gill of wine, to every wounded in Third Division one glass of lemonade, some bread, and preserves and tobacco—as much as I am opposed to the latter, for they need it very much, they are so exhausted.

I feel very thankful that this was a successful battle; the spirit of the men is so high that many of the poor fellows said today, "What is an arm or leg to whipping Lee out of Penn?" I would get on first-rate if they would not ask me to write to their wives; *that* I cannot do without crying, which is not pleasant to either party. I do not mind the sight of blood, have seen limbs taken off and was not sick at all.

*

We have been two days on the field; go out about eight and come in about six—go in ambulances or army buggies. The surgeons of the Second Corps had one put at our disposal. I feel assured I shall never feel horrified at anything that may happen to me hereafter. There is a great want of surgeons here; there are hundreds of brave fellows, who have not had their wounds dressed since the battle. Brave is not the word; more, more Christian fortitude never was witnessed than they exhibit, always say, "Help my neighbor first, he is worse." The Second Corps did the heaviest fighting, and, of course, all who were badly wounded were in the thickest of the fight, and, therefore, we deal with the very best class of the men—that is, the bravest.

*

It took nearly five days for some three hundred surgeons to perform the amputations that occurred here, during which time the Rebels lay in a dying condition without their wounds being dressed or scarcely any food. If the Rebels did not get severely punished for this battle, then I am no judge. We have but one Rebel in our camp now; he says he never fired his gun if he could help it, and, therefore, we treat him first-rate. One man died this morning. I fixed him up as nicely as the place will allow; he will be buried this afternoon. We are becoming somewhat civilized here now and the men are cared for well.

*

Miss Dix was in camp today and stuck her head in the tents, but she does not work at all, and her nurses are being superseded very fast. I think we have some excellent nurses; we must have at least thirty women in the whole hospital. I have one tent of Johnnies in my ward, but I am not obliged to give them anything but whiskey.

I have no doubt that most people think I came into the army to get a husband. It is a capital place for that, as there are very many nice men here, and all men are required to give great respect to women. There are many good-looking women here who galavant around in the evening, and have a good time. I do not trouble myself much with the common herd. There is one man who is my right-hand man; he is about nineteen years old—is a hospital steward and will do anything to accommodate.

3

Meanwhile Sallie Robbins Broadhead agreed to take three visitors into her home.

July 9. A man called today and requested me to take into my home three wounded men from one of the field hospitals. I agreed to take them, for I can attend to them and not be compelled to leave my family so long every day as I have done. I am quite anxious to learn the condition of that man at the Seminary whose wife I sent for. I was thinking of her when the cars, for the first time since the destruction of Rock Creek bridge, came into town, the road having been repaired.

The Government can now forward supplies in abundance, and the poor fellows can be better provided for in every way. I talked with some wounded Rebels at one of the hospitals, and they are very saucy and brag largely. They are very kindly treated, and supplied in all respects as our men are.

July 10. This morning I again visited the Seminary and was rejoiced to see the improvements that had been made in the arrangements for the patients. Nearly all have been provided with beds and clean clothing, and a more comfortable look pervades the whole building. I miss many faces that I had learned to know, and among them the man whose wife I had written to. A lady stayed with him until he died and cut off a lock of his hair, which she gave me for his wife. At five o'clock our men were brought to our home, and I prepared them as nice a supper as I could, and they appeared quite cheerful, notwithstanding their dirty persons, having been lying in a field hospital three miles from town without a change of clothing since before the battle, and with very imperfect attendance.

July 11. This day has been spent in caring for our men. We procured clean clothes from the Sanitary Commission, and having fixed them up, they look and feel better, though their wounds are very painful.

Our town, too, begins to look more settled, and more like its former self.

The atmosphere is loaded with the horrid smell of decaying horses and the remains of slaughtered animals, and, it is said, from the bodies of men imperfectly buried. I fear we shall be visited with pestilence, for every breath we draw is made ugly by the stench.

July 12. Today the lady I sent for came to see her husband. I never pitied anyone as I did her when I told her he was dead. I hope I may never again be called upon to witness such a heart-rending scene.

The only comfort she had was in recovering the body, and in tears she conveyed it to the resting place of her family. I had some satisfaction from the fact that I had marked the grave, without which she might not have recovered it. Many persons have called today wanting lodging, but we cannot accommodate all. The town would not hold all who, from various motives visit the battlefield, even if there were no wounded in it.

This is Sunday, but since the battle we have had no Sunday. The churches have all been converted into hospitals, and the cars come and go as on other days, and the usual bustle and confusion reign in the streets, and there is nothing but the almanac to remind us of the day of rest. One of my patients grows worse and worse, and is gradually sinking to his long home.

July 13. This day has passed much as yesterday and the day before. The town is as full as ever of strangers, and the old story of the inability of a village of twenty-five hundred inhabitants, overrun and eaten out by two large armies, to accommodate from ten to twelve thousand visitors, is repeated almost hourly. Twenty are with us tonight, filling every bed and covering the floors. To add to my anxiety, the nurse has just informed me that our sickest man will die soon. It is sad; and even we, who have known him so short a time, will miss him. What our soldiers are in the army I cannot say, but when they are wounded, they all seem perfect gentlemen, so gentle, patient, and kind, and so thankful for any kindness shown them.

July 14. It is now one month since I began this journal, and little did I think when I sat down to while away the time, that I would have to record such terrible scenes as I have done.

Had anyone suggested any such sights as within the bound of possibility, I would have thought it madness. No small disturbance was occasioned by the removal of our wounded to the hospital. We had but short notice of the intention, and though we pleaded hard to have them remain, it was of no use. So many have been removed by death, and recovery, that there was room; and the surgeon having general care over all ordered the patients from private homes to the General Hospital. A weight of care, which we took upon us for duty's sake, and which we had learned to like and would have gladly borne, until relieved by the complete recovery of our men has lifted off our shoulders, and again we have our house to ourselves.

4

On the day that Sallie ended her journal the Army of Northern Virginia succeeded in crossing the Potomac. For a week the tension had mounted as the country waited for Meade to overtake Lee's ragged army and smash it forever. Aghast at the news that Lee had escaped, Lincoln met with his Cabinet, but the moment seemed too glum for serious deliberation. The diary of Secretary Welles reports the closing incidents of that meeting.

The President said he could not take up anything in Cabinet today. I retired slowly. The President hurried and overtook me. He said, with a voice and countenance I shall never forget, that he had dreaded, yet expected, this; that there had seemed to him for a full week a determination that Lee, though we had him in our hands, should escape with his force and plunder. "There is bad faith somewhere!" he exclaimed. "What does it mean, Mr. Welles? Great God! What does it mean?"

5

But Frank Arteas Haskell, writing his letter to his brother

at about this time, struck out savagely at the critics who thought the Army of the Potomac had been remiss in its duty.

Men there are who think that nothing was gained or done well in this battle because some other general did not have the command, or because any portion of the army of the enemy was permitted to escape capture or destruction. As if one army of a hundred thousand men could encounter another of the same number of as good troops and annihilate it! Military men do not claim or expect this; but the McClellan destroyers do, the doughty knights of purchasable newspaper quills; the formidable warriors from the brothels of politics, men of much warlike experience against honesty and honor, of profound attainments in ignorance, who have the maxims of Napoleon, whose spirit they as little understand as they do most things, to quote, to prove all things; but who, unfortunately, have much influence in the country and with the Government, and so over the army.

It is very pleasant for these people, no doubt, at safe distances from guns, in the enjoyment of a lucrative office or of a fraudulently obtained government contract, surrounded by the luxuries of their own firesides where mud and flooding storms and utter weariness never penetrate, to discourse of battles and how campaigns should be conducted and armies of the enemy destroyed. But it should be enough, perhaps, to say that men here or elsewhere who have knowledge enough of military affairs to entitle them to express an opinion on such matters, and accurate information enough to realize the nature and the means of this desired destruction of Lee's army before it crossed the Potomac into Virginia, will be most likely to vindicate the Pennsylvania campaign of General Meade and to see that he accomplished all that could have been reasonably expected of any general of any army. Complaint has been, and is made specially against Meade, that he did not attack Lee near Williamsport before he had time to withdraw across the river. These were the facts concerning this matter:

The thirteenth of July was the earliest day when such an

attack, if practicable at all, could have been made. The time
before this, since the battle, had been spent in moving the
army from the vicinity of the field, finding something of the
enemy and concentrating before him. . . . The Potomac,
swelled by the recent rain, was boiling and swift and deep, a
magnificent place to have drowned all the Rebel crew. I have
not the least doubt but that General Meade would have liked
to drown them all if he could, but they were unwilling to be
drowned and would fight first. To drive them into the river
then, they must be routed.

General Meade, I believe, favored an attack upon the
enemy at that time, and he summoned his corps commanders
to a council upon the subject. . . . Of the eight generals there,
Wadsworth, Howard, and Pleasonton were in favor of immediate attack, and five, Hays, French, Sykes, Sedgwick, and
Slocum were not in favor of attack until better information
was obtained of the position and situation of the enemy.

Of the *pros* Wadsworth only temporarily represented the
First Corps in the brief absence of Newton, who, had a battle
occurred, would have commanded. Pleasonton, with his
horses, would have been a spectator only, and Howard, with
the *brilliant Eleventh Corps*, would have been trusted nowhere
but a safe distance from the enemy—not by General
Howard's fault, however, for he is a good and brave man.
Such was the position of those who felt sanguinarily inclined.

Of the *cons* were all of the fighting generals of the fighting
corps, save the First. This, then, was the feeling of these
generals—all who would have had no responsibility or part
in all probability, *hankered* for a fight—those who would have
had both part and responsibility did not. The attack was
not made. At daylight on the morning of the fourteenth,
strong reconnaissances from the Twelfth, Second, and Fifth
Corps were the means of discovering that between the enemy,
except a thousand or fifteen hundred of his rear guard who
fell into our hands, and the Army of the Potomac, rolled the
rapid, unbridged river. The Rebel General, Pettigrew, was
here killed. The enemy had constructed bridges, had crossed

during all the preceding night, but so close were our cavalry and infantry upon him in the morning that the bridges were destroyed before his rear guard had all crossed.

Among the considerations influencing these generals against the propriety of attack at that time were probably the following: The army was wearied and worn down by four weeks of constant forced marching of battle, in the midst of heat, mud, and drenching showers, burdened with arms, accoutrements, blankets, sixty to a hundred cartridges, and five to eight days' rations. What such weariness means few save soldiers know. Since the battle the army had been constantly diminished by sickness or prostration and by more straggling than I ever saw before. Poor fellows—they could not help it. The men were near the point when further efficient physical exertion was quite impossible. Even the sound of of the skirmishing, which was almost constant, and the excitement of impending battle had no effect to arouse for an hour the exhibition of their wonted former vigor. The enemy's loss in battle, it is true, had been far heavier than ours; but his army was less weary than ours, for in a given time since the first of the campaign it had marched far less and with lighter loads. These Rebels are accustomed to hunger and nakedness, customs to which our men do not take readily. And the enemy had straggled less, for the men were going away from battle and toward home, and for them to straggle was to go into captivity, whose end they could not conjecture. The enemy was somewhere in position in a ridgy, wooded country, abounding in strong defensive positions, his main bodies concealed, protected by rifle pits and epaulements, acting strictly on the defensive. His dispositions, his position even, with any considerable degree of accuracy were unknown, nor could they be known except by reconnaissances in such force, and carried to such extent, as would have constituted them attacks liable to bring on at any moment a general engagement, and at places where we were least prepared and least likely to be successful. To have had a battle there then, General Meade would have had to attack a cunning enemy in the dark, where surprises, undiscovered rifle pits and batteries, and unseen bodies of men might have met his forces at every point. . . .

Of course the army, both officers and men, had very great disappointment and very great sorrow that the Rebels *escaped* —so it was called—across the river; the disappointment was genuine, at least to the extent that disappointment is like surprise; but the sorrow to judge by looks, tones and actions, rather than by words, was not of that deep, sable character for which there is no balm.

Would it not be an imputation upon the courage or patriotism of this army if it was not rampant for fight at this particular time and under the existing circumstances? Had the enemy stayed upon the left bank of the Potomac twelve hours longer, there would have been a great battle there near Williamsport on the fourteenth of July.

Epilogue: "Flowers Shall Bloom Upon These Graves"

ON THE sixth of July, while Haskell's bullet bruise was still too inflamed and sensitive for him to be of service on the field, he decided to revisit Gettysburg. His division that day was halted four miles down the Baltimore Pike, and he found that by shortening his right stirrup strap to favor his bruised leg he could ride his horse at a walk without serious discomfort.

It seemed very strange upon approaching the horseshoe crest again not to see it covered with the thousands of troops and horses and guns, but they were all gone—the armies, to my seeming, had vanished—and on that lovely summer morning the stillness and silence of death pervaded the localities where so recently the shouts and the cannon had thundered.

The recent rains had washed out many an unsightly spot, and smoothed many a harrowed trace of the conflict; but one still needed no guide save the eyes to follow the track of that storm which the storms of heaven were powerless soon to entirely efface. The spade and shovel, so far as a little earth for the human bodies would render their task done, had completed their work. . . . But still one might see under some concealing bush or sheltering rock what had once been a man, and the thousands of stricken horses still lay scattered as they had died. The scattered small arms and the accoutrements had been collected and carried away, almost all that were of any value; but great numbers of bent and splintered muskets, rent knapsacks and haversacks, bruised canteens, shreds of caps, coats, trousers of blue or gray cloth, worthless belts and cartridge boxes, torn blankets, ammunition boxes, broken wheels, smashed limbers, shattered gun carriages, parts of harness, of all that men or horses wear or use in battle, were scattered broadcast over miles of the field. From these one could tell where the fight had been hottest.

The rifle pits and epaulements and the trampled grass told

238

where the lines had stood, and the batteries—the former being thicker where the enemy had been than those of our own construction. No soldier was to be seen, but numbers of civilians and boys, and some girls even, were curiously loitering about the field, and their faces showed not sadness or horror, but only staring wonder or smirking curiosity. . . .

Never elsewhere upon any field have I seen such abundant evidences of a terriffc fire of cannon and musketry as upon this. Along the enemy's position, where our shells and shot had struck during the cannonade of the third, the trees had cast their trunks and branches as if they had been icicles shaken by a blast. . . . Along the slope of Culp's Hill . . . the trees were almost literally peeled from the ground up some fifteen or twenty feet, so thick upon them were the scars the bullets had made. Upon a single tree, not over a foot and a half in diameter, I actually counted as many as two hundred and fifty bullet marks. The ground was covered by the little twigs that had been cut off by the hailstorm of lead. . . .

All along through these bullet-stormed woods were interspersed little patches of fresh earth raised a foot or so above the surrounding ground. Some were very near the front of the works; and nearby, upon a tree whose bark had been smoothed by an axe, written in red chalk would be the words, not in fine handwriting, "75 Rebels burried here." "☞ 54 Rebs. there." And so on. Such was the burial and such the epitaph of many of those famous men once led by the mighty Stonewall Jackson. Oh, this damned Rebellion will make brutes of us all if it is not soon quelled!

Our own men were buried in graves, not trenches; and upon a piece of board or stave of a barrel or bit of cracker box placed at the head were neatly cut or penciled the name and regiment of the one buried in such. This practice was general, but of course there must be some exceptions for sometimes the cannon's load had not left enough of a man to recognize or name. . . .

A full account of *the battle as it was* will never, can never be made. Who could sketch the changes, the constant shifting of the bloody panorama? It is not possible. The official reports may give results as to losses, with statements of attacks and repulses; they may also note the means by which results were attained, which is a statement of the number and kind of the forces employed, but the connection between means and results, the mode, the battle proper, these reports touch lightly. . . . By and by, out of the chaos of trash and falsehood that the newspapers hold, out of the disjointed mass of reports, out of the traditions and tales that came down from the field some eye that never saw the battle will select, and some pen will write what will be named *the history*. With that the world will be and, if we are alive, we must be content.

Already, as I rode down from the heights, nature's mysterious loom was at work, joining and weaving on her ceaseless web what the shells had broken there. Another spring shall green these trampled slopes, and flowers planted by unseen hands, shall bloom upon these graves; another autumn and the yellow harvest shall ripen there—all not in less but in higher perfection for this poured-out blood. In another decade of years, in another century or age, we hope that the Union, by the same means, may repose in a securer peace and bloom in a higher civilization. Then what matters it if lame Tradition glean on this field and hand down her garbled sheaf—if deft story with furtive fingers plait her ballad wreaths, deeds of her heroes here? or if stately history fill, as she list her arbitrary tablet, the sounding record of this fight? Tradition, story, history—all will not efface the true, grand epic of Gettysburg.

References

Chapter One

1: Broadhead, *Diary*, Ms., 1-3.
2: Dooley, *War Journal*, 97-100
3: *Ibid.*, 56, 62-3, 51, 96-7
4: Cooke, *Annals*, 671-74
5: *Rebellion Record*, VII, 325-26
6: Blackford, *With Jeb Stuart*, 224-27
7: Bayly, *Stories of the Battle*, Ms., unpaged

Chapter Two

1: Haskell, *Gettysburg*, 1-5
2: Reid, *Rebellion Record*, VII, 84-5.
3: Haskell, *Gettysburg*, 5-7
4: Meade, *Annals*, 208
5: Rusling, *Civil War Days*, 72-3
6: Reid, *Rebellion Record*, VII, 88
7: Broadhead, *Diary*, Ms., 3-5

Chapter Three

1: Dana, *Philadelphia Weekly Times,* Feb. 22, 1878
2: Bayly, *Stories of the Battle,* Ms., unpaged
3: Broadhead, *Diary*, Ms., 5-6
4: Doubleday, *Chancellorsville and Gettysburg*, 124-36
5: Halstead, *Battles & Leaders,* III, 285
6: Howard, *O. R.,* Ser. I, XXVII, 704
7: Haskell, *Gettysburg*, 11-6
8: Doubleday, *Chancellorsville and Gettysburg*, 151; Howard, *Autobiography*, 418; Halstead, *Battles & Leaders,* III, 285

Chapter Four

1: Rodes, *S.H.S.P.,* II, 145
2: *Ibid.,* 147
3: *Ibid.,* 148
4: Buell, *Story of a Private Soldier*, 66-73
5: Schurz, *O. R.,* Ser. 1, XXVII, 728-29
6: Doubleday, *Chancellorsville and Gettysburg*, 147-50

7: Broadhead, *Diary*, Ms., 6-7
8: Haskell, *Gettysburg*, 11
9: Alleman, *At Gettysburg*, 43-5
10: Freemantle, *Three Months in the Southern States*, 251-56
11: Bayly, *Stories of the Battle*, Ms., unpaged

Chapter Five

1: Whittier, *Civil War Papers*, 75-6
2: Haskell, *Gettysburg*, 17-9, 23-7
3: Longstreet, *Annals*, 420-22
4: Broadhead, *Diary*, Ms., 7
5: Bayly, *Stories of the Battle*, Ms., unpaged
6: Haskell, *Gettysburg*, 27-35
7: Longstreet, *Annals*, 422-24
8: Hood, quoted in Oates, *The War Between the Union and the Confederacy*, 208-10
9: Freemantle, *Three Months in the Southern States*, 257-60
10: Haskell, *Gettysburg*, 35-41

Chapter Six

1: Tremain, *Two Days of War*, 60-5
2: Graham, *On to Gettysburg*, 9-10
3: Oates, *The War Between the Union and the Confederacy*, 210-11
4: Perry, quoted in *Ibid.*, 228-29
5: *Ibid.*, 212-14
6: Prince, quoted in *Ibid.*, 215
7: *Ibid.*, 217-19
8: Gerrish, *Army Life*, 109-10
9: Oates, *The War Between the Union and the Confederacy*, 219-21
10: Graham, *On to Gettysburg*, 10-12

Chapter Seven

1: Lamar, quoted in McLaws, *M.V.H.S.P.*, 74
2: McNeily, *M.V.H.S.P.*, 267
3: Tremain, *Two Days of War*, 236-37
4: Reid, quoted in McNeily, *M.V.H.S.P.*, 248
5: Meade, *With Meade at Gettysburg* 127-28
6: Haskell, *Gettysburg*, 45-51
7: *Ibid.*, 52-4

Chapter Eight

1: Broadhead, *Diary*, Ms., 7-8
2: Bayly, *Stories of the Battle*, Ms., unpaged
3: Jacobs, *Notes on the Rebel Invasion of Maryland and Pennsylvania*, 37-8
4: Haskell, *Gettysburg*, 58-63
5: Gibbon, *Battles & Leaders*, 231
6: Haskell, *Gettysburg*, 63-5

Chapter Nine

1: Whittier, *Civil War Papers*, 103-06
2: Haskell, *Gettysburg*, 69-75
3: *S.H.S.P.*, 104-06
4: Alexander, *Battles & Leaders*, III, 357
5: Dooley, *War Journal*, 101-03
6: Haskell, *Gettysburg*, 76-82

Chapter Ten

1: Haskell, *Gettysburg*, 83-6
2: *Ibid.*, 86-90
3: *Ibid.*, 90-3
4: Wood, *Phila. Weekly Times*, August 11, 1877
5: Haskell, *Gettysburg*, 95-100

Chapter Eleven

1: *Rebellion Record*, VII, 114
2: Haskell, *Gettysburg*, 101-07
3: *Ibid.*, 107-11
4: Dooley, *War Journal*, 106-07
5: *Rebellion Record*, VII, 114
6: Haskell, *Gettysburg*, 111-13
7: Alexander, *Battles & Leaders*, III, 366-67
8: Freemantle, *Three Months in the Southern States*, 265-67
9: Haskell, *Gettysburg*, 117-19

Chapter Twelve

1: Brooke-Hawle, *Annals*, 481-83
2: Broadhead, *Diary*, Ms., 8-9
3: Bayly, *Stories of the Battle*, Ms., unpaged
4: Pickett, *The Heart of a Soldier*, 97-100
5: Haskell, *Gettysburg*, 139-42, 144-48

6: Alleman, *At Gettysburg*, 71-4
7: Basler, *Collected Works*, VI, 314
8: Broadhead, *Diary*, Ms., 9-10

Chapter Thirteen

1: Broadhead, *Diary*, Ms., 10-12
2: Hancock, *South After Gettysburg*, 7-18
3: Broadhead, *Dairy*, Ms., 12-15
4: Welles, *Diary*, 369-70
5: Haskell, *Gettysburg*, 126-33

Epilogue

Haskell, *Gettysburg*, 146-50, 156, 158

Bibliography

ALEXANDER, E. PORTER. See *Battles and Leaders of the Civil War.*

ALLEMAN, MRS. TILLIE (PIERCE), *At Gettysburg, or What a Girl Saw and Heard of the Battle.* New York: Privately Printed. 1889.

Annals of the War, The. Philadelphia: The Times Publishing Company, 1879.

BASLER, ROY P. (ed.), *The Collected Works of Abraham Lincoln.* New Brunswick: Rutgers University Press. 1953. 9 vols.

Battles and Leaders of the Civil War. Edited by Robert Underwood Johnson and Clarence Clough Buel. New York: The Century Company, 1884-88. 4 volumes.

BAYLY, WILLIAM HAMILTON. *Stories of the Battle.* (Typescript at the Library of the Gettysburg National Military Park.)

BLACKFORD, W. W. *War Years With Jeb Stuart.* New York: Charles Scribner's Sons, 1946.

BROADHEAD, SALLIE ROBBINS. *Diary.* (Originally published in *The Gettysburg Compiler.* References cited in this work are taken from a typescript copy in the Library of the Gettysburg National Military Park.)

BROOKE-RAWLE, WILLIAM. See *Annals of the War, The.*

BUELL, AUGUSTUS. *The Cannoneer—Story of a Private Soldier.* Washington: The National Tribune, 1890.

Civil War Papers Read Before the Commandery of the State of Massachusetts, Military Order of the Loyal Legion of the United States, Volume I. Boston: Printed for the Commandery, 1900.

COOKE, JOHN ESTEN. See *Annals of the War, The.*

DANA, H. E. See Philadelphia *Weekly Times.*

DOOLEY, JOHN. See DURKIN, JOSEPH T.

DOUBLEDAY, ABNER. *Chancellorsville and Gettysburg (Campaigns of the Civil War,* Volume VI). New York: Charles Scribner's Sons, 1882.

DURKIN, JOSEPH T., (ed.), *John Dooley Confederate Soldier His War Journal.* Washington: Georgetown University Press, 1945.

FREMANTLE, ARTHUR JAMES LYON. *Three Months in the Southern States, April-June, 1863.* London: William Blackford & Sons, 1863.

GERALD, G. B. See McNEILY, J. S.

GERRISH, THEODORE. *Army Life, A Private's Reminiscences of the Civil War.* Portland: Hoyt, Fogg and Donham, 1882.

GIBBON, JOHN. See *Battles and Leaders of the Civil War.*

GRAHAM, ZIBA B. *On to Gettysburg, Two Days From my Diary of 1863.* Detroit: Winn and Hammond, 1889.

HALSTEAD, E. P. See *Battles and Leaders of the Civil War.*

HANCOCK, CORNELIA. *South After Gettysburg, Letters of Cornelia Hancock from the Army of the Potomac, 1863-1865.* Edited by Henrietta Stratton Jaquette. Philadelphia: University of Pennsylvania Press, 1937.

HASKELL, FRANK ARTEAS. *The Battle of Gettysburg,* edited by Bruce Catton. Boston: Houghton, Mifflin Company, 1958. [Earlier editions: "about 1880," 1898, 1908 and 1910.]

HOOD, JOHN B. See OATES, WILLIAM COLVIN.

HOWARD, OLIVER OTIS. *Autobiography of Oliver Otis Howard.* New York: The Baker and Taylor Company, 1908. 2 volumes.

JACOBS, MICHAELS. *Notes on the Rebel Invasion of Maryland and Pennsylvania.* Gettysburg: Star and Sentinel, 1884.

LAMAR, G. B., JR. See Lafayette McLaws in *Southern Historical Society Papers.*

LINCOLN, ABRAHAM. See BASLER, ROY P.

LLOYD, J. C. See McNEILY, J. S.

LONGSTREET, JAMES. See *Annals of the War, The.*

McNEILY, J. S. See *Southern Historical Society Papers.*

MEADE, GEORGE. *The Life and Letters of General George Gordon Meade.* New York: Charles Scribner's Sons, 1913. 2 volumes.

MEADE, GEORGE G. See *Annals of the War, The.*

Mississippi Valley Historical Society Papers.

MOORE, FRANK (ed.). *The Rebellion Record: A Diary of American Events.* New York: G. P. Putnam and D. Van Nostrand Company, 1861-68. 11 volumes.

OATES, WILLIAM COLVIN. *The War Between the Union and the Confederacy and Its Lost Opportunities.* New York and Washington: The Neale Publishing Company, 1905.

Official Records. See *War of the Rebellion.*

PERRY, W. F. See OATES, WILLIAM COLVIN.

Philadelphia *Weekly Times.*

PICKETT, GEORGE EDWARD. *The Heart of a Soldier, as Revealed in the Intimate Letters of General George E. Pickett, C. S. A.* New York: Seth Moyle, Inc., 1913.

PRINCE, HOWARD L. See OATES, WILLIAM COLVIN.

Rebellion Record. See MOORE, FRANK.

REID, WHITELAW. See MCNEILY, J. S.

RODES, ROBERT EMMETT. See *Southern Historical Society Papers.*

RUSLING, JAMES F. *Men and Things I Saw in Civil War Days.* New York: Eaton & Mains, and Cincinnati: Curts & Jennings, 1899.

SCHURZ, CARL. See *Official Records.*

Southern Historical Society Papers.

TREMAIN, HENRY EDWIN. *Two Days of War, a Gettysburg Narrative and Other Excursions.* New York: Bonnell, Silver & Bowers, 1905.

War of the Rebellion . . . Official Records of the Union and Confederate Armies. Washington, D.C., Government Printing Office, 1880-1901. 128 volumes.

WELLES, GIDEON. *The Diary of Gideon Welles, Secretary of the Navy Under Lincoln and Johnson.* Edited with an introduction by John T. Morse, Jr. Boston: Houghton Mifflin Company, 1911. 3 volumes.

WHITTIER, EDWARD N. See *Civil War Papers.*

WOOD, W. W. See Philadelphia *Weekly Times.*

Index

James I. Robertson, Jr., is Alumni Distinguished Professor of History at Virginia Tech. His numerous writings have won many awards and include *General A.P. Hill* (1987); *Soldiers Blue and Gray* (1988); and *Civil War! America Becomes One Nation* (1992). He appears frequently on the A&E network's weekly program "Civil War Journal" and has completed a full-length biography of Confederate General "Stonewall" Jackson.